C000134375

"This is an important book that anyone
of contemporaries who are deeply aliena
with much profit. Distilled out of twenty years of personal evangelism, this book reflects both a deep grasp of biblical theology and
a penetrating compassion for people—and finds a way forward in
wise, probing questions. How very much like the Master himself!"

—D. A. CARSON
Research Professor of New Testament
Trinity Evangelical Divinity School

"*Questioning Evangelism* provides an absolutely unique blend of
apologetic information and practical evangelistic advice. Newman
is a skilled practitioner and this book is must reading for those who
want to learn how to bring apologetics into evangelism in a biblical
and relationally sensitive sort of way."

—J. P. MORELAND
Distinguished Professor of Philosophy
Talbot School of Theology, Biola University

"Randy Newman goes way beyond how-tos and apologetics, bringing
back the lost art of listening, dialogue, and the heart of evangelism
in the spirit of Christ."

—MARC V. RUTTER
National Director, Human Resource Leadership
Campus Crusade for Christ International

"Randy Newman has penned a valuable resource for all of us who
are trying to share the good news of Jesus with our contemporaries."

—MITCH GLASER
President
Chosen People Ministries

"Asking questions, the right questions, is an essential skill needed by all Christians. Next time I share my faith, I'm going to be asking some 'gospel-paving' questions!"

—LIEUTENANT GENERAL R. L. VAN ANTWERP
Former Chief of Engineers, United States Army
President of the Officers' Christian Fellowship

"Newman's purpose is not to explain what the saving message is. . . . He focuses instead on asking good questions to get the listener engaged in conversation, rather than a monologue, as so often happens in evangelism. . . . Why not give questions a try? You might find that you like it."

—*Journal of the Grace Evangelical Society*

"Exciting. . . . Randy Newman attacks [ordinary evangelical] ideas with very fresh questions to continue the conversation. . . . [This] is one of the very best books on questioning."

—*The Lamplighter*

QUESTIONING
EVANGELISM

THIRD EDITION

QUESTIONING EVANGELISM

Engaging People's Hearts the Way Jesus Did

RANDY NEWMAN

Foreword by Lee Strobel

KREGEL
PUBLICATIONS

Library of Congress Cataloging-in-Publication Data
Names: Newman, Randy, 1956- author.
Title: Questioning Evangelism : engaging people's hearts the way Jesus did / Randy Newman.
Description: Third edition. | Grand Rapids, MI : Kregel Publications, 2023. | Includes bibliographical references.
Identifiers: LCCN 2022037078 (print) | LCCN 2022037079 (ebook) | ISBN 9780825447808 (paperback) | ISBN 9780825469640 (kindle edition) | ISBN 9780825470240 (epub)
Classification: LCC BV4520 .N46 2023 (print) | LCC BV4520 (ebook) | DDC 248/.5--dc23/eng/20220826
LC record available at https://lccn.loc.gov/2022037078
LC ebook record available at https://lccn.loc.gov/2022037079

ISBN 978-0-8254-4780-8, print
ISBN 978-0-8254-7024-0, epub
ISBN 978-0-8254-6964-0, Kindle

Printed in the United States of America
23 24 25 26 27 28 29 30 31 32 / 5 4 3 2 1

To my Jewish mother,
Rhonda Newman,
who, at the ripe young age of seventy-five,
found answers to her many questions
and became a follower of Jesus,
Savior, Rabbi, Redeemer, and Lord.

Contents

Foreword

The email was snarky, with decidedly hostile and mocking undertones. At the end, the person—someone I didn't know—posed a pointed question: "If your God is loving, why does He allow so much pain and suffering in the world?"

I wasn't in a good mood when I read the missive. Part of me wanted to answer in a similarly negative style, but I quickly realized that wouldn't be the right approach. So I started to write a detailed five-point answer to the pain-and-suffering question—you know, the kind of theologically sound response you learn when you study Christian apologetics.

I paused. I deleted what I had written. Instead, I simply typed, "Of all the questions in the universe, why did you choose to ask that one?" I hit Send.

The answer came the next day. This second email had a totally different tone—the anger was gone, and the writer was much more sincere. He described his impressive academic achievements and how he had climbed to success in his career—only to lose his eyesight and health to diabetes. His job evaporated. His friends drifted away. Now he was living on welfare and food stamps. He was suffering from depression, loneliness, bitterness, and fear.

My heart went out to him. As for him, he responded that he felt heard and valued. Suddenly, the door was open to a fruitful spiritual conversation.

This, in short, is the power of a question. And that's what this book is about—how to share God's message of hope and grace through probing questions. That's right—sort of like Jesus did.

Nobody teaches the art of question-asking better than my friend Randy Newman. When you meet Randy in person, you're immediately drawn to his self-deprecating humor, his undeniable intellect, and his big heart for God and people—all of which bleed through the pages of this must-read book.

Years ago, Christian apologists would figuratively line up the targets of their evangelism and machine-gun them with facts, evidence, and arguments. That no longer works. For the most part, evangelism happens through relationships, which are better nurtured by provocative questions than a memorized gospel speech.

Let Randy teach you how to be a more effective ambassador for Jesus in the twenty-first century by doing more listening than talking, by validating the other person as being made in the image of God, and by respecting their spiritual journey.

And, of course, by asking good questions—like Randy learned from the Master Himself.

LEE STROBEL
Author of *The Case for Christ* and *The Case for Heaven*
Founding Director of the Lee Strobel Center
for Evangelism and Applied Apologetics
Colorado Christian University

Preface to the Third Edition

Our world is getting hotter. No, I'm not talking about global warming or climate change of our physical planet. I'm referring to the social, cultural climate into which we proclaim the good news about Jesus. That emotional temperature is rising dramatically. If there ever was a time when many people were receptive to the gospel (perhaps in the 1950s) or coolly neutral toward our message (perhaps the 1980s), today the tone has morphed into one of hostility. At one time, people said, "Come to your Bible study? Sure, I'm open-minded." Then, they switched to, "Hey, what's true for you is true for you but not for me. You can believe whatever you want." Today, they say, "You believe what? How can you be so closed-minded and bigoted? You're what's wrong with the world!"

When I first wrote *Questioning Evangelism* almost twenty years ago, the evangelistic temperature was already beginning to climb. Today, it's scorching. But along with the heat has come a hunger. The unavoidable suffering of a pandemic has intensified people's longing for answers—for both their heads and their hearts. The fruit of godless living has yielded a level of pain and relational alienation that cries out for comfort. Into this difficult time, the gospel is even better news than we may have realized in previous years.

Thus, I offer more questioning of how we do evangelism. I've also added a chapter on science because that challenge to our faith has gotten particularly hot in recent years. As with the previous two editions, I am certainly not questioning whether we should evangelize. I'm questioning how. But behind and beneath that questioning lies a certainty, a conviction, and yes, even an eagerness to spur us all on to tell people what they must hear. May God embolden us beyond all we ask or imagine.

Acknowledgments

The word *grateful* prompts joy and warm affection for the many people who encouraged me during the writing of this book—listening to my ideas, reading a chapter or two (or more!), helping me formulate the flow of an argument, or telling me what really didn't connect. I owe a lot of thanks to Ellen Beauchamp, Jim Beavers, Barbara Brand, Mike Calkin, David Case, Dave Fossum, Mitch Glaser, Derrick Lovick, Mark Lundquist, Dave McGaw, Mike Metzger, Jim Roembke, Joe Scimecca, Stan Wallace, David Walnut, and George Selden for their time and suggestions.

I'm grateful to the members of the Pentagon Prayer Breakfast, Burke Community Church, Barcroft Bible Church, McLean Bible Church's Life Builders' class, and the faculty fellowships at George Mason University and the University of Maryland for allowing me to "try out" my ideas in messages to them.

Thank you to my greatest encouragers and challengers—Lin Johnson, Spencer Brand, Patrick Dennis, Don Carson, and J. P. Moreland—for taking the time to evaluate my writing and urging me to keep going.

I am delighted to say to my three sons—Dan, David, and Jon—that Dad will be more available now that this project is complete. It would be a display of God's grace if this book helps you reach out to your peers—people I can't even begin to figure out!

Most of all, I'm grateful to my wife, Pam, for loving me and cheering me on. At times, you believed in me and this work more than I did. Writing the chapter on marriage was a delight—because of you.

Introduction

You may think that this book is just plain weird. When it comes to evangelism, I think differently than a lot of people. I ask questions that other people don't ask. I come up with answers that many people don't think of. And answers that a lot of people find knock-down, drag-out invincible leave me unconvinced.

Maybe you think like I do. Or maybe you know people who ask the same kinds of questions that I ask. Or maybe our world has changed so significantly that we need to rethink evangelism.

The questions that I ask are not unreasonable. People often say, "Good question." When I say that certain answers are unconvincing, it's as if I've shouted something about the emperor's new clothes. And in response to the answers that I offer, people often tell me, "Gee, I wish I'd thought of that."

For a long time, I wondered if I should just keep quiet and cling to the proverb, "Even a fool, when he keeps silent, is considered wise" (Prov. 17:28 NASB1995). Wishing to find another option, I tried out my questions and answers on some real live non-Christians. In the course of writing this book, I met with dozens of amazingly kind and thoughtful people who were making progress on their own spiritual journeys. They were gracious in allowing me to join them for part of the trip. Some of them were students, a few were professors, and most were ordinary folks from various walks of life. One of the first people to share his uncertainties with me (and allow me to share some of my ideas with him) was a fireman who read Nietzsche!

Along the way, I received enough encouragement to write this book.

My prayer is that readers will be encouraged and aided in the task of telling others the best news ever announced. I'm not calling into question the validity of evangelism. I'm calling Christians to use questions in the venture of evangelism. I have two fears, however.

The first is that some people might see *Questioning Evangelism* as a criticism of other books on evangelism or apologetics. Such landmark works as Josh McDowell's *More Than a Carpenter*, Paul Little's *Know Why You Believe*, or C. S. Lewis's *Mere Christianity* come to mind. It would be the height of presumption for me to criticize such works. These books (and many others like them) are gifts from God to His church, and He has used them in amazing ways. I give away copies as often as I can, because they're very effective—with certain people.

I also like several newer books in the evangelistic arsenal. Lee Strobel's *The Case for Christ* and *The Case for Faith* are best sellers for a good reason. They are well-written, well-reasoned, and compelling works that our Lord has used and will continue to use to bring many into the kingdom. Two recent additions to our apologetic toolbox deserve careful study and wide dissemination: Timothy Keller's *The Reason for God* and Rebecca McLaughlin's *Confronting Christianity*.

A diverse audience, though, requires diverse approaches. *Questioning Evangelism* offers another approach. If Jesus teaches us anything about evangelism, it's that He used a variety of methods with a variety of people.

Any evangelistic approach, though, requires three skills. The first and most basic involves *declaring* the gospel, including the ability to clearly and concisely articulate the message of salvation. A tool such as Cru's "Knowing God Personally" is helpful in presenting the message clearly while avoiding unnecessary distractions or confusing rabbit trails. Declaring the gospel also includes the sharing of one's own story or testimony. Every Christian needs fluency in articulating how the Lord changed his or her life and the difference that change makes daily.

The second evangelistic skill is *defending* the gospel. Anticipating common questions, acquainting oneself with helpful discoveries from the past, and planning how to deliver this information in a logical sequence have to be part of "always being ready to make a defense" (1 Peter 3:15 NASB1995).

The third skill—and this is where *Questioning Evangelism* fits in—is built upon the foundations of declaring and defending the gospel. That skill is called *dialoguing* the gospel. Often neglected and difficult to master, but absolutely essential, this skill of giving and taking—asking questions and bouncing ideas back and forth—might be just what our postmodern audience needs. We need all three skills if we're to be Christ's ambassadors in the twenty-first century.

My second fear is that some people might view *Questioning Evangelism* as a technical handbook. If so, they might be tempted to use its approach to evangelism in a cookie-cutter, mechanical way. Doing so, however, would prove unfruitful and frustrating. I don't want people to respond to my examples by saying, "I've got to memorize this so the next time someone asks me that question, I'll say these words, use these phrases, ask these questions," and so forth.

Instead, I hope that readers will develop a different way of thinking about people, their questions, and our message. And because of that difference, our evangelistic conversations will sound less content/persuasion driven and more relationship/understanding driven. They'll sound more like rabbinic dialogues than professorial monologues. They'll be an exchange of ideas that lead both participants to the truth of the gospel. For one participant, it will be the first arrival at that point; for the other participant, it will be a rediscovery and a new appreciation of the message of the cross.

The goal of *Questioning Evangelism* is to help people know *how* to think about an issue more than *what* to think. This book will help followers of Jesus to develop their minds ("the mind of Christ") more than their methodologies, giving readers a sense of what to *say*. More important, though, readers will grow in confidence, knowing what to *ask*, because this book is about questions—questions that Christians can ask to move the conversation in a Christ-ward direction, questions that non-Christians are asking (either directly or indirectly), and questions that Christians can use as answers!

Some of the questions that people ask today are the same old questions that people have asked for millennia. For example, "Why does a good God allow evil and suffering?" But people today ask that question as we struggle to emerge from a pandemic while grieving the loss of millions (that's not an overstatement) of lives, making the question less sterile than it might have been in the past.

Some of the questions have been asked before, but the temperature in the tone is hotter now. When someone asks, for example, "Can Jesus really be the only way to God?" it might be more an accusation than a sincere inquiry. After all, the eternal state of the proverbial "heathen in Africa" is no longer the issue. Rather, it refers to the Hindu who lives next door, the Muslim whose desk is next to yours, the Jew who coaches your son's soccer team, or the New Age, crystal-clinging, tie-dyed T-shirt-wearing unmarried couple living together down the street.

Some of the questions *are* new. Twenty years ago, few people brought up the issue of homosexuality in the context of an evangelistic conversation. Now, however, people raise that question often, and frequently word it as an attack: "Why are you Christians so homo-phobic?" And it's not just about homosexuality (a rather old-fashioned term which has been completely replaced by "gay"). Today we speak of LGBTQ+ and are open to adding several more letters after that.

A number of questions that lurk within evangelistic chats are unspoken. At one time, only a few rogue fraternity brothers had the boldness to ask why they should stop sleeping with their girlfriend(s!). And even then, their questions were more defense than honest inquiries, with a fair amount of guilt mixed in. Today, because of the sexual revolution, marital fidelity and chastity are on the defen-sive and modern questioners might wonder (aloud or in their jaded hearts), "What's so great about marriage?" or, "If I believe in this God you talk about, will I have to go along with His [your?] antiquated, stifling, and unhealthy ideas about sex?" or, "Why should I have sex with just one person for the rest of my life?"

Whether the questions are old or new—or angry varieties of either—we should be more engaging and less confrontational in our sharing of the good news. We must find new hinges upon which to swing open new doors. We must be disciples of our Lord and rabbi, Jesus of Nazareth, so that more and more people will join us in that great gathering of worshippers around the Lamb. If He sees fit to use this book toward that end, giving you confidence along the way, I will be grateful.

PART 1
WHY ASK QUESTIONS?

CHAPTER 1

Why Are Questions Better Than Answers?

I'll never forget his name.[1] It was one that I'd never heard before—Artyum. He was from Ukraine and was possibly the most sincere seeker I've ever met. I just didn't know what to do with him. We struck up a conversation on the center lawn of the American University in Washington, DC, on a springlike day in November. It wasn't supposed to be that warm. But there we were, Artyum and I, basking in the sunshine, when the calendar said that we should have been inside sipping cups of hot chocolate.

We talked about the weather, classes, hometowns, and things like that. Then he asked me what I did on campus. When I worked for an organization with the name Campus Crusade for Christ (now known in the United States as Cru) and people asked, "What do you do?" it didn't take long to steer the conversation toward the gospel. It's one of the perks of being a crusader.

As a trained evangelist, I steered our chat to the point where a little green booklet became the focal point of our conversation. "Knowing God Personally" is an adaptation of Bill Bright's "The Four Spiritual Laws" and is a good evangelistic tool for sharing the gospel. I still believe that as much as ever. But what happened that day at the American University changed my thinking about some of the ways we do evangelism.

---

1. Portions of this chapter originally appeared in Randy Newman, "Stop Answering Questions," *Discipleship Journal*, January/February 2002: 24–29. Unless otherwise noted, all scenarios are drawn from actual encounters and many are composites.

I'd been trained and had conducted seminars in how to introduce the booklet, how to progress through the booklet, how to avoid distractions during the booklet, how to bring someone to the point of decision at the end of the booklet, and how to walk him or her through that eternity-changing moment of conversion after concluding the booklet. I could state the advantages of using such a tool (and there are many). I could show the drawbacks of just winging it and not using such a focused tool (and there are many). And I could share stories of how God has used it to lead many people to the Savior.

I read the first point: "God loves you and created you to know Him personally." I don't remember pausing at that point. I don't think I even breathed. But somehow Artyum interrupted.

"What do you mean when you say the word *God*?" he wondered aloud. "And what do you mean when you say the word *love*? And, most importantly, how do you know all this is true?"

It was a difficult moment for me. All of my training had told me to sweep away any and all questions with, "That's a good question. How about we come back to that when I'm done reading the booklet?" That line had worked well many times for me. The inevitable result was that the questions would be forgotten and never brought up again. That's because many questions that are asked early during an evangelistic presentation are not real questions—they're smoke screens. The questioner is trying to avoid the conviction that is sure to come when one confronts the gospel.

So they stop the presentation before it gets uncomfortable with, "Well, we can't really believe the Bible; it's got too many contradictions in it," or "There are so many religions in the world, how can anyone know which one's right?" or a million other pretentious comments that *should* be swept away with the "that's-a-good-question" line.

But Artyum's questions were different. They weren't smoke screens. I know the difference between an honest inquirer and a truth avoider. Artyum's questions were foundational. Could I progress to the second page in the booklet and read, "People are sinful and separated from God," if he was stuck on the words *God* and *love*? What would be in store for us when we hit the word *sin*?

I mentally reviewed the background data that I'd gathered earlier in our chat and connected it to our present discussion. Being from Ukraine, Artyum had been reared in an atheistic, communist world, reading Nietzsche and Marx and thinking deeply about life. He was a history major who loved philosophy and was bothered by the intellectual shallowness displayed by most Americans. He wasn't annoyed by my initiation of evangelism. He genuinely wanted to work through his questions. Unlike me, however, he didn't feel any pressing need to work through the booklet. He did feel, though, a sense of importance about working through real interaction about weighty questions.

What followed was a ninety-minute discussion, revolving around questions that strike at the foundation of faith: "How do we know what we know?," "What do we know for certain?," and "What difference does it all make?" Toward the end of the conversation, I was asking more questions of him than he was of me.

Artyum helped me rethink the task of evangelism. *Questioning Evangelism* is the result of that process. And in all of the examples in this book, Artyum's is the only name that I haven't disguised. Although I refer to real people in real conversations, all other names have been changed. But I've kept Artyum's name, hoping that someday he'll see this book and contact me, telling me that he's come to faith in Christ. He didn't that day on American University's lawn. I lost track of him soon after the weather returned to normal November temperatures.

Why Are We Frustrated?

I came away from that conversation both excited and frustrated. Communicating at that level of intensity and truth-seeking was invigorating. That level of excitement was relatively new, but the frustration was all too familiar. Another nondecision. People don't as readily "pray the prayer" with me as they do with famous speakers I've heard. Those natural evangelists are always sitting down next to someone and sharing the gospel. And they always lead every person to a salvation decision. (And it's always on an airplane!)

Some people have told me that my lack of evangelistic fruit results from lack of prayer. I certainly don't pray enough, but I wonder if that's all there is to it. Other people have told me that I don't push hard enough in "closing the sale." I don't know how to respond to that; the gospel isn't a product that we sell. On introspection, I've wondered what I haven't said to work the same magic as so many others.

I've found that I'm not alone in my frustration. In fact, frustration might be the most common emotion that Christians associate with evangelism (followed closely by guilt, confusion, and despair). Our frustration is multifaceted. We're frustrated that our message doesn't yield more decisions, genuine fruit, cultural impact, or advancing of God's kingdom in the way Jesus talked about.

First, we just don't have as many evangelistic conversations as we know we should. The message that has gripped our hearts and forms the centerpiece of our lives remains unspoken, unshared, and unproclaimed. We miss opportunities to tell people what Jesus means to us. Our culture's secularism has silenced us when we should be sharing. We wonder why the topic that is so often on our minds is so seldom on our lips.

Second, most of us don't hold a candle to people who are gifted by God as evangelists. And when we actually do step out in faith and share Christ, not as many people as we'd like bow their heads and pray "the sinner's prayer." So hearing about the successes of a Billy Graham only adds to our frustration. Instead of motivating us to be bold, the success stories discourage us. That's not an excuse, though. Paul told Timothy, who was a timid nonevangelist, to "do the work of an evangelist" (2 Tim. 4:5). So we find ourselves clinging to the promise that God forgives even the greatest of sinners—assuming that *sinners* means those who are evangelistic failures—and hoping for a method of evangelism for nonevangelists.

Third, we're frustrated by the lack of lasting fruit. If you've ever "led someone to Christ" and then later found that person totally uninterested in spiritual growth, you know the pain I'm referring to. True, not all the seeds in Jesus's parable landed on good soil. Still, we wonder why some plants spring up and then wither in the sun, or on the rocky soil, or under the distractions of this world. We wonder why, for all of our evangelistic efforts, the number of people who go to church has decreased dramatically while the number who say that they have no religious faith continues to rise.

Fourth, we're frustrated by our lack of saltiness—that is, cultural impact. If we're supposed to be the "salt of the earth," a preservative, why is our culture decaying?

These frustrations are realized in an environment of such religious diversity that many of us question some of our basic assumptions about Christian belief. Different religions are not theoretical concepts practiced in other countries; they're embraced by the people next door.

Our local library advertises seminars on yoga, meditation, crystal usage, and the teachings of Mormonism.

The reality of pluralism (the existence of differing points of view) tempts us to consider the assertions of relativism (the validity and truthfulness of all points of view). In our most honest moments, we wonder how we can hold to Jesus's claim that "no one comes to the Father except through me" (John 14:6). Our frustration and intimidation, then, lead to a condition that borders on evangelistic paralysis, or what one speaker referred to as "spiritual lockjaw."

Is There a Better Way to Evangelize?

We can have better results from our evangelizing. Our efforts can produce more fruit, advancing the kingdom further than has been recently achieved. A better way exists, and it looks, sounds, and feels more like Jesus, the rabbi, than like Murray, the used-car salesperson. It involves more listening than speaking, inviting rather than demanding a decision. Perhaps the most important component to this kind of evangelism is answering questions with questions rather than giving answers.

Maybe I think this way—responding to questions with questions—because I'm Jewish. I grew up with dialogues that went like this:

RANDY: How's the weather down there?

GRANNY BELLE: How could the weather be in Florida in the middle of
         July?

Or

RANDY: So, how have you been?

UNCLE NAT: Why do you ask?

Or

RANDY: How's your family?

AUNT VIVIAN: Compared to whom?

I'd like to think, though, that I answer questions with questions
because I'm following the example of Jesus. It's uncanny how often
our Lord answered a question with a question.

A rich man asked Jesus, "Good teacher, what must I do to inherit
eternal life?" That question was a great setup for a clear, concise gospel
presentation. I can almost hear a disciple whispering in Jesus's ear,
"Take out the booklet." How could Jesus not launch into the most
perfect model for every evangelistic training seminar for all time?
But how did he respond? He posed a question, "Why do you call me
good?" (Mark 10:17–18).

When religious leaders asked Jesus if it was right to pay taxes,
Jesus referred to a coin and asked, "Whose image is this?" (Matt.
22:20). When the Pharisees, "looking for a reason to bring charges
against Jesus," asked Him, "Is it lawful to heal on the Sabbath?"
Jesus's response was a question: "If any of you has a sheep and it falls
into a pit on the Sabbath, will you not take hold of it and lift it out?"
(Matt. 12:10–11).

I once did a study of how Jesus answered every question that was
asked of Him in all four Gospels. Answering a question with a question was the norm. A clear, concise, direct answer was a rarity.

So when I answer a question with a question, I'd like to think I'm following the example of Jesus. But to be honest, I most likely do it because I've become tired. After years of answering the questions of nonbelievers, I've grown tired of my answers being rejected.

At times (far too many, I'm afraid), I've answered questions with biblically accurate, logically sound, epistemologically watertight answers, only to see questioners shrug their shoulders. My answers, it seemed, only further confirmed their opinion that Christians are simpletons. My answers had, in fact, hardened them in their unbelief rather than softened them toward faith. I realized that, instead of moving people closer to a salvation decision, an answer can push them further away. Rather than engaging their minds or urging them to consider an alternate perspective, an answer can give them ammunition for future attacks against the gospel.

So I started answering questions with questions, and have gained far better results.

Once a team of skeptics confronted me. It was during a weekly Bible study for freshmen guys that we held in a student's dorm room. The host of the study, in whose room we were meeting, had been telling us for weeks of his roommate's antagonistic questions. This week, the roommate showed up—along with a handful of like-minded friends.

The frequently asked question of exclusivity arose, more an attack than a sincere inquiry.

"So, I suppose you think all those sincere followers of other religions are going to hell!"

"Do you believe in hell?" I responded.

He appeared as if he'd never seriously considered the possibility. He looked so puzzled, perhaps because he was being challenged when he thought that he was doing the challenging. After a long silence, he said, "No. I don't believe in hell. I think it's ridiculous."

Echoing his word choice, I said, "Well, then why are you asking me such a ridiculous question?"

I wasn't trying to be a wise guy. I simply wanted him to honestly examine the assumptions behind his own question. His face indicated that I had a good point, and that he was considering the issues of judgment, eternal damnation, and God's righteousness for the first time in his life.

The silence was broken by another questioner, who chimed in, "Well, I *do* believe in hell. Do you think everyone who disagrees with you is going there?"

I asked, "Do you think anyone goes there? Is Hitler in hell?" (Hitler has turned out to be a helpful, if unlikely, ally in such discussions.)

"Of course Hitler's in hell."

"How do you think God decides who goes to heaven and who goes to hell? Does He grade on a curve?"

From there, the discussion became civil for the first time, and serious interaction about God's holiness, people's sinfulness, and Jesus's atoning work ensued. Answering questions with questions turned out to be a more effective, albeit indirect, way to share the gospel.

Another time when questioning worked better than answering was during a lunchtime conversation with an atheist philosophy professor. He was the faculty advisor for the campus philosophy club, and I was a campus minister for Campus Crusade. Together, we had cosponsored a debate about the problem of evil, and afterward we met to evaluate how the event had gone.

After some discussion of such things as how we could have publicized the event better, and what topics we could address in future forums, I asked him his opinion about the content of the debate.

I realized that I was in way over my head and that nothing I could articulate about the Christian perspective on evil could top what some brilliant philosophers had said the previous evening. But I wanted to see if I could get the conversation out of the philosophical realm and onto a personal level. I was concerned about this person's soul.

He told me that he still thought that Christians failed to present a decent answer for the problem of evil. So I posed the question to him. After confirming that he was an atheist, I asked, "What's your atheistic explanation for why terrible things happen?"

He paused and finally said quietly, "I don't have one."

I told him that this wasn't just some academic issue for me. As someone with a Jewish heritage, I had to wrestle with the reality of the Holocaust. I recounted my last visit to the United States Holocaust Memorial Museum and how emotionally difficult it was for me. I asked him again if there was an atheistic way to make sense out of the Nazis' slaughter of six million of my people.

Again, his answer was a nonanswer.

I told him that the Christian answer to the problem of evil definitely has its shortcomings and that I, for one, am not intellectually or emotionally satisfied with it. But I also told him that my incomplete answer was better than no answer at all. The rest of our lunchtime consisted of a productive and respectful tête-à-tête that moved us closer to each other and, I hope, moved him closer to seeing some flaws in his own worldview.

Answering a question with a question, then, often has significant advantages over using direct answers. It brings to the surface the questioner's assumptions. It also takes the pressure off you—the one being asked—and puts the pressure on the one doing the asking. Shifting the burden of the response is important because as long as we're on the defensive, the questioners are not really wrestling with issues. They're just watching us squirm.

For example, the chief priests and the teachers of the law once challenged Jesus: "'Tell us by what authority you are doing these things,' they said. 'Who gave you this authority?' He replied, 'I will also ask you a question. Tell me: John's baptism—was it from heaven, or of human origin?'" (Luke 20:2–4).

The Gospel writers give us insight into the real motivations of the religious authorities. After a short consultation together to work out a maneuver, they realized their predicament. Given John's popularity, if they answered that his message was from heaven, then Jesus would ask them why they didn't believe him. On the other hand, if they said that John's message was "of human origin," that is, nothing more than a mere man's ramblings, they'd have a riot on their hands. So they told Jesus that they didn't know. Jesus showed them that their insincere nonquestion deserved an appropriate nonanswer: "Neither will I tell you by what authority I am doing these things" (v. 8).

Responding to a question with a question paves the way for a concept that the questioner might not otherwise consider. When I asked my dormitory interrogators if they believed in hell, I paved the way for the concept of divine judgment. Many ideas that are central to our gospel message—God's holiness, people's sinfulness, Christ's atoning work on the cross, and people's responsibility—are alien today for many people. Questions bring these concepts into clearer focus for consideration and even acceptance.

Jesus's conversation with the woman at the well (John 4:1–26) fits this pattern although He never actually asked a question. The woman's notions of righteousness, sin, and worship had to be challenged before she would accept Jesus's way of seeing those concepts. Without His challenging comments, it is doubtful she ever would have arrived at the point of saving faith.

On a practical note, answering a question with a question might alleviate some hostility. When people ask questions that are really attacks in disguise, responding with a question deflects the heat. People usually don't like the temperature and tend to adjust the thermostat accordingly, which helps create a more productive conversation.

To be sure, a direct answer is at times preferable. Some questioners are sincere and would benefit most from a clear, concise statement of what the Bible says. On quite a few occasions, Jesus didn't beat around the bush. Consider, for example, His direct answer to the teacher of the law who asked, "Of all the commandments, which is the most important?" (Mark 12:28).

But more and more we should hold back our answer, and with a question pave the way to receptivity. When your coworker asks in an accusatory tone, "Why do you still believe in God in light of people dying of COVID?," ask him, "How do *you* explain so many deaths?" Or when your cousin asks, "Why are you so narrow-minded as to believe that all Buddhists are going to hell?" ask her, "Have you become a Buddhist?" or "Have you studied Buddhism enough to become convinced that its adherents are worthy of heaven?" or "What have you found about Buddhism that impresses you so?" Those questions might be a better way to respond than to indignantly quote, "No one comes to the Father but through Me" (John 14:6 NASB1995).

When your neighbor asks, "Why do you think that Jesus was anything more than just a good moral teacher?" don't take out your C. S. Lewis–inspired Lord-liar-lunatic diagram just yet. Wait a few seconds and ask her, "What makes you think that Jesus was a good teacher? Have you read a lot of His teachings? Which messages impress you the most about Jesus's teaching ability? What would you say was Jesus's main message?"

Recently, a pastor urged his congregation to open the door to evangelism by challenging the prevailing slogans of our day. "The next time someone at work says, 'Image is everything,'" he told them, "respond, 'No, it's not! Image isn't everything! The glory of God is everything!'"

Although I agree with his theology, his methodology may be flawed. It would be better to respond with a puzzled look and a one-word question, "Really?" After getting the coworker's attention, a follow-up question could be, "Do you really think that image is everything?" I think that many people would see the point. Then a few gospel-paving questions could be added: "What do you think *is* everything? What would you say is the most foundational thing in life?"

What Is Rabbinic Evangelism?

Answering a question with a question is part of a different style of sharing the good news, one that I call rabbinic evangelism. Rabbis, using this style of debate, train their disciples to think critically about God and life. The method was used in Jesus's day and is similar to what happens today in training schools called "yeshivas." This analytical method is sometimes called "pilpul."

Moishe Rosen, the founder of Jews for Jesus, encourages this style of dialogue in his book *Share the New Life with a Jew*. Rosen shows how seeing both sides of a question can help people think, which is a necessary but often neglected component in the evangelism process. One of his illustrations is worthy of imitation:

> A rabbi posed a question to a Gentile inquirer, trying to illustrate this different style of thought.

"I will ask you some questions," he said, "to see if you can logically come to the right answers. Two men fell down a chimney. One was dirty, and the other was clean. Which one washed?"

"The dirty one, of course," replied the Gentile.

"Wrong!" exclaimed the rabbi. "The dirty one looked at the clean one and thought to himself, *Amazing! We just fell down a chimney but we didn't get dirty.* But the clean man saw the dirty man, presumed that they were both dirty, and immediately went to wash up."

The Gentile smiled. "Oh, I see."

"No, you don't," said the rabbi. "Let me ask you the second question: Two men fell down a chimney; one was clean and the other—"

The Gentile was puzzled. "You already asked me that question," he said.

"No," contended the rabbi. "The other one was dirty. Which one washed?"

"The clean one," said the Gentile.

"Wrong again," said the rabbi. "It was the dirty one. He looked at the clean man and thought, *It's amazing that he should fall down the chimney and remain clean,* whereupon he looked at his own hands and realized that he was dirty, and went and washed. And now, for my third question. Two men fell down a chimney; one was dirty and the other was clean. Which one went and washed?"

The perplexed Gentile shrugged. "I don't know whether to say it was the dirty one or the clean one."

"Neither!" said the rabbi. "The whole question is ridiculous! How can two men fall down a chimney together, and one come out dirty and the other come out clean?"[2]

Although this illustration has elements of absurdity, such an

---

2. Moishe Rosen, *Share the New Life with a Jew* (Chicago: Moody, 1976), 47.

exercise teaches people to think critically. Such rabbinic reasoning is needed and should be used today in evangelism as we engage the hearts and minds of non-Christians.

I believe that Paul used such a style of evangelism in his synagogue preaching, which is mentioned many times in the book of Acts. In Acts 17:2–3, for example, we read, "As was his custom, Paul went into the synagogue, and on three Sabbath days he *reasoned* with them from the Scriptures, *explaining* and *proving* that the Messiah had to suffer and rise from the dead. 'This Jesus I am proclaiming to you is the Messiah,' he said" (emphasis added; similar statements are found in Acts 17:17; 18:4, 19; and 24:25).

Those three verbs—*reason, explain*, and *prove*—convey the give-and-take that occurred in those sessions. In the original Greek, the first verb, *reason*, has an intensity that may well be best stated in the *Revised Standard Version* translation—"he *argued!*"

Perhaps those arguments sounded something like this:

> PAUL: So, you see that Jesus is the Messiah, just as our Holy Scriptures foretold.

> SYNAGOGUE TEACHER: How can that be? He was a blasphemer!

> PAUL: What makes you say such a thing?

> SYNAGOGUE TEACHER: He claimed to be the Holy One, blessed be His name.

> PAUL: So? Doesn't the Scripture say that the Messiah will be divine?

> SYNAGOGUE TEACHER: Where does it say that?

> PAUL: In Isaiah, the prophet, he's called "Wonderful Counselor, Mighty God, Everlasting Father,

Prince of Peace." In Micah, we're told that he has always existed, "from the days of eternity." King David called him "my Lord."[3] Who could fulfill these Scriptures except God Himself?

SYNAGOGUE TEACHER: True. But this Jesus you speak of—he died. How can the Eternal One, blessed be His name, die?

PAUL: Don't our own Psalms tell us, in chapter 16, that our Messiah would come back from the dead?

SYNAGOGUE TEACHER: There you go again with that resurrection stuff. Why do you always come back to that?

PAUL: Because I'm still waiting for you to show me the dead body. Have you found it yet?

SYNAGOGUE TEACHER: Who let this man in here?

What Rabbinic Evangelism Is *Not*

Rabbinic evangelism is not simply a rational, logical argument. We must avoid the danger of thinking that a person's reception of the gospel is simply based upon his or her ability to reason. If that were the case, nonbelievers would only need to be convinced of the truthfulness and sensibility of our message and they'd walk the aisle. But faith is more than intellectual assent to the facts. Far too many Christians have come away from an evangelistic presentation shaking their heads in wonder at the stupidity of their unsaved friends. "What could be holding them back?" they wonder.

If we think that the gospel is simply a good deal that any reasonable person would accept, we'll not only be amazed at how many people turn it down, but we may actually distort the message in the process of proclaiming it. We might strip the gospel of its

---

3. Respectively, these references appear in Isaiah 9:6; Micah 5:2 (NASB1995); and Psalm 110:1.

supernatural and convicting elements, talking about the offer of a free gift, or going to heaven, or living forever, or feeling the freedom of forgiveness, or the need to make a decision as if these were parts of a benefits package. To be sure, these are important components of the gospel message. But without the context of God's holiness, the horror of our sinfulness, the need for repentance, and the necessity of the cross instead of just a guidebook to better behavior, we'll terribly misrepresent the gospel. People need to hear the bad news in our message before they can appreciate the good news. Not only do the minds of nonbelievers need to be persuaded, but also their knees need to buckle.

For years, I presented the gospel using a pen to help illustrate. I wanted to ensure that my listeners understood Ephesians 2:8-9: "For it is by grace you have been saved, through faith—and this is not from yourselves, it is the gift of God—not by works, so that no one can boast."

To explain what was meant by the word *gift*, I would hold out a pen and tell the person, "I'd like to give you this pen as a gift." Then I'd ask, "What would you need to do to make this pen yours?"

"Take it," they'd say. Everyone got this question right.

But no one, absolutely no one, ever got the point that I was trying to make. I finally figured out why. Salvation isn't a pen!

Certainly, salvation is free. It is a gift that must be accepted, not worked for or earned. But the reason I'd accept the gift of a pen is different than the reason I'd accept the gift of salvation. I don't need a pen. I could find something else to write with. I could even live my entire life without using a pen. I probably already have a lot of pens, ones that I might like better than the one I'm being offered. I might accept a pen as a token of the giver's generosity or as a display of friendship.

But accepting salvation is different. If I correctly understand what I'm being offered by the Messiah's death on a cross, I know that it's something that I can't live without (eternally, that is). I'm lost without it. I'm dead in my sins. I must accept this free gift to avoid total and eternal alienation from a holy, righteous God. I need to accept such an unspeakably gracious offer with the acknowledgment that I deserve exactly the opposite. So my attitude of accepting the gift is one of humility and repentance. Illustrating such a profound offer by giving someone a pen misrepresents the heart of the message.

Rabbinic evangelism also is not a sales pitch. If we were to try to convince someone to "buy" the gospel, we'd shy away from some difficult words that need to be said. Confronting a prospect with unpleasant truths doesn't work in sales, but it is essential in evangelism.

My encounter with Warren brought this reality home to me. As a successful businessperson, Warren was frequently invited to luncheons sponsored by evangelistic organizations. He had heard the testimonies of many top executives, and he had been given a library full of evangelistic books. He knew the arguments for the historicity of the biblical documents better than some seminary professors. He was more convinced than anyone I had ever met that Jesus actually did rise from the dead! And his car was filled with evangelistic recordings that people had given him for the many long road trips required in his work.

But Warren just couldn't commit. He knew all of the right answers, and he knew the *shoulds*, *musts*, and all of the other urgent verbs used in late-night pleas from evangelistic friends. So what was Warren's problem? Why had he left so many would-be evangelists in his wake, shaking their heads and wondering what was holding him back? Why had the sales-style approach not worked?

Warren's "problem" was his girlfriend. She kept saying yes. She was more than willing to sleep with him, even though he'd made it clear to her that he wasn't interested in marriage. She kept hoping that her "yes" would someday lead to his "I do." Although they lived four hours apart, nine years later their situation hadn't changed. He kept staying over at her house on the weekends and then returning to his place on Monday through Friday. Neither wanted to leave their high-paying jobs, so "for economic reasons," their situation remained the same.

One day I had lunch with Warren at a Mexican restaurant. I asked him (me and my pesky questions!), "Would you marry her if economics wasn't a factor?" He didn't even pause between chips. "Why should I?" he responded to my question with a question. He had all that he wanted from this relationship—sex and companionship on the weekends, and freedom from obligation during the week.

I explained that he also had another kind of freedom, one that wasn't all that good: freedom from integrity. He was joining himself physically and emotionally with a woman he was unwilling to commit himself to volitionally (that's what marriage is). By doing so, he was creating a disintegration in his soul that prevented his being a whole person. That's why the Creator of sex is so negative about the expression of sex outside the commitment of marriage. Sex isn't just a physical act. When we divorce it from other components of our personhood, we adulterate ourselves.

I explained this to Warren, knowing that these concepts are so rarely expressed. An element of rabbinic evangelism is that it confronts where a sales pitch won't. Yet some of it was getting through. I could tell; he stopped eating the chips.

His immorality prevents his turning to Christ. As John puts it in the third chapter of his Gospel, "People loved darkness" (3:19). That's why Warren hasn't come to Christ even though he keeps going to (and enjoying!) those evangelistic businessmen's luncheons. I suspect that he never will come to faith until he breaks up with or marries his girlfriend.

This book offers a solution for our evangelistic frustration. I'm suggesting that we do more than just "proclaim the simple gospel" and wring our hands when the results don't come pouring in. I'm proposing a style of evangelism that is a dialogue more than a sales pitch. I'm pleading for conversations that lead to conversions, rather than impersonal presentations that lead nowhere. I'm encouraging the use of questions more than the use of answers. The apostle Paul found validity in adding reasoning, explaining, and proving to his arsenal of evangelistic weapons. So should we.

CHAPTER 2

Solomonic Soulwinning: What Does the Book of Proverbs Teach Us About Questions?

Our family once joined a gym. We became part of that vast horde of Americans who sweat, pump iron, and count calories. We used terms such as *reps, sets, pecs, aerobic capacity,* and *optimum heart rate.* We got on bikes, treadmills, and elliptical trainers, and watched little LCD screens that told us how our cardio-fitness ratio was developing.

Before getting educated about the weight-control process, I sank in discouragement when I saw that after thirty minutes of huffing and puffing I'd burned off only 378 calories (but who's counting?). I thought, *All that sweat and I didn't even make a dent in last night's cheesecake!* After a little work on a calculator, I concluded that I'd need 14,247 consecutive hours on these machines to make me look like the people in the gym's promotional material. Something had to be wrong with my figuring.

I later learned that there's more to the fat-burning cardio exercise process than just the number of calories you burn while you're on the equipment. That's, in fact, only a small part of the equation. During a gym-sponsored seminar designed to help us get the most from our workouts, I learned about increasing my rate of metabolism. If you work out consistently, the presenter said, you increase the rate of your normal metabolism—your everyday, relaxed, sitting-on-the-couch-watching-television burning of energy. With increased metabolism, you could burn off last night's dessert more efficiently even while sitting still (or even sleeping!). Consistent periods of exercise change the way your body works at all other times.

A similar dynamic works in our spiritual lives. If we think that Christian spirituality is just what happens while we're reading the Bible, praying, or singing worship songs in church, we have a truncated view of faith. We wouldn't be alone, however, in our error. Many Christians crowd their schedules with religious activities and minimize all of the "secular" stuff to be more "spiritual."

A healthier, more biblical pattern includes spiritual disciplines— Bible reading, prayer, worship, fasting, solitude, and other such exercises—but results in a transformation of all of life. We take on Christlikeness and grow in wisdom and compassion (among other things), and then these qualities change the way we do everything else—including the "secular" stuff.

The task of evangelism looks different if we think in this transformed way. Rather than trying to learn all the right words, have all of the right booklets, anticipate all of the right questions, and memorize all of the right intros and Scripture, we should approach evangelism with wisdom. This means that we become people who incarnate the gospel and speak of it freely because our hearts and minds have been captivated by it. Becoming people of wisdom and compassion is the prerequisite for any evangelistic technique.

This chapter is about wisdom, with the book of Proverbs as the primary text. Later chapters address issues of compassion, listening, and anger (also important themes in the book of Proverbs). As we study these pithy statements by Solomon and others, we grow in wisdom. We develop lenses through which to see the world. We construct grids through which to interpret reality. And we sound more like a rabbi than a used-car salesperson.

To be sure, Proverbs teaches us how to handle specific situations. But as physical exercise makes our bodies more adept at burning calories, immersing ourselves in Proverbs makes us become more adept at applying wisdom to a wide variety of situations, not just the specific ones that Solomon addressed.

What proverb or Scripture could you apply, for example, to the following conversation with a disturbed young man named Adam? After hearing me speak to a church group about rabbinic evangelism, he approached me with a serious look on his face. He seemed not to be happy—with me or anyone else in the world.

"On what do you base your reality?" he asked, without introduction or greeting.

"I'm sorry. Could you repeat the question?" I was stalling. Having just finished speaking, I was tired—both physically and mentally—and I was trying to muster some strength for what looked like a tough conversation.

"On what do you base your reality?" he repeated.

I reached out my hand and introduced myself and asked his name. I told him that knowing his name would be helpful for me before we delved into such deep waters.

After exchanging names, I said, "I'm not sure I'm the one who bases reality on anything. That would be God's job. Do you mean, on what do I base my understanding of reality?" I was praying for wisdom and compassion as I spoke to this guy: wisdom because his question was complex and I sensed emotional issues behind the intellectual question; and compassion because I didn't want to talk to anyone just then, let alone some depressed, difficult, intellectual interrogator.

"Okay. You could word the question that way."

"I guess my perception of reality is based on truth, as God has revealed it. At least, that's my goal—to try to be as close to the truth as possible. Why? On what do you base *your* reality?"

What followed was one of the most difficult conversations I've ever had with anyone. Adam was a man in pain. An intellectually rigorous dialogue about metaphysics was not his real agenda. He told me that no one had ever loved him. His family had alienated themselves from him, and no woman had ever grown close enough to him to consider marriage. He freely shared these things even though we'd just met. When I talked about Jesus suffering for our sins, he told me that he'd suffered far more than Jesus ever had.

Although I could have provided answers, answers weren't what Adam needed. Although many of the things that Adam said were foolish, he was not the kind of fool described in the book of Proverbs. I couldn't point to any one verse of Scripture that described Adam's situation or prescribed a remedy for him. But the wisdom I've gathered from Scripture and the compassion that has come from meditating on God's grace helped me connect with this troubled man. We still dialogue, and he seems to be getting closer to light and further from darkness.

Four Lessons From Solomon

As we seek to build wisdom within our souls, Solomon *can* teach us four specific lessons about specific situations.

1. Avoid an Argument

I easily could have had an argument with Adam. Solomon, though, warned us, "Starting a quarrel is like breaching a dam; so drop the matter before a dispute breaks out" (Prov. 17:14). Or "Whoever loves a quarrel loves sin; whoever builds a high gate invites destruction" (17:19). Solomon even tells us why such avoidance is prudent: "A brother wronged is more unyielding than a fortified city; disputes are like the barred gates of a citadel" (18:19).

Many an evangelizing Christian has won the battle but lost the war by not avoiding an ugly argument. In Acts 17, Paul gives us insight about healthy arguing, while Proverbs teaches us about the destructive kind of arguing. We must discern the difference. A believer might prove to a coworker that Jesus really did rise from the dead, that the Bible really has archaeological evidence to support it, or that the Christian church really has been a force for good in the world. But along the way, that evangelizer might alienate that colleague to such an extent that he or she might never want to hear about God again. Our Christian had the content right but failed to exercise wisdom.

Remember the old saying, "The man convinced against his will is of the same opinion still."

2. Recognize a Fool

This second lesson shows us that some dialogues should stop, and others should never start. Recognizing these situations before it's too late is crucial.

Solomon told us, "Stay away from a fool, for you will not find knowledge on their lips" (Prov. 14:7), and he advises us not to "speak to fools, for they will scorn your prudent words" (23:9). As he often does, Solomon tells us why we need to avoid wasting our breath: "Fools find no pleasure in understanding but delight in airing their own opinions" (18:2). (Note: The vital lessons about answering a fool, found in Proverbs 26:4–5, are addressed at length in chapter 5 of this book.)

A young woman named Shelly met a fool for lunch. That was not her intention. In fact, the fool in this case was her father, Bill. She had hoped for a pleasant father-daughter conversation about her new job, his new house in the retirement community, and light things such as the weather.

But, as was his custom, Bill took the opportunity to attack Shelly's Christian faith. He'd been doing a lot of reading, he told her, and had even put some of his thoughts into writing. He couldn't believe how "stupid" the Christian preachers on television were and how "biased" the best-selling Christian authors were. Out came a file folder of his written diatribes against the spokespeople of the faith. The folder was thick, evidence of many hours of work and a lot of energy expended.

"Dad, this seems like a really big deal to you. You must spend hours reading and writing this stuff," Shelly said, trying not to sound exasperated. "Why do you do this?"

"Here, look at this article," he blurted, ignoring her question. "Listen to what this preacher says about Noah's ark." He was unstoppable. After a long quote of a rather anti-intellectual-sounding article, Bill asked his daughter, "Is that the stupidest argument you've ever heard?"

"Dad, that's not fair. You only choose stupid people to refute. You should answer the best defenders of the Christian faith, not the easiest ones to knock down."

"Like this guy?" he countered. He quickly pulled another sheet from his file. He quoted another, less extreme Christian writer and started to attack his logic.

Shelly interrupted, "Is this really how you want to spend our lunchtime?"

Again, no response to her question. Shelly wasn't surprised. This had been going on for years. There'd been a time when she actually tried to answer his arguments, but she now saw that he was never interested in true dialogue.

That day's lunch sounded like so many others. He never responded to her questions. He simply brought out another article, book, story, or letter to the editor that supported his agnosticism.

She asked if he'd ever read that book she sent him for his birthday, C. S. Lewis's *Mere Christianity*.

He almost made eye contact with her.

"Yeah. I read it."

"What did you think?"

"It was okay. I don't remember too much about it."

She doubted his honesty but couldn't figure out how to accuse him of lying. Lewis's arguments deserved better attention than Bill gave to them. Lewis, an Oxford professor, embodied a more formidable foe for him. Bill's lack of interaction with Lewis convinced Shelly that her dad was less interested in the truth and more interested in airing his own opinions.

"Dad, let's continue this conversation when we have Lewis's book in front of us and we can discuss his arguments."

"But what about this book that I found at the library?"

Shelly called for the waiter and asked for their check.

In our zeal (or is it desperation?) for evangelistic conversations, we sometimes think that any conversation about God is a good conversation. If we're with a fool, however, we would be better off, as Shelly did, to walk away.

Consider what Jesus told us about some conversation partners: "Do not give dogs what is sacred; do not throw your pearls to pigs" (Matt. 7:6). Our message is too precious to be treated with ridicule and derision. When we simply let fools wallow in their foolishness, we run the risk that they'll "trample them [the sacred pearls, that is, the gospel message] under their feet, and turn and tear you to pieces."

Shelly was right for calling a halt to her father's foolish onslaught. Faced with a similar situation, we should try to bring the true nature of someone's arguments to the surface by posing questions.

"Why are you bringing up these things?"

"Are you asking these questions because you really want an answer?"

"If I give you an answer to this question, would you be convinced that Christianity is true?"

"What's the biggest issue that prevents you from being a Christian?"

"Are you willing to read something that I think answers your question?"

Until someone is more interested in truth than in airing his or her own opinions, it's best to talk about the weather.

3. Remember That People Are People

Proverbs presents a multifaceted picture of people. We're not just rational beings to be informed and educated, spiritual beings to be evangelized and enlightened, or physical beings to be fed and satiated. We are whole beings, called to love God with our whole heart, soul, strength, and mind.

This lesson hit home at two o'clock on a Saturday afternoon as I spoke at a weekend retreat. The way the students took notes during the third evangelism training session surprised me. The first session, on Friday night, was about how to make a clear presentation of the gospel. I suggested ways to begin a conversation and demonstrated how to present the gospel in a succinct way. The students yawned all the way through it.

"Tell us something we haven't heard a million times." Their bored faces said it all.

Saturday morning's session received a similar response. I spoke about clarifying misconceptions about the gospel, offering illustrations that had worked many times for me. They'd heard them all before.

So I dreaded Saturday afternoon's session. Even if it weren't the worst time of day to speak, I wondered if I had anything new to teach them.

I asked them how many had read Dale Carnegie's *How to Win Friends and Influence People.* They laughed.

"Isn't that a secular book that salesmen use to help them make more money?" one of them asked.

"Well, some people use the book that way," I answered, "but Carnegie has a lot of wisdom that we can apply to a more eternally significant task than just making sales."

They didn't seem convinced, so I told them about David. I'd met David during the first week of that school year. He was a freshman and seemed lost on the big urban campus. He attended one of our meetings (because a friend invited him), and I had the opportunity to share the gospel with him. He wasn't interested in the gospel. My message made sense, he said, but seemed irrelevant to his life. What difference did some guy's martyrdom thousands of years ago make in his life today?

I tried my best to answer his question, but nothing seemed to connect. He showed a bit of a response when I told him what difference the gospel made in my life. Unlike many other testimonies that I'd shared before, I didn't dwell on the content of the gospel—what my life was like before I became a Christian, what convinced me to become a Christian, or how I can be sure I'm going to heaven. Instead, I shared what I now call my "so-what testimony." I talked about my experience of being a Christian: how I now sense a purpose and meaning to life, how I never feel alone, and how—because I feel accepted by God—I more willingly accept other people. I told how being a Christian makes my marriage better, gives me a clear conscience, and fills me with a sense of optimism and hope.

Then I changed the subject and asked how he was adjusting to his new environment. I was genuinely concerned. I listened. Through his rambling answer, he indicated that he hadn't made many friends, that he liked classical music, and that he hated the cafeteria food.

I told him that I too liked classical music; that, in fact, I had been a music major in my undergraduate days. We talked about Beethoven,

Debussy, and Dvořák. I told him that students were entitled to free tickets for on-campus concerts. Then I invited him to play volley-ball with us the next night. He could meet some people, eat some watermelon, and have some fun—and we wouldn't even be doing any preaching.

He came to the volleyball night and then, shortly thereafter, started attending a Bible study one of the students led in his dorm. David was moving closer to the point of decision each day.

What does David's story have to do with *How to Win Friends and Influence People*? The things I learned from Dale Carnegie did more to move David closer to the cross than anything I'd learned from evangelism seminars.

Now the students at the Saturday afternoon seminar were ready to listen. They knew David! They knew he was going to Bible studies, but they didn't know how he got there. They took out their notebooks and pens.

I listed Dale Carnegie's nine guidelines for relating better to people. These guidelines pave the way for sharing the gospel more fruitfully. I didn't use much illustration because the guidelines are self-explanatory:

1. Don't criticize, condemn, or complain.
2. Give honest, sincere appreciation.
3. Arouse in the other person an eager want. (That's what a so-what testimony can do.)
4. Become genuinely interested in other people.
5. Smile.
6. Remember that a person's name is to that person the sweetest and most important sound in any language.
7. Be a good listener. Encourage others to talk about themselves.
8. Talk in terms of the other person's interests.
9. Make the other person feel important—and do it sincerely.[1]

---

1. Dale Carnegie, *How to Win Friends and Influence People* (New York: Simon & Schuster, 1936), 80, 142.

The students wrote as fast as I could speak. Each of them had attended numerous seminars on evangelism, but they all remarked that they'd never before heard these concepts. They now seemed more eager than ever to share their faith when they returned to campus. Then I opened my Bible. I told them that Carnegie wasn't as original as they might have thought.

Long before Carnegie wrote *How to Win Friends and Influence People,* Solomon observed, "When the LORD takes pleasure in anyone's way, he causes their enemies to make peace with them" (Prov. 16:7). Solomon went even further; beyond mere business sense, he gave instruction for conveying grace to others. In words that the New Testament repeats, he told us, "If your enemy is hungry, give him food to eat; if he is thirsty, give him water to drink. In doing this, you will heap burning coals on his head, and the LORD will reward you" (25:21–22).

Solomon understood the complex nature of people. He realized that conveying content makes up only a small part of the communication process. Being sensitive to a person's heart comprises a much larger portion. Thus, Solomon tells us, "The purposes of a person's heart are deep waters, but one who has insight draws them out" (20:5). And "Each heart knows its own bitterness, and no one else can share its joy" (14:10). Solomon recognized the mundane realities of life: "If anyone loudly blesses their neighbor early in the morning, it will be taken as a curse" (27:14). And long before holistic medicine became popular, the Holy Scriptures connected our spiritual nature with our physical body: "A heart at peace gives life to the body, but envy rots the bones" (14:30).

4. Remember the Power of the Tongue

The fourth lesson in Solomonic soulwinning warns us of the power of words. On the positive side, the "mouth of the righteous" and the "speech of the upright" can bring forth wisdom (Prov. 10:31; 12:6), rescue the wicked (12:6), bring healing (12:18; 15:4; 16:24), commend knowledge (15:2), "promote instruction" (16:21, 23), and have "the power of life and death" (18:21). No wonder that "one who loves a pure heart and who speaks with grace will have the king for a friend" (22:11). On the negative side, "a lying tongue hates those it hurts" (26:28), is "like a scorching fire" (16:27), "gushes folly" (15:2), pierces like a sword (12:18), and lies "in wait for blood" (12:6).

Heeding these warnings will lead us to use words "with restraint" (17:27) and to guard our mouths and keep ourselves from calamity (21:23). It will lead us not to speak in haste, for "there is more hope for a fool" than for one who speaks before thinking (29:20). It will chasten us to choose words that are respectful and avoid words that hurt.

This doesn't mean that total silence is always golden. One campus minister set up a "Listening Post" on a campus, and students could come to the post and talk. He placed a literal wooden post on a table in the middle of a heavily trafficked part of the campus. The minister sat on a chair on one side of the table, facing an empty chair on the other side of the table. A large sign urged students to sit down and talk, guaranteeing, "I'll just listen in silence." He did just that. I watched. I also noticed that many students left, wearing disappointed frowns.

One student blurted in disgust, "What the @#&*'s the point of that!" Instinctively, the students knew more than the minister. They hungered for "an honest answer [that] is like a kiss on the lips" (24:26). They knew that "a person finds joy in giving an apt reply—and how good is a timely word!" (15:23). After years of counseling some of these students, I've seen the wisdom that "whoever rebukes a person will in the end gain favor rather than one who has a flattering tongue" (28:23). Just sitting in silence and nodding your head might convey a tacit affirmation that serves the same function as flattery. But somewhere between total silence and nonstop talk lies wisdom.

He Who Wins Souls Is Wise

By combining two seemingly unrelated aspects of a godly life—internal righteousness and external outreach—Proverbs 11:30 says something very significant. The verse begins, "The fruit of the righteous is a tree of life" (NKJV). If we reflect upon that image—that of not just bearing fruit but also being the tree that produces the fruit—we each grow in our desire to be a righteous person, to be a tree of life. The fruit of that tree might be a positive outlook, or that we resist temptation to sin because holiness has a hold on our inner lives, or that we gravitate toward honesty and justice because our hearts have been touched by those qualities. As a tree of life, we bear fruit the way a pear tree bears its fruit.

The second half of the proverb, however, goes in an unexpected direction: "and he who wins souls is wise." A connection is made between our own internal righteousness and our influence upon others. To "win souls" in the Old Testament doesn't refer to a Billy Graham–type sermon in a stadium or an open Bible presentation of the gospel in a prison cell. Rather, it refers to influencing someone's heart and mind.

Absalom's "[stealing] the hearts of the people of Israel" (2 Sam. 15:6) is a negative example of winning souls for a sinful cause. Solomon would have us win hearts for a righteous end. We'd be wise to influence someone's soul and make that person righteous—in right standing before God and right in his daily dealings with others.

I tried to do this with the men of Lambda Chi Alpha. As a young campus minister, I was invited to speak to their newly formed chapter at Maryland's Towson University. My topic, "The Real Meaning of Christmas," was selected by their education committee, which consisted of several Christian guys I knew.

These young zealots wanted me to come and preach the gospel to their heathen fraternity brothers. So I did what they asked and almost got run out of town. I could tell that this presentation wasn't coming across as good news. They were polite, but their body language spoke loudly and clearly. As you might guess, we didn't have anyone walk the aisle that night.

It was almost a miracle that the Christians on the education committee convinced their officers to invite me back. They asked me to make another presentation—"The Real Meaning of Easter." Different time of year, same temperature of fire and brimstone—same number of converts.

I wondered if there might be another way to present the gospel to a fraternity. I prayed that Lambda Chi Alpha would be struck with collective amnesia, and if they ever invited me back, I'd try a different approach.

The education committee asked me to come one more time but said, "Try to do something less religious." I suggested the topic of "Chapter Unity," a talk that might help them bring their fifty-plus members into closer relationships. They were willing to give it a try and told me to keep it to less than twenty minutes.

When I got up to speak, I could tell that I needed to dig myself out of a hole. I began by thanking them for inviting me and complimenting them for their open-mindedness. To relieve some of the tension, I cracked a few jokes about some things that had happened on campus that week.

I told them my topic for the night was "Chapter Unity," and I talked about the need for unity and harmony in our society. I shared the experience of my neighborhood watch committee and the unity in our common desire for safety for our families. I think they were pleasantly surprised that I was involved in something that wasn't religious, and they seemed more open to listening.

The first suggestion to aid unity was a common goal. I didn't offer what I thought it should be, but I asked, "What is your purpose for having a fraternity?" They should all agree on what their purpose is, and they should be able to state it concisely and clearly. They were with me.

The second aid was clear communication. They should have some skills for ensuring that they understood one another. I shared some funny quotations from insurance claim forms that displayed bad communication, and the laughter helped my cause.

The third ingredient was forgiveness. They wouldn't need this if everyone in their fraternity was perfect, but . . .

They got my point without my having to finish the sentence. I shared how forgiveness made my marriage work, and how important forgiveness is for two people who want an intimate relationship. Without forgiveness, there is no intimacy. I could tell that they were interested.

"There is a lot more I can say about forgiveness," I said, "but I want to stay within my time limit. Let me just say that, as a Christian, I think there is a correlation between a person's forgiveness by God and the ability that person will have in expressing forgiveness to others."

My last suggestion for chapter unity was the need for encouragement. I told them that positive, uplifting words are healing and unifying, whereas sarcasm and insults are divisive and painful. I could tell that I'd touched a nerve. I wasn't surprised. What college guys don't cut each other down with sarcasm and insults!

I concluded my talk, saying that I'd appreciate their feedback about my presentation since this was a bit different than the other talks I'd given. They smiled, remembering that the real meaning of Christmas and the real meaning of Easter hadn't been such big hits with them. They applauded and several of them wanted to ask questions. When I told them that I was available for discussion, some of them actually wrote down my phone number.

I had many good conversations with several guys as a result of that presentation. Most significantly, several new guys started showing up at the chapter's Bible study hosted by the Christian guys on the education committee. A few of them came to faith in Christ, and several others who'd strayed from Christ rededicated their lives to the Lord.

I can give Solomon some credit that my third talk to Lambda Chi Alpha was better received. "Chapter Unity" displayed more wisdom and compassion, showed more awareness that people are people, and won more souls than other approaches I'd tried. The previous two talks reinforced the group's suspicion that religion had nothing new to say to them. Popular culture, though, has always been suspicious of Christianity. And in the days to come, that will be even more pronounced. We'll need, then, to remember, "If you want to gather honey, don't kick over the beehive."[2] We'll cause our enemies to make peace with us (Prov. 16:7).

---

2. Dale Carnegie, *How to Win Friends and Influence People* (New York: Simon & Schuster, 1936), 31.

CHAPTER 3

How Do Questions Pave the Way for Answers?

Not many people have heard of the "plug theory." Even fewer people believe it. Nevertheless, my son Dan proclaims it with boldness. He sounds convinced that it holds the keys to understanding international politics, world history, and military strategy.

The plug theory contends that every country has a plug, located somewhere near its geographic center, that prevents the country from sinking. Obviously, it's in a nation's best interest to prevent anyone from pulling its plug. Thus, keeping its plug location a secret remains a top priority for a nation's military, security, intelligence, and political forces. Pull the plug, and any other concern becomes meaningless.

Dan guesses that the plug of America sits somewhere in Kansas. His theory has some intriguing implications: Atlantis didn't protect its plug very well; Holland had its plug pulled but rescued its land from submersion by reinserting the plug and building a series of dikes; Vatican City is itself a plug; Lesotho is the plug for South Africa.

Dan waxes eloquent about the plug theory at family gatherings. The response is always the same—laughter and entertainment. No one ever believes him, tells him that he's right, or thanks him for enlightening them. Dan's listeners never write to their congressmen and women, urging the protection of our plug, thereby keeping the world safe for democracy.

Dan's theory amuses but never persuades. For anyone to believe his notion, Dan would need to demonstrate support from, and correlation to, other things that people already accept. If anyone had ever seen one of these plugs, for example, that would help. Or if anyone who serves in our government ever gave credence to the idea, that would make people listen more seriously.

Supporting facts and ideas build "plausibility structures," making belief in something more probable. Without plausibility structures, an idea is unlikely to get even a hearing, let alone adherents.

For many people, believing in Jesus is as likely as believing in the plug theory. In their minds, neither idea has much plausibility. The propositions—that there is a God, that He is personal and knowable, that He hates sin, that He sent His Son to earth, and that His Son's death gives us freedom from guilt and gets us into heaven after we die—all sound as reasonable as the idea that a big plug in the middle of Kansas keeps our country afloat.

This doubt arises, in part, because the gospel used to have more plausibility structures supporting it than it does today. People believed that such a thing as truth existed, and that we could find out what it was. People believed in words, that they had meaning, and that the intention of a message was determined by its author, not by a reader. People accepted the law of noncontradiction and were bothered when someone espoused two ideas that contradicted each other. People believed in a correlation between life and beliefs, and quickly pointed out hypocrisy when they saw it. People believed the gospel because, given the many other things that they believed, it was believable.

Today, many of those plausibility structures have been dismantled. More than one hundred years ago, J. Gresham Machen declared prophetically:

> False ideas are the greatest obstacles to the reception of the gospel. We may preach with all the fervor of a reformer and yet succeed only in winning a straggler here and there, if we permit the whole collective thought of the nation or of the

world to be controlled by ideas which, by the resistless force of logic, prevent Christianity from being regarded as anything more than a harmless delusion.[1]

The church's calling, then—in addition to proclaiming the gospel, feeding the poor, building up families, and encouraging the downtrodden—must also include intentional efforts to build plausibility structures.

Consider the apostle Paul's outline of his ministry agenda in 2 Corinthians 10:3–5. After defending himself against his critics, who wondered why he did things the way he did, he states:

> For though we live in the world, we do not wage war as the world does. The weapons we fight with are not the weapons of the world. On the contrary, they have divine power to demolish strongholds. We demolish arguments and every pretension that sets itself up against the knowledge of God, and we take captive every thought to make it obedient to Christ.

We can imagine some of the "weapons of the world" that Paul had in mind—jargon, rhetoric, flashy images, emotional manipulation, and sales techniques—things that have as much appeal as those annoying pop-up ads on the internet. Weapons he *would* endorse include praying for people, quoting Scripture, giving literature, and proclaiming boldly the good news.

But certain weapons—the ones that are able to "demolish strongholds," "demolish arguments," and "take captive every thought"— differ from those in the more common arsenal. Such weapons include dialogue, discussion, challenging questions, well-crafted explanations about life's difficulties, and thought-provoking articles about various topics addressed from a Christian perspective. These

---

1. Address delivered on September 20, 1912, at the opening of the one hundred and first session of Princeton Theological Seminary. Reprinted in J. Gresham Machen, *What Is Christianity?* (Grand Rapids: Eerdmans, 1951), 162.

weapons topple the weak scaffolds people are standing on, so they see their need for something more solid. They take thoughts prisoner and make them submissive to a new master—the logic of scriptural truth. They tear apart ideas people have trusted in (that is, their "strongholds") so that they see the tenuousness of their situation.

To employ these weapons, we must understand five principles and employ five operative questions. But demolishing strongholds is not easy. We pave the way for belief with questions that build plausibility structures, but we must be on our toes and ready for a struggle. The tone of Paul's words—*wage war, weapons, fight, demolish, pretension, make obedient, take captive*—indicate that the struggle isn't going to be a picnic.

Principle Number One: Reveille Precedes Revelation

Put more simply, we must awaken people. In many cases, people have been lulled into believing the illogical, and rousing them from sleep must happen before we present any gospel content.

When people say things that, given some thought, would prove to be nonsense, we must help them see the fallacy of their statements.

- "I think all religions are the same."
- "I think all people are basically good."
- "I would never tell anyone their religion is wrong."

People who say such things are in desperate need of an alarm clock.

To quote the title of Neil Postman's 1985 book, we are "amusing ourselves to death."

C. S. Lewis referred to the role of amusement in *The Screwtape Letters*, the 1942 classic that remains in print. In the very first imaginary letter from the senior demon to a new trainee, Screwtape instructs Wormwood about tripping up his "patient" and ruining his faith:

> It sounds as if you supposed that *argument* was the way to keep him out of the Enemy's [i.e., God's] clutches. That might have been so if he had lived a few centuries earlier.

At that time the humans still knew pretty well when a thing was proved and when it was not; and if it was proved they really believed it. They still connected thinking with doing and were prepared to alter their way of life as the result of a chain of reasoning. But what with the weekly press and other such weapons we have largely altered that. Your man has been accustomed, ever since he was a boy, to have a dozen incompatible philosophies dancing about together inside his head. He doesn't think of doctrines as primarily "true" or "false," but as "academic" or "practical," "outworn" or "contemporary," "conventional" or "ruthless." *Jargon, not argument, is your best ally in keeping him from the Church.* . . . The trouble about argument is that it moves the whole struggle onto the Enemy's own ground.[2]

A good way to move "the whole struggle onto the Enemy's own ground" is to start with a one-word question: "Really?" This can help sound the reveille before revelation begins.

When people say, for instance, "I think all religions are the same," we could respond with, "Really?" Then, after people begin to awaken, we can elaborate by asking, "Do you really think your religion is the same as all others? How about people who say their religion requires them to kill people or crash airplanes into buildings or blow themselves up? They thought that it was going to take them to heaven. Do you *really* think that *their* religion is the same as yours?" The ensuing discussion could explore which religions are credible and why.

When people say, "I think all people are basically good," we could respond with, "Really? Does that include terrorists or child molesters or people who fire bullets randomly into a crowd?" If they are willing to concede that they didn't mean *all*, it's worth exploring where the lines are drawn between good, not so good, pretty bad, and downright evil.

This process might hurt. Waking up, whether physically or

---

2. C. S. Lewis, *The Screwtape Letters* (New York: HarperCollins, 1942, 2001), 1 (emphasis added).

intellectually, is seldom pleasant. It would help if we say the word *really* with as little sarcasm in our voice as possible.

Principle Number Two: Some Things Can't Be True

If I were to write the sentence, "I cannot write a single word in English," you'd know that something was odd. That statement, written in English, can't be true; it's self-refuting. One day, my son gave me a piece of paper on which was written, "The statement on the other side of this paper is true." I, of course, turned it over, only to find this sentence: "The statement on the other side of this paper is false." Over and over I turned it, much to my son's delight, only to see that this conundrum was unsolvable. The combination of statements could not work.

Many things people say about religion are self-refuting. "All religions are true" is a common example. Despite the frequency of this pronouncement—or its many variations—all religions *can't* be true. If one religion claims to be the only correct path to God (as Christianity, Judaism, Islam, and most other religions do), then a religion that contradicts it cannot be true.

People resist such logic, but without it, all dialogue is nonsense. Such resistance is why people picked up stones to throw at Jesus instead of inviting Him to their next interfaith dialogue. His claims of exclusivity have always negated other points of view, and that has never been popular.

To overcome resistance, we must soften hearts before anyone will listen to "no one comes to the Father but by Jesus." We can soften hearts by asking the question, "Can you explain that [your statement] to me?"

Asking this question demonstrates an unwillingness to be put on the defensive. In fact, it has a certain amount of offense to its posture. Far too often, Christians assume a defensive posture and allow themselves to be backed into a corner. But our message is coherent, plausible, and beneficial. Other people should defend their messages. In so doing, the foolishness or impossibility of their religion will be demonstrated. We can take an offensive posture without being rude or mean-spirited or insulting. (See chapter 11 for more about this topic.)

A conversation along these lines might sound like this:

NON-CHRISTIAN: I don't think anyone has the right to say that their religion is right and someone else's is wrong. I think that all religions are right.

CHRISTIAN: I'm not sure I understand. Can you explain that to me?

NON-CHRISTIAN: What do you mean?

CHRISTIAN: Well, I used to believe that myself—that all religions were right and that no one's faith was better than anyone else's.

NON-CHRISTIAN: So what happened to you?

CHRISTIAN: Someone challenged me to think about it a little. I started finding out what different religions believed. I found that religions that disagree on such basic things can't all be right.

NON-CHRISTIAN: They don't disagree about *basic* things. They just disagree about unimportant things like what kinds of clothes to wear or whether to worship on Sunday or Saturday or some other day.

CHRISTIAN: I disagree! Different religions differ on *major* things.

NON-CHRISTIAN: Like what?

CHRISTIAN: Like what God is like or if there even is a god. Or what we humans are like, what the whole meaning of life is, whether we're supposed to try to connect with God (or whatever) through action or by withdrawing. And then there's the whole thing about the afterlife. Do we go to heaven, or do we just die and that's it? And what difference does any of this make? You'd be amazed at how different the answers are to those questions.

NON-CHRISTIAN: Whoa. Slow down. Those things are all so theoretical. When it comes to things that are down to earth, like loving your neighbor, all religions agree about that, don't they?

CHRISTIAN: Not really. For example, should we care for people dying in the streets, the way Mother Teresa did, or should we let them die so we don't mess up their karma, the way her Hindu critics did? Or how about this: Judaism says that God chose the Jewish people, the descendants of Isaac, to get the land of Israel. Muslims believe that Allah chose them because they're the descendants of Ishmael, and *they* should get the land (and they call it Palestine!). There's a lot of rocks being thrown at each other because of this disagreement, and they can't *both* be right.

NON-CHRISTIAN: Well, they should just split the land.

CHRISTIAN: That's a great idea! But that's not what either side is saying. If they were to split the land, they'd *both* have to change their beliefs.

NON-CHRISTIAN: What's so bad about that? Isn't compromise a good thing?

CHRISTIAN: Of course it is. But that would mean that they'd have to say, "Hey, we're wrong," and they'd have to say that you, someone who's neither a Jew nor a Muslim, are right.

NON-CHRISTIAN: Now you're mixing religion and politics. You can't do that.

CHRISTIAN: Do you mean that it would be *wrong* to mix religion and politics?

NON-CHRISTIAN: Yes!

CHRISTIAN: So you'd tell someone who mixed religion and politics that they're wrong?

NON-CHRISTIAN: Of course I would.

CHRISTIAN: So you, with your religious perspective—that religion shouldn't be mixed with politics—would tell someone else that their religious perspective—that mixes religion and politics—is wrong?

NON-CHRISTIAN: Hmm. Well, I think no one should *ever* discuss religion or politics. Can we change the subject?

Asking the question, "Can you explain that to me?" helps build the plausibility structure that some things can't be true. People can then search for criteria to determine which things can be true.

Principle Number Three: Some Things Can Be Partially True

Quite often, a non-Christian will tell us that other religions contain truth just as Christianity does and that Christians should not claim any kind of superiority. Jesus was just another guru like Muhammad, Buddha, or Deepak Chopra. How should we respond? Far too often, we try to show all of the flaws in other religions.

We don't need to do that. Nothing is wrong with admitting that other religions get some things right. Again, C. S. Lewis had valuable insight. In *Mere Christianity*, he wrote:

If you are a Christian you don't have to believe that all the other religions are simply wrong all through. If you are an atheist you do have to believe that the main point in all the religions of the whole world is simply one huge mistake. If you are a Christian, you are free to think that all those religions, even the queerest ones, contain at least some hint of the truth. When I was an atheist I had to try to persuade myself that most of the human race have always been wrong about the question that mattered to them most; when I became a Christian I was able to take a more liberal view. But, of course, being a Christian does mean thinking that where Christianity differs from other religions, Christianity is right and they are wrong. As in arithmetic—there is only one right answer to a sum, and all other answers are wrong; but some of the wrong answers are much nearer being right than others.[3]

When conceding that another religion contains truth, we can add the single-word question, "So?"

Someone may tell us, for example, that Buddhists are right about the reality of a spiritual realm and that we should be more aware of the unseen universe. We can say, "I agree," and then add lovingly, not sarcastically, "So?"

Surprised that you didn't attack Buddhism defensively, they might or might not see your point. You can clarify by elaborating, "So? Buddhism's right that there's a spiritual realm. There's still a whole lot more to finding a faith. We need one that meets all of our needs—both in this life and in the afterlife. I think that Buddhism gets some of that right. In fact, we'd almost expect every religion to get some things right. The question is to find the one that gets it *all* right. I have a lot of unanswered questions about Buddhism. Have you studied it very much?"

From there, the conversation can progress past the level of cliché and dig into more satisfying substance.

---

3. C. S. Lewis, *Mere Christianity* (New York: HarperCollins, 1952, 2001), 35.

Asking the question, "So?" helps build the plausibility structure that some things can be partially true without being fully true. As in a court of law, when it comes to finding a faith that meets all of our needs, we must find the truth, the *whole* truth, and nothing but the truth.

Principle Number Four: Some Things Might Be True

I learned this principle from a guy named Bobby. As we sat in the dormitory cafeteria eating lunch, I sensed that his question was sincere.

"Why should we believe what the Bible says about Jesus, or Moses, or anyone else? It's probably been changed so many times over the years. It's just like the game of telephone."

I was well acquainted with the telephone-game analogy. One person decides what message he or she wants to send through several people who are sitting in a line. The first person whispers the message into the ear of the person who's sitting in the next chair. Without repeating it or answering any clarifying questions, the second person passes the message along to the third person, and so on down the line.

The message invariably gets distorted along the way. What begins as "Mary had a little lamb" becomes "Mary had a little ram" and then "Mary had a little Spam," all the way down the line until it's "Harry had a Yiddish ham."

"That's just the way it must be with the Bible, right?" The volume of Bobby's voice was attracting attention. "Who knows how the story of the feeding of the five thousand really happened?"

"Well, that could be one way to explain how we got the Bible," I offered.

He waited for more preaching on my part, perhaps a sermonette about God's holy, infallible Word, a diatribe that he'd heard before. But I just waited for him to consider some alternatives.

"How else could it have happened?" he wondered.

I felt the force of his doubt. Perhaps there was a time when Bobby truly expected answers to his questions. When he first started making his telephone analogy about the Bible, he might have hoped that someone would offer a satisfying response to his challenge. But the more people kept missing his target, the more hardened he became in his unbelief. There was in his voice almost a sense of "I dare you to prove my telephone theory wrong."

So I opted for a partial victory rather than the total one.

"Isn't it possible that the God who first inspired the Bible also preserved it?"

Silence.

"Do you see what I'm asking?"

"Not really."

"Let's just say that there is a God and that He wants to communicate with us. That's possible, theoretically, isn't it?"

"Theoretically."

"And let's just say that He's chosen to do so by inspiring people to write stuff down. The written word does have some advantages over the oral tradition, right?"

"Yeah, I guess."

"So, God inspires people to record certain events that occurred in Jesus's life, or certain messages that Moses preached, or things like that.

"Then, this same God who inspires the words, and makes sure they get written down the way He wants them to, *also* makes sure they stay that way. Isn't that possible?"

"Yes. It's possible."

"That's what I believe happened. The telephone analogy is possible but, as I've looked at discoveries, archaeology, and other things, I think the telephone thing is a less likely explanation of how we got the Bible than the way I've sketched out."

Bobby had more questions. But at least this one had finally been responded to in a way that softened him a little.

"Isn't it possible?" may be one of the most important ways to begin a question. It helps people consider that something *might* be true so that they ultimately can accept that it *is* true. Some of the applications of this phrase might sound like this:

- "Isn't it possible that Jesus did rise from the dead?"
- "Isn't it possible that God did part the Red Sea?"

- "Isn't it possible that the kind of God who parts a Red Sea could also make a virgin have a baby?"
- "If God can suspend the laws of nature in one place, isn't it possible that He could do so anywhere?"
- "Isn't it possible that there really is only one right way to get to God and that all the other ways are 'close but no cigar'?"
- "Isn't it possible that Jesus really is the one who fulfills all of those Old Testament prophecies? That He really is the Messiah?"
- "Isn't it possible that there is a God who exists somewhere but He's beyond your level of knowledge at this point? You wouldn't say that you've got all knowledge, right? Isn't it possible that you could find out something tomorrow that would make a belief in God at least worth considering?"

One caution, however, when dialoguing with the principle of "some things might be true." Rather than leading people to partial acceptance, the dialogue sometimes exposes their level of irrational disbelief. They might be so committed to their position that no amount of evidence or reasoning can sway them.

Such people may be committed to preconceived *un*belief, or blind doubt. They insist that something *isn't* true simply because they've decided it *can't* be true.

Consider the man who thought that he was dead. He was convinced that he'd already died. He declined invitations to dinner, to play golf, or to go anywhere because, he said, "I'm dead."

His friends tried to show him the error of his ways. They brought months' worth of obituary pages to him, none containing his name. He insisted that the editors had missed his passing. His friends did everything they could think of to show him that he was alive, but no amount of evidence could counter his primary assumption.

One friend finally thought of a possibility. "Do dead men bleed?" he asked.

"No," responded the "dead" man.

So he grabbed a pin and pricked the "dead" man's finger. Sure enough, blood came out, and his friends thought that they had now shown to him irrefutable proof that he was alive.

His response exposed his intractability. "I can't believe it!" he shouted. "Dead men *do* bleed!"

Noted philosopher and author Dallas Willard offered this advice for our interaction with such a person: "Often a good starting point when trying to help those who do not believe in God or accept Christ as Lord is to get them to deal honestly with the question: Would I *like* for there to be a God? Or, would I *like* it if Jesus turned out to be Lord? This may help them realize the extent to which what they *want* to be the case is controlling their ability to see what *is* the case."[4]

Not all unbelief, then, is intellectual at its core; therefore, reason alone will fail to sway such unbelief. We would do well to remember Jesus's evaluation: "This is the verdict: Light has come into the world, but people loved darkness instead of light because their deeds were evil" (John 3:19). In his book *Ends and Means*, Aldous Huxley illustrates his own flawed motive for his beliefs:

> I had motives for not wanting the world to have a meaning; consequently I assumed that it had none, and was able without any difficulty to find satisfying reasons for this assumption. . . . The philosopher who finds no meaning in the world is not concerned exclusively with a problem in pure metaphysics. He is also concerned to prove that there is no valid reason why he personally should not do as he wants to do, or why his friends should not seize political power and govern in the way that they find most advantageous to themselves. . . . For myself, as, no doubt, for most of my contemporaries, the philosophy of meaninglessness was essentially an instrument of [political and sexual] liberation.[5]

---

4. Dallas Willard, *Renovation of the Heart: Putting on the Character of Christ* (Colorado Springs: NavPress, 2002), 111.
5. Aldous Huxley, *Ends and Means: An Inquiry into the Nature of Ideals and into the Methods Employed for Their Realization* (Westport: Greenwood, 1970), 270.

Asking a question that begins with "Would you like it if . . . ?" helps expose a flawed plausibility structure—one that says we sometimes believe things because we want to, not because they're true.

Principle Number Five: Somebody Sees the Whole Elephant, or We Can Know the Truth

Some arguments gain authority simply by repetition. The more they're offered as support, the more accepted the arguments become—regardless of how reasonable or unreasonable they might be. The story of the blind men and the elephant is a case in point. It's a favorite in boardrooms and classrooms. Depending on which website you consult, the story is either Hindu or Buddhist in origin and started in India, Pakistan, or somewhere in Africa. It goes like this . . .

A group of blind men wanted to know what an elephant looked like. They found one, and each man zeroed in on a different part of the elephant's body. The one who found its side concluded that an elephant is like a wall. The one who felt its tusk declared that an elephant is like a spear. In turn, each one offered a different description. Holding the tail led to a comparison with a snake, the knee with a tree, the ear with a fan, and so forth. But none of them had access to the entire animal, so none could say legitimately what the whole elephant looked like.

By application, the blind men are likened to followers of different religions. The moral is that no religion can claim to have the whole truth. Something about this call for humility is very appealing. At a university colloquium on conflict resolution, a professor implored emotionally for people of all faiths to stop claiming they have all the answers, and just listen to one another. "If we combine all our insights, together we'll arrive at the truth," he assured us.

The professor's sentiment suggests that no one religion has claim of truth, and that sentiment is expressed well in the last two stanzas of John Godfrey Saxe's nineteenth-century poem "The Blind Men and the Elephant":

And so these men of Indostan
   Disputed loud and long,
Each in his own opinion
   Exceeding stiff and strong,
Though each was partly in the right,
   And all were in the wrong!

So, oft in theologic wars
   The disputants, I ween,
Rail on in utter ignorance
   Of what each other mean,
And prate about an elephant
Not one of them has seen![6]

Although people love this parable and its message of humility, its problem is its own arrogance! The blind men are condemned for claiming to perceive the whole elephant. But the only way the teller of the parable could say that the blind men are wrong is if the *teller* sees the whole elephant—the very thing that he or she says no one can do.

In the process of condemning religious people for being arrogant, the nonreligious person turns out to be the most arrogant of all. Whether uttered by an impassioned professor or a clever poet, the self-contradiction becomes plain to see. Do you hear the tone of Saxe's strong words "utter ignorance" and his conclusion that "all were in the wrong"? Even choosing blind men to be the representatives of religion has a certain condescension to it, does it not?

So when a well-meaning friend tells us the parable of the blind men and the elephant or declares that no religion has the whole picture, we should ask him or her the fifth question: "How do you know that?"

This might be the most important question we can ask because it gets below the surface. It digs into the underlying issue of how we

---

6. John Godfrey Saxe, "The Blind Men and the Elephant," in *The Best Loved Poems of the American People*, ed. Hazel Felleman (New York: Doubleday, 1936), 521–22.

know what we know. Philosophers call this aspect of truth "episte-mology." They would tell us that questions of epistemology must precede questions of content. In other words, determining *how* we know something must come before deciding *what* we know.

Although dialogues of epistemology are important, they are often frustrating. Asking people "How do you know that?" might get a blank stare or a dirty look in response. Few people have ever thought on this level. After a doubter tells "the blind men and the elephant" story, a conversation might sound like this:

NON-CHRISTIAN: You see, different religions are just like all of those blind men. None of them has the whole truth.

CHRISTIAN: How do you know that?

NON-CHRISTIAN: Huh?

CHRISTIAN: How do you know that none of the blind men has the whole truth?

NON-CHRISTIAN: Well, it's just a story.

CHRISTIAN: I know. And it's not a bad one—except I still wonder how the person who first told it could say with such certainty that none of the blind men got it right.

NON-CHRISTIAN: I guess it's because he wasn't blind. What's your point?

CHRISTIAN: My point is that someone sees the whole elephant! In this case it's you.

NON-CHRISTIAN: What's so bad about that?

CHRISTIAN: You're the one who said *no one* sees the whole elephant! That's what's so bad about it. You're breaking your own rule. You're claiming to have more knowledge than any of those blind men. Are you sure you want to make that claim?

One can ask, "How do you know that?" in a variety of ways. Each way can aid in the task of plausibility construction.

- "What makes you believe that?"
- "What convinces you of that?"
- "Where have you heard that?"
- "What is the strongest case for that?"
- "Has someone persuaded you of this perspective?"
- "Have you read some things that have sold you on this?"

The plausibility structure erected by these questions makes a more solid foundation for people's beliefs than just a hackneyed illustration or story.

The great news we proclaim is that God sees the whole elephant. He has told us what it looks like, and that's why we can know the truth! This claim doesn't mean that we know everything. The Bible itself delineates the parameters of our knowledge: "The secret things belong to the LORD our God, but the things revealed belong to us and to our children forever, that we may follow all the words of this law" (Deut. 29:29).

We're not arrogant, then, to claim this level of knowledge. It's only by God's grace that He reveals it to us. He wants us to know it, be enlightened by it, find salvation in it, and build our lives upon it.

This is good news, but in our zeal to share it, we sometimes fail to pave the way for belief. If we want to see people transformed by God's truth instead of being amused by it, we must find ways for them to hear it as something more plausible than the plug theory.

PART 2
WHAT QUESTIONS ARE PEOPLE ASKING?

CHAPTER 4

Why Are Christians So Intolerant?

I was looking for an escape hatch. I felt the pressure building in my chest and wondered how red my face was. As the participants shared who they were and why they were there, I wondered, *Who am I and what in the world am I doing here?*

I'd been invited to the university's Institute for Conflict Analysis and Resolution (ICAR), which sponsored a two-day seminar titled "Conflict Resolution and Religious Proselytizing." When a friend from the program invited me, he said that they were having difficulty attracting evangelical Christians.

"Does that surprise you?" I asked him. "The seminar's title has as much appeal as one on 'How to Stop Beating Your Wife.'"

I agreed to attend but asked my friend to keep working at getting other "proselytizers" to join in the fun. No such luck. As I arrived at the seminar, I met the moderator, who offered a relieved smile.

"We're so glad you're able to make it," he said. "It turns out you're the only evangelical who's able to attend. You're going to provide an important balance."

I politely shook his hand and lied: "I'm glad to be here."

After the thirty-three participants had been seated around the large conference table, we took turns introducing ourselves, sharing why we were there. The first participant gave his Indian name and said, "I'm from the Hindu Council on Interfaith Relations. My purpose in being here is to learn how to stop Christian missionaries from converting people in India. It's an alien religion, and it disrupts our society."

Great start, I thought.

The second participant was an ordained minister and leader in the national "peace movement." He was there to help promote understanding and eliminate the intolerance that "lurks behind" attempts to convert people from one religion to another.

Is it hot in here, I thought, *or is it just me?*

Introductions progressed around the table (I would hear more than half before it was my turn), reflecting a wide range of faith perspectives. The two people before me set the stage for my introduction. The local rabbi was there to learn how to help his congregation's young people resist proselytizers in their schools. The member of the Catholic diocese was there to report on their document stating that Catholics no longer need to evangelize Jews.

Do I identify myself as a Jewish believer in Jesus, I wondered, *or do I play it safe and simply tell them that I'm representing a crusade?* Talk about bad options.

"My name is Randy Newman, and I'm on staff with Campus Crusade for Christ here at this university," I began. "You might guess from that title that we're an evangelistic organization and that the topic of this seminar, proselytizing, is important to us. I'm not crazy about that term, but I guess you could say that I'm here to represent that side of the discussion."

No one looked happy. I deliberately turned so that the rabbi would be out of my peripheral vision for this next part. I decided that it was time for a joke.

"I should tell you, I'm not that crazy about the term *crusade* either. A friend of mine once suggested that we change our name to something equally friendly—like Campus Jihad for Jesus."

This line had always gotten laughs. Today, no one so much as cracked a smile. That's when I wondered about the escape hatch.

"The reason I'm here," I continued in a simple, businesslike manner, "is to learn ways for religious dialogue to take place where all sides get to say what they really believe. I should let you know that this is a very important topic to me because I came to my belief in Jesus from a Jewish background."

Long pause.

The moderator (a Jewish sociologist and the author of a book that argues that Jesus was *not* the Messiah!) broke the silence. He acknowledged that I was the only one representing a group that sought to win converts and so provided an important part of the workshop. I was grateful when the attention turned to the introduction of the next participant, the campus Buddhist chaplain. He had grown up in a Catholic home, tried Protestantism for a while, and now called himself a disciple of the Dalai Lama.

For the next two days, we discussed, debated, and tried to dialogue. The prevailing viewpoint saw proselytizing as unnecessary because all paths lead to the same God. They argued not only that proselytizing was unnecessary but also that evangelism reflects an archaic and unenlightened way of thinking that causes unfortunate amounts of conflict and pain. For two days, I messed up any chance for unanimity.

The Difficulty of This Question

Such a scenario is unusual, but holding the minority opinion on the exclusivity of Christianity is not. As Christians, we follow the One who declared the ultimate in political incorrectness: "I am the way and the truth and the life. No one comes to the Father except through me" (John 14:6). How are we to hold to such a narrow proposition in a day that exalts "openness," "diversity," and "tolerance"?

As the greatest challenge of our day, this question comes not only from theoretical-philosophical types. Instead of the sterile "Is Jesus the only path to God?" we are assaulted by almost everyone with the more potent "How can you believe you're the only ones going to heaven?" The underlying accusation is, "Why are Christians so intolerant?"

This charge packs a punch for at least three reasons. Demographically, more people pose this objection than they do any other. Emotionally, this issue generates more heat than others. (Just as they would not *want* to be a member of the Ku Klux Klan—an organization that thinks that one race is superior to all others—no one would *want* to believe that one religion is superior to all others.) And rationally, most people cannot even begin to comprehend such a position. It seems obvious that along with diversity of skin color, nationality, cultural customs, style of clothing, and flavors of ice cream comes diversity of religion.

"God is too big to be confined to just one religion," they say.

To make things more difficult, Christians find themselves in an equally immovable position. To be a believer of the New Testament is to pledge allegiance to bold proclamations such as, "Salvation is found in no one else, for there is no other name under heaven given to mankind by which we must be saved" (Acts 4:12). When we think deeply about it, we become more convinced of the logical consistency of our position and the contradictions and impossibility of our detractors.

The gap between us and non-Christians seems wider on the issue of exclusivity than on other points of contention. But before defaulting to "What can we say?" it is worthwhile to reflect on the strength of our arguments, the reasons behind those arguments, and the need to *build* our case rather than merely *proclaim* it.

The Strength of Our Arguments

When I was a college sophomore, I read the New Testament for the first time. The Jesus I discovered there was different from the one I'd expected to find. His claims were radical. Why didn't anyone tell me that He was such a fanatic?

It wasn't just His claim of being "the way and the truth and the life" (John 14:6) that struck me. He had the audacity to forgive someone's sins (Mark 2:1–12). He boasted that if you didn't believe in Him, you'd die in your sins (John 8:24) because you were condemned already (John 3:18). He asserted that He existed before Abraham because He was the great I AM (John 8:58 NKJV). He honestly believed that He would live forever (Matt. 28:20) and be in the very midst of people who would believe in Him centuries later (Matt. 18:20). He called Himself the Resurrection and the Life, the Bread of Life, the Good Shepherd, and the Living Water, and He declared unashamedly, "I and the Father are one" (John 10:30).

The more I read of Jesus's claims, the less He seemed merely a rabbi or a prophet. The classifications of megalomaniac or Messiah surfaced as the only likely options.

Then when I read the following words by C. S. Lewis, I felt both good and bad:

> I am trying here to prevent anyone saying the really foolish thing that people often say about Him: "I'm ready to accept Jesus as a great moral teacher, but I don't accept His claim to be God." That is the one thing we must not say. A man who was merely a man and said the sort of things Jesus said would not be a great moral teacher. He would either be a lunatic—on a level with the man who says he is a poached egg—or else he would be the devil of hell. You must make your choice. Either this man was, and is, the Son of God: or else a madman or something worse. You can shut Him up for a fool, you can spit at Him and kill Him as a demon; or you can fall at His feet and call Him Lord and God. But let us not come with any patronizing nonsense about His being a great human teacher. He has not left that open to us. He did not intend to.[1]

I felt good because, in light of all that I'd read in the Gospels, these words made so much sense. I felt badly because I knew that I could no longer stay on the fence. Lewis's paragraph both intrigued and haunted me.

My rabbi told me that Jesus was a prophet. My history teacher told me that He was a rabbi. But after reading the Gospels, I thought that calling Jesus a prophet or a rabbi missed the point by a mile. It would be like calling Babe Ruth an outfielder without ever mentioning those other things that he did in his baseball career (all 714 of them!).

---

1. C. S. Lewis, *Mere Christianity* (New York: HarperCollins, 1952, 2001), 52.

It didn't get any easier for me when I read the rest of the New Testament. In addition to Peter's "no other name under heaven" proclamation (Acts 4:12) are many of Paul's lofty praises of Jesus, the most extensive being this:

> The Son is the image of the invisible God, the firstborn over all creation. For in him all things were created: things in heaven and on earth, visible and invisible, whether thrones or powers or rulers or authorities; all things have been created through him and for him. He is before all things, and in him all things hold together. And he is the head of the body, the church; he is the beginning and the firstborn from among the dead, so that in everything he might have the supremacy. For God was pleased to have all his fullness dwell in him, and through him to reconcile to himself all things, whether things on earth or things in heaven, by making peace through his blood, shed on the cross. (Col. 1:15–20)

"All things were created through him *and for him*." Such things have no place on a mere mortal's resume.

The strength of our argument stems, then, from the weight of the claims made by Jesus and the New Testament writers. If we sound intolerant to relativists, how much more narrow must the New Testament sound!

Many others have spelled out convincing arguments for an exclusive salvation.[2] Central to these arguments in distinguishing Christianity from all other religions is the significance of the resurrection.[3]

As strong as they are, however, these arguments fall mainly on deaf ears if we don't also articulate the reasons behind them.

---

2. Just one of many examples is Paul Little, *Know Why You Believe*, rev. ed. (Downers Grove, IL: InterVarsity Press, 2008), 181–99.
3. See, for example, J. P. Moreland, *Scaling the Secular City* (Grand Rapids: Baker, 1987), 159–83.

The Truths Behind the Arguments

Try asking nonbelievers, "If Jesus is not the only way to salvation, why, then, did He have to die?" You'll likely draw blank stares or create tied tongues. But until one understands the answer to that question, one will not see the reasonableness of Jesus's "I am the way" claim.

That answer must include both of these nonnegotiable truths of the gospel:

1. God is more holy than we think.
2. We are more sinful than we think.

God's holiness is a foreign concept for many non-Christians. *What's the big deal?*, they wonder. *No one's perfect.* People have trouble grasping why God was so hacked off that He demanded the death of His Son.

Fortunately, few people have the nerve just to dismiss God. As a result, when they can't answer our question, they're more likely to listen to a brief explanation such as the following.

"Something within us cries out for goodness and moral purity, doesn't it? We might live in a world that compromises and cheats. But something within us tells us that's not the way it's supposed to be. We want justice and fairness and goodness. The God of the Bible is that kind of God. His most central quality is that of holiness—being absolutely good and right about everything He does. Doesn't that sound appealing?"

The second aspect of the answer, the depth of our sinfulness, needs clarification as well. Although most people are quick to admit that everyone makes mistakes, they can't see what difference it makes. We must show that making a mathematical error in a checkbook is not the essence of sin; cooking the books or cheating someone is!

It doesn't help that some Christians have tried to illustrate sin as an archery term.

"*Sin* is simply missing the mark," they say. "The same Greek word for *sin* is used as an archery term, so we're all just 'target-missers.'"

Well, the same Greek word might be used, but the two concepts couldn't be further apart. When the Bible describes the nature of our rebellion against God, it paints an uglier picture than our simply missing a bull's-eye (see Rom. 3:10–18). Rather than aiming carefully at God's target, we turn our backs and shoot arrows everywhere else. Wanting to please ourselves, we ignore the true bull's-eye and set our affections on seductive targets that cannot satisfy, sanctify, or save. We are not primarily target-missers; we are self-centered false-target worshippers.

I wouldn't suggest saying any of that to a non-Christian, but I would avoid the archery illustration. Following such faulty reasoning, a thoughtful seeker might wonder why God would go to all of the trouble of the cross simply because we aren't spiritual Robin Hoods.

Only the cross takes seriously both God's holiness and our sinfulness. If we could reach God by having our good deeds outweigh our bad deeds (something that is impossible to measure), the Almighty must be a bargain-basement deity. He'll lower His standards to match our final offer.

On the other hand, if some people were able to reach God without Christ's work on the cross, they must have less of a sin problem than those who can benefit from only more drastic measures. To put it the way the apostle Paul did, "If righteousness could be gained through the law, Christ died for nothing!" (Gal. 2:21). It doesn't seem too strong to conclude that either Christ is the *only* way to God or He is *no* way at all.

What We Shouldn't Say About the Only Way

What I've said so far might not convince everyone. But mentioning these reasons might build plausibility for exclusivity, which might otherwise sound ridiculous. Consider the alternatives to those reasons.

When asked if Jesus is the only way, some Christians only turn up the volume: "Absolutely! He's the way, the truth, and the life. He said it, I believe it, and that settles it."

Others simply sound sarcastic: "Well, Jesus isn't just another choice on the menu! Check out Buddha's or Muhammad's or some other religious leader's tomb. Is it empty? No. But is Jesus's body in His tomb? Nooooooo."

And some Christians have compromised. Frustrated by the difficulties of the minority position, they've developed a more palatable message. A friend recently told me, "I've had a lot of success in evangelism by saying something like this: 'Nobody's religion is perfect, and no one has the whole truth. Every religion contains some truth and some falsehood. So what we need to pursue is a faith that humbly admits that it doesn't know everything.'"

I can see why people find this approach less objectionable. But somehow I think that Jesus would object! This sounds more like the "blind men and the elephant" story than anything I read in the New Testament. This kind of faith has no stumbling block. Nor does it have any compelling reason to believe it. And the tragedy is, like any other false gospel, it cannot save. Just because it's less offensive doesn't mean that it's the answer to the question of intolerance.

How Do We Say "One Way" When People Say "No Way"?

When people get stuck at "There can't be just one way to God," we must use dialogues as a crowbar. These dialogues must have three elements: surprise, despair, and gradual progress.

Fairly convinced that Christians are narrow-minded bigots, skeptics expect us to try to sell Christianity as the best product on the market. They assume that we'll do so while describing the intensity of the flames of hell. They shake their heads in amazement and call us "spiritual Neanderthals." (That's what one rabbi, speaking on a popular television show, called a Southern Baptist pastor for believing that Jews need to believe in Jesus.) We have to say something that makes them do a double take.

Depending on your level of chutzpah or the closeness of the friendship, you might try something like this:

NON-CHRISTIAN: I can't believe you're so intolerant as to believe that Christianity is the only way.

CHRISTIAN: What's so bad about intolerance?

NON-CHRISTIAN: What's so bad about intolerance! Are you crazy? It leads to hatred and racism and—how can you be so ridiculous?

CHRISTIAN: You sound pretty upset.

NON-CHRISTIAN: Well, of course, I'm upset.

CHRISTIAN: Actually, you sound intolerant.

NON-CHRISTIAN: What!

CHRISTIAN: You sound intolerant of my intolerance.

NON-CHRISTIAN: I'm not intolerant.

CHRISTIAN: Everyone's intolerant of something. We have to be. Wouldn't you say that you're intolerant of some things? I would hope so.

Or

NON-CHRISTIAN: I can't believe you believe that Christianity is the only way.

CHRISTIAN: Then why do you think Jesus said such a narrow-minded thing?

NON-CHRISTIAN: I don't think Jesus was narrow-minded.

CHRISTIAN: Me neither. Why do you think that He claimed the things He did about Himself? He was the one who said that He's the only way to God.

NON-CHRISTIAN: Are you sure He said that, or is that just something His followers made up?

CHRISTIAN: No, I'm really sure that He said those things. It's not just a few isolated phrases either. He said, "I am the way and the truth and the life," and He implied similar things many other times.

[Some slowly dispensed doses of Scripture and apologetics could prove helpful here.]

NON-CHRISTIAN: Well, I don't understand the Bible all that well. I don't know why Jesus would say those things.

CHRISTIAN: Would you like to hear what I think He meant?

Or

NON-CHRISTIAN: What's so great about Christianity that makes it the only way to God?

CHRISTIAN: Well, I think it's a voice of humility in an age of arrogance.[4]

NON-CHRISTIAN: Humility! What's so humble about claiming to be the only right way?

---

4. I am indebted to Tim Downs for this argument. His views about evangelism have been significant in shaping my thinking. Tim Downs, *Finding Common Ground* (Chicago: Moody, 1999).

CHRISTIAN: Let me ask you a question. Do you think you're going to heaven?

NON-CHRISTIAN: I guess. I'm not totally sure.

CHRISTIAN: Do you think everyone goes to heaven?

NON-CHRISTIAN: I'm not sure of that either.

CHRISTIAN: Do you think that everyone *deserves* to go to heaven? Do you think that Hitler is in heaven?

NON-CHRISTIAN: No. I guess he's not. And I guess some other people go to hell.

CHRISTIAN: Why do you think that *you're* likely to go to heaven?

NON-CHRISTIAN: Well, I'm a pretty good person. I've never killed anyone.

CHRISTIAN: So, you'll get to heaven because you've been pretty good, but some people will go to hell because they've been pretty bad?

NON-CHRISTIAN: Yes. I think so.

CHRISTIAN: So, you think that you're better than the people who go to hell?

NON-CHRISTIAN: Hmm. I guess.

CHRISTIAN: You see? That's why I say that Christianity is a voice of humility in an age of arrogance. I think that your belief is pretty much what most people think. But Christianity says that *no one* is good enough to get to heaven.

NON-CHRISTIAN: No one?

CHRISTIAN: No one. The only way people get to heaven is by accepting a gift—not by earning a reward. That's humble. Thinking that you deserve to go to heaven is arrogant.

Dialoguing to the Point of Despair

Once we've caught people by surprise, we should dialogue with them until they're at the point of despair. They must come to the painful realization that their notion of how people get to heaven (i.e., being good enough, never killing anyone, treating others nicely, etc.) doesn't work. No one is ever that good. God will never be that compromising. Their foundation must crumble before they'll consider rebuilding.

Consider Jesus's example. After His dialogue with the rich man in Mark 10, He said to His disciples, "How hard it is for the rich to enter the kingdom of God!" (v. 23). To give His lesson some punch, He added, "It is easier for a camel to go through the eye of a needle than for someone who is rich to enter the kingdom of God" (v. 25).[5] Jesus led the disciples right to the point of despair, made evident when they said to each other, "Who then can be saved?" (v. 26). They had to see that no amount of riches (material or religious) could save anyone. Only then could they hear the message of grace: "With man this is impossible, but not with God; all things are possible with God" (v. 27).

A dialogue that leads gradually to despair might sound like this:

---

5. Appealing to a little-known "fact" of a short gate in a city wall known as the "eye of a needle," some people have argued that a camel would have to get down on its knees to fit through it. Thus, by application, only by getting down on their knees (i.e., humbly repenting, removing any excess baggage, giving away all except the barest of necessities, etc.) could the rich enter the kingdom of heaven. Gordon Fee and Douglas Stuart rightly dismiss this interpretation. We have no solid archaeological evidence for any such gate. Nor do we have any written record of this interpretation until the eleventh century AD. Most significantly, this interpretation misses Jesus's point completely. If this is what Jesus meant, why would any of His hearers be "amazed at his words" and wonder, "Who then can be saved?" See Gordon D. Fee and Douglas Stuart, *How to Read the Bible for All Its Worth* (Grand Rapids: Zondervan, 1993), 21.

NON-CHRISTIAN: I just can't believe that you think that Christianity is the only way.

CHRISTIAN: I can't believe that there's any other way that works!

NON-CHRISTIAN: Why not?

CHRISTIAN: I can't see how *anyone* can get to heaven!

NON-CHRISTIAN: You don't think that *anyone's* good enough to get to heaven?

CHRISTIAN: No. Do you know anyone who has kept all of God's commandments?

NON-CHRISTIAN: Well, no . . . but nobody's perfect.

CHRISTIAN: Exactly! Why in the world should God let *anyone* into heaven? Or, better yet, if God did let sinful people into heaven, what kind of a god would He be?

NON-CHRISTIAN: You don't think that someone like Mother Teresa is in heaven?

CHRISTIAN: I'm not so sure that she thought she was good enough.

NON-CHRISTIAN: Really?

CHRISTIAN: No. She talked pretty openly of her sinfulness.[6]

NON-CHRISTIAN: Wow. So, if Mother Teresa's not good enough—

---

6. A balanced, short biography of Mother Teresa illustrates this point in David Aikman, *Great Souls: Six Who Changed the Century* (Lanham, MD: Lexington Books, 2002), 191–249.

CHRISTIAN: That doesn't bode well for you or me.

NON-CHRISTIAN: This sounds terrible. You really don't think that Mother Teresa's in heaven?

CHRISTIAN: That's not what I said.

NON-CHRISTIAN: Yes, you did.

CHRISTIAN: I said that Mother Teresa isn't *good enough* to get into heaven.

NON-CHRISTIAN: You're giving me a headache.

CHRISTIAN: There's a difference between being good enough to get into heaven and being in heaven for some other reason.

NON-CHRISTIAN: Like how?

CHRISTIAN: Like God's grace. That's the only way anyone gets into heaven. If you have to be good enough, and even Mother Teresa wasn't, then no one's getting in.

I'll admit, this is a difficult process. But for people who are unmoved by any other presentation of the gospel, this might be the way for them to see the Way.

Here are a few other possible responses to the same type of accusation:

NON-CHRISTIAN: How can you believe that your way is the only way?

CHRISTIAN: Well, you believe that *your* way is the only way, don't you—the way that says that exclusive ways are wrong?

Or

NON-CHRISTIAN: How can you be so intolerant as to believe that Christianity is the only way?

CHRISTIAN: Is your intolerance better than mine?

Or

NON-CHRISTIAN: Don't you think that *all* religions are true?

CHRISTIAN: You certainly don't believe that, do you? *All* religions? Surely you think that some of them are wacko?

Or

NON-CHRISTIAN: Don't you think that all religions are just different roads that lead up to the top of the same mountain?

CHRISTIAN: Maybe. They might *lead* that way. The question is, "Do they all make it to the top?"

No Way to Avoid "One Way"

I was told about a certain powerful church leader who, when asked about his job's frustrations, replied, "Everywhere the apostle Paul went, they had a riot. Everywhere I go, they serve tea."

We'd rather find some pleasant middle ground, wouldn't we? We don't want our neighbors to think that we're intolerant, but neither do we want them to deem our message irrelevant. Isn't there some way to be winsome without being wimpy?

We do need to strike a balance. But maybe there's no way to avoid the charge of intolerance. By showing respect, listening, and showing compassion, we must remove every stumbling block except the one—the cross. There still remains the thing that got Jesus into hot water. Maybe there's no way to avoid a "one way" mess.

I wrestled with that possibility as the ICAR conference that I mentioned at the beginning of this chapter came to a close. Trying to arrive at some point of resolution, our moderator asked a final question: "In light of all that we've discussed these past two days, how can religious proselytizing take place without conflict?"

Hands went into the air. Suggestions started flying. You can imagine the pleas for tolerance, acknowledgment of truth in all religions, and so forth.

"I don't think we *can* eliminate conflict," I blurted out.

Our moderator asked me to explain.

"Maybe we've got an unrealistic goal. I'm not opposed to some of these suggestions. My religious tradition emphasizes that all people, no matter what they believe, are created in the image of God. So we always should show respect, listen well, and validate each other. When some religions explain their stand, there could very well be no conflict at all. But with Christianity, I'm afraid conflict is inevitable."

I checked to ensure that people were with me.

"A lot of religions have a message that sounds like, 'Try this. You might like it,' or 'This could help you achieve success and peace,' or 'You're okay. This will help you improve.' But evangelical Christianity says, 'You're *not* okay. You shouldn't just try this. You have to believe it or you're lost.' That makes it a message that always sparks conflict. After all, Jesus bothered people everywhere He went."

There was another long pause.

This time, the silence was broken by the Buddhist chaplain.

"I think he's right. Whenever I put up a poster about some Buddhist activity on campus, no one gets upset. Every time an evangelical group puts up a poster, it gets torn down, or people tell the university to stop them. I don't think Christians are doing anything wrong. I just think the nature of their message makes some people hostile."

I had the sense that the two-day conference was a success.

Before people benefit from the good news, they're likely to be bothered by the bad news. If our goal is to avoid conflict, we need a different message. If, on the other hand, our goal is to be truthful (something more difficult than open-minded) and loving (something far better than tolerant), then we have the perfect message and the ideal model of how to proclaim it.

What About Those Who Have Never Heard?

Sometimes the topic of intolerance leads people to inquire about the fate of those who've never heard the gospel. Although the question has no easy answer, the asking reveals that the logic of the gospel is getting through to the questioner.[7]

People pose this question as a smoke screen, an expression of confusion about the gospel, or a sincere inquiry about God's fairness. A few sample dialogues might prove instructive.

Scenario 1: The Question Posed as a Smoke Screen

Some questioners really don't care about those who've never heard. They just want to get themselves off the hook by poking holes in our faith. Turning the question around is appropriate.

Non-Christian: What about all those people in parts of the world that never hear this? Is God going to send them to hell just because they never had anybody tell them?

Christian: What do you think?

Non-Christian: I don't know. You tell me!

Christian: Do you think God would just say, "Tough luck"?

Non-Christian: No. I think God is fairer than that. But you said Jesus is the only way.

---

7. For a full treatment of the theological issues behind this question, see J. Robertson McQuilkin, "The Narrow Way," in *Perspectives on the World Christian Movement: A Reader*, ed. Ralph D. Smith and Stephen C. Hawthorne (Pasadena, CA: William Carey Library, 1981), 127–34.

CHRISTIAN: I agree with you that God is fair. So I'd think that God takes these kinds of things into account.

NON-CHRISTIAN: But that's not what you said. You said, "The only way—"

CHRISTIAN: I know. But I'm not so sure that God has told us everything about how He takes care of every situation. I don't think He needs to. I'm sure that He'll do the right and fair thing. What He has made clear is how He'll judge people who have heard and have decided that they didn't want any part of Jesus.

NON-CHRISTIAN: That makes sense.

CHRISTIAN: So, how about you? You've heard about Jesus. What do you think about Him?

SCENARIO 2: THE QUESTION EXPRESSING A NEED FOR CLARIFYING THE GOSPEL

NON-CHRISTIAN: If what you say is true, what's going to happen to people who've never heard about Jesus?

CHRISTIAN: What do you think?

NON-CHRISTIAN: I don't know. It sounds like they're going to hell. But that doesn't seem fair.

CHRISTIAN: I think you're right that fairness is part of the issue. My understanding of the Bible is that God will judge people on what they *do* know, not on what they *don't* know.

NON-CHRISTIAN: That seems fair.

CHRISTIAN: But people know more than we think!

NON-CHRISTIAN: What do you mean?

CHRISTIAN: Let me first make sure that we're talking about the same thing. Let's step back and talk about God's judgment in general. Do you think anyone goes to hell?

NON-CHRISTIAN: Yes. I think that some people deserve to go there.

CHRISTIAN: So do I. Why do you think so?

NON-CHRISTIAN: Because they've done evil things or they've killed someone or something like that.

CHRISTIAN: Anything else?

NON-CHRISTIAN: Lots of things, like stealing or cheating.

CHRISTIAN: Would you say that the Ten Commandments cover a lot of it?

NON-CHRISTIAN: Yeah.

CHRISTIAN: Me too. Have you ever broken any of the Ten Commandments?

NON-CHRISTIAN: I don't know. I don't think so.

CHRISTIAN: I know I have. I've taken the Lord's name in vain. I've put some things higher than God on my priority list.

NON-CHRISTIAN: Where's that in the Ten Commandments?

CHRISTIAN: It's the very first one! "You shall have no other gods before me."

NON-CHRISTIAN: Uh-oh.

CHRISTIAN: Yeah. Me too. And if I take seriously the stuff Jesus said, then I'm guilty of murder and adultery too. He said that hatred or lust in our hearts is the place where murder and adultery begin.

NON-CHRISTIAN: So how does anyone get to heaven?

CHRISTIAN: Not by being good enough! If that were the case, heaven would be empty. I certainly don't think there'll be any bragging when people stand before a holy God.

NON-CHRISTIAN: I'm confused.

CHRISTIAN: Sorry. I didn't mean to mix you up. I just think that what the Bible says about grace is so important.

NON-CHRISTIAN: Grace? What do you mean by that?

CHRISTIAN: I'll tell you. But I don't want to ignore your question about those who haven't heard about Jesus. Let me tell you how I think anyone gets to heaven, and then we'll go back to people who haven't heard. How's that?

SCENARIO 3: THE QUESTION POSED AS A SINCERE INQUIRY ABOUT THE FATE OF THE UNEVANGELIZED

NON-CHRISTIAN: It sounds like you're saying that anyone who hasn't heard about Jesus is going to hell. That doesn't sound fair.

CHRISTIAN: You're right. It doesn't. But maybe there's another way to look at this question.

NON-CHRISTIAN: How?

CHRISTIAN: Your question presupposes two things. One is that there actually is a message to hear. The second is that some people haven't heard it.

NON-CHRISTIAN: Right.

CHRISTIAN: The Bible would say yes to the first presupposition—there is a message to be heard. But the Bible would say no to the second presupposition—there really aren't any people who haven't heard it.

NON-CHRISTIAN: You've got to be kidding me. There are millions of people who haven't heard about Jesus.

CHRISTIAN: Let's take one thing at a time. The Bible says there certainly is a message that everyone must hear. I'd summarize it in four points.

1. There is a loving, righteous, knowable God.
2. There's something about us that separates us from that God.
3. God has provided a means to reconcile us—Jesus's death on the cross.
4. Each person needs to trust in that means of reconciliation for him- or herself.

NON-CHRISTIAN: I agree that summarizes the Christian message. I don't know if I buy it, but I think it's accurate. But how can you say that everyone's heard that?

CHRISTIAN: Don't get ahead of me. Make sure that you see what's behind this message. God has provided the means to reconcile people to Him. It's not people earning their way to God based on what they do. This is what distinguishes Christianity from all other religions.

NON-CHRISTIAN: I see that.

CHRISTIAN: The Bible says that every single person on the planet already knows the first two points of this four-point outline. They see evidence of God in nature or in their own hearts [see Rom. 1:19–20; Ps. 19:1–2; Acts 14:15–17; Eccl. 3:11].

NON-CHRISTIAN: Okay. But what about points three and four?

CHRISTIAN: This requires a little bit of putting two and two together. But I think the Bible says that everyone either rejects or accepts points one and two. People look either at the stars or in their hearts and wonder, "Is there some kind of Creator behind it all?" or they don't. They also look in their own hearts and say either "I'm in trouble" or "I'm okay."

NON-CHRISTIAN: Where are you getting this from?

CHRISTIAN: I think that the best place to study this is in the first two chapters of Romans in the New Testament. Maybe you should read it for yourself before we continue this conversation.

NON-CHRISTIAN: I will read it. But I'd like you to go on.

CHRISTIAN: Okay. I think that these two chapters argue that some people reject this little amount of revelation (that there is a God and that we fall short of His perfection) by suppressing it. If that's true, then it's not God who rejects them but they who reject God. It says that they are without excuse.

NON-CHRISTIAN: Why would they suppress it?

CHRISTIAN: For the same reason that anyone rejects God. He's holy, and we're not. We'd rather not deal with a God who makes demands on us. That's why people like other gods—the ones that aren't so holy or so demanding, or the ones that say we're not accountable.

NON-CHRISTIAN: Okay. Stop preaching. Suppose they don't suppress it?

CHRISTIAN: I don't think God explicitly tells us how He's going to handle every situation, because that's His job, and He doesn't need to consult with us on anything.

NON-CHRISTIAN: That's a good way of putting it.

CHRISTIAN: It makes sense to me if I think of it like this: revelation rejected brings darkness; revelation received brings light.

NON-CHRISTIAN: You might have lost me there.

CHRISTIAN: If people reject the first two points of revelation, God is simply giving them what they ask for—a life separated from Him. Darkness. They'll stay in darkness unless something radical happens. But for the people who say, "Yes, there must be something bigger than me, and I don't match up," I think God will get the rest of the story to them.

NON-CHRISTIAN: If they say yes to points one and two, he'll send them three and four?

CHRISTIAN: Yes.

NON-CHRISTIAN: Where does the Bible say that?

CHRISTIAN: Lots of places in the Bible say things such as, "You will seek me and find me when you seek me with all your heart" [Jer. 29:13], or "You, LORD, have never forsaken those who seek you" [Ps. 9:10; see also 1 Chron. 28:9; 2 Chron. 15:2; 16:9; Ps. 145:18; Luke 19:10].

NON-CHRISTIAN: So, how does God get points three and four to them?

CHRISTIAN: Most of the time it's through other people, but God is also capable of bringing the rest of the story any way He wants—through visions or dreams, for example.

NON-CHRISTIAN: Or other religions?

CHRISTIAN: I don't think so. If those other religions proclaimed these four points, well, then they wouldn't be other religions—they'd be Christianity! If they proclaimed something else, they'd be saying that it was some form of self-effort. That's exactly the opposite of Christianity.

NON-CHRISTIAN: Buddhism is self-effort?

CHRISTIAN: Yes. You achieve Nirvana by meditation or some other discipline. Every religion says some form of "Do this and you'll get there." They might describe "there" differently, and they have different lists of what to do, but it's all self-effort.

Non-Christian: Okay. You already gave me that works-versus-grace sermon.

Christian: The bottom line is that I don't really know how God will get points three and four to someone, but His usual plan is for people to tell people. That's why there's so much in the Bible about people going all over the world to announce this message. That's why I'm telling you all of this.

Non-Christian: I think I'll have to read that book of Romans.

CHAPTER 5

Why Does a Good God Allow Evil and Suffering and Things Like Pandemics?

A s I began to write this chapter, our world was re-engulfed in yet another wave of the COVID-19 pandemic, the latest in an ongoing series of strangely named variants. We all thought that by this time we'd be finished with mask-wearing, social distancing, and canceling travel plans. We're also hearing reports of out-of-control wildfires, record shattering heat waves, terrorist attacks, and sexual abuse charges that seem to never end.

The so-called problem of evil has always been a difficult question for Christians.[1] Our critics have called it the Achilles' heel of our faith. "How can a good God allow such evil and suffering?" It's the ultimate *why* question. There will always be people who'll want to know, "Why?" We must answer them and not just by regurgitating what someone might write on a Philosophy 101 exam.

Over the course of more than twenty years as a campus minister, I've conducted a lot of surveys. As freshmen move into their new homes away from home, many of us ministers have stood outside dormitories, asking new students to take a few moments to fill out a short questionnaire. It's been a good way for us to identify those students who are interested in joining a Bible study or those who are willing to talk and to hear our presentation of the gospel.

---

1. Portions of this chapter originally appeared in Randy Newman, "Living Without an Answer," *Discipleship Journal*, September/October 2002: 28–34.

To find out what issues we should address on campus, we started including this question: "If you could ask God any one question, something that has never been answered to your satisfaction, what would you ask?"

Some of the answers have been funny—obvious attempts to avoid our question: "Why didn't You make the Packers win the Super Bowl this year?" "Why did You make men so stupid?" "Why are women so hard to figure out?"

Some of the questions were attacks: "Why do You let Christians hand out surveys outside my dorm?"

Most noteworthy to me, though, was the trend that occurred over the years. When we began to ask this question, the most frequent responses were intellectual inquiries about religion: "Why does the Bible have so many contradictions in it?" "Why are there so many religions if there's only one God?" "How can we know what You are like?"

Years later, the temperature got hotter. The tone became more hostile, as reflected in the various wordings of the most frequently asked question: "Why do Christians think theirs is the only right way?;" "Why are Christians so intolerant?;" "How can you think that you're the only ones going to heaven?"

That lasted only a short time, although I'm sure that the sentiments still linger. Most recently, the question that most often appears on our survey addresses the problem of evil, the ultimate *why* question: "Why do some people suffer so much?" "Why does a good God allow things such as COVID or cancer?"

Many of the questions were worded more personally: "Why did my grandmother die of COVID?" "Why is my aunt dying of cancer?"

Although the handwriting on some of the surveys was almost illegible, the emotions behind the words were starkly clear.

The Nonanswers That Some Christians Offer

How are we—followers of Christ and people who say that God is good—to respond when people ask why bad things happen? Whether the question is expressed as "How can a good God allow evil and suffering?" or "Where is God during the pandemic?," the challenge is formidable.

Many of the so-called answers don't work. Or they really don't address the question the way it deserves to be answered—by delving into the depths of intellectual confusion as well as empathizing with the pain of despair.

Do we say that we live in a fallen world and that things are not as God intended? Surely this is true. But why are some people affected by the fallenness of our world so much more than others? Why do some parents make regular commutes with their child to cancer treatments while other parents have carefree drives with their children to soccer practices or clarinet lessons?

Do we say that we inherited the consequences of sin from our spiritual forebears, Adam and Eve, and that's why evil happens? Again, I wonder why the consequences of that day in the garden of Eden seem, in our world today, so random and arbitrary.

One well-meaning Christian circulated an email attempting to explain "where God was on September 11, 2001." It proclaimed that God was very busy that day—keeping a lot of people off the flights, delaying a lot of people in traffic so they didn't get to the World Trade Center, and so forth. Even more than twenty years after that horrific day, such "explanations" seem moronic. This was supposed to comfort people and attract nonbelievers to the gospel? What kind of weak god is that—a god who tried his best to stop this tragedy but came up short?

I could go on, citing other answers that have been offered. Each one would prove more shallow than the last.

The truth is, we don't have an adequate answer for the problem of evil. No one does. We simply must have the honesty to admit it. That's what we'd do if we were to take seriously what God has revealed to us in the book of Job.

The Nonanswer of Job
Of all of the possible ways to address the existence of evil, to help us cope with this most difficult topic of life (what C. S. Lewis called

"the problem of pain"), God gave us the book of Job. Job seems to be, at first glance, an odd way to answer our question. It's a book of poetry, not of philosophy; it records dialogues filled with emotions rather than diatribes packed with proclamations, a barrage of questions rather than a series of answers. And it's long. And it still doesn't answer our question.

Consider the fact that it's poetry. Poems are not what most of us turn to for answers. We turn to them for comfort, strength, or inspiration. If we were in Job's place, we wouldn't have asked for a poetry reading. We'd have demanded quick, rational explanations for what was happening to us. We'd have wanted God to tell us in no uncertain terms (just as Job demanded) why we were going through that hell. We wouldn't have wanted a book like Lamentations—poetic, emotional, and slow-moving. We'd have wanted a document that read like the book of James—blunt, clear, and to the point.

But God didn't give us that kind of document. He gave us poems. He gave the nation of Israel the book of Lamentations—one extensive poem—to help them process their national grief when their beloved (but neglected) Jerusalem was destroyed. He gave us the book of Job to do the same thing on a personal level.

So in reading the book of Job, we *feel* on a greater level than we comprehend. Don't your emotions plummet with Job's when you read the following words?

> Why did I not perish at birth,
>   and die as I came from the womb?
> Why were there knees to receive me
>   and breasts that I might be nursed?
> For now I would be lying down in peace;
>   I would be asleep and at rest
> with kings and rulers of the earth,
>   who built for themselves places now lying in ruins,
> with princes who had gold,
>   who filled their houses with silver.

Or why was I not hidden away in the ground like a still-
born child,
like an infant who never saw the light of day? (3:11–16)

Don't you feel the depths of his emotion when he tries to quantify
his pain?

If only my anguish could be weighed
and all my misery be placed on the scales!
It would surely outweigh the sand of the seas—
no wonder my words have been impetuous.
The arrows of the Almighty are in me,
my spirit drinks in their poison;
God's terrors are marshaled against me. (6:2–4)

Don't you feel his desperation as he acknowledges his sin while
making a plea for God to be merciful? Sure he has sinned, he freely
confesses. But does this level of punishment really fit the crime?

If I have sinned, what have I done to you,
you who see everything we do?
Why have you made me your target?
Have I become a burden to you?
Why do you not pardon my offenses
and forgive my sins? (7:20–21)

This is not the place in Scripture to formulate a theology of forgiveness. It *is* a place to realize how the processes of confession and
intercession feel. It's also a place to cultivate intense emotions about
the misuse of theology. Don't you feel like slugging Job's idiot friends
after they offer such horrible words as, "Does God pervert justice?
Does the Almighty pervert what is right? When your children sinned
against him, he gave them over to the penalty of their sin" (8:3–4)?

Job felt intense indignation toward them! And so should we. If we
don't feel the power of his sarcasm, we've missed the point in responses

such as, "Doubtless you are the only people who matter, and wisdom will die with you!" (12:2).

When people simply respond to pain with cold, calculated statements of theology, they deserve the title that Job gave his friends—"miserable comforters" (16:2). And God's evaluation of their theological expertise was even less flattering: "I am angry with you . . . because you have not spoken the truth about me, as my servant Job has" (42:7). And I think that God wants us to feel what Job felt when he asked his friends, "Will your long-winded speeches never end? What ails you that you keep on arguing?" (16:3).

Consider, too, that the book of Job is a series of dialogues. Surely, God could have inspired a writer to address this topic in the style of an elaborate, well-crafted argument—like the book of Romans. Instead, the drama consists of cycles of interchanges between Job and his friends. The cycles are marked by a great deal of repetition—almost painstaking repetitions. Nor are the cycles balanced. The third cycle is not as complete as the previous two, as though it got interrupted.

And then comes a disturbing exchange with a fourth friend, Elihu. In some ways, it's similar to the exchanges with Eliphaz, Bildad, and Zophar. Yet this last exchange is different than the others. It's hard to tell what we should think and feel about Elihu. The effect is one of confusion. Consequently, a great deal of debate has occurred in commentaries about whether Elihu was correct (as the other three men surely were not).

Rather than sounding like the fine-tuned drama that we'd prefer, these dialogues combine to more resemble a series of recordings from psychotherapy sessions.

And maybe that's exactly how the book of Job is supposed to sound. Maybe God gave us this magnificent book not so we'd impress philosophers with erudite answers, but so we'd process grief and come through it as Job did—with a stronger faith, a humble heart, and a hand held over our mouths (see 40:4). We lie on the couch, so to speak, with Job and travel with him through a process of argument, despair, self-examination, defense, lamentation, philosophizing, anger, and a host of other honestly expressed emotions to which his friends were oblivious. We come to incomplete conclusions, disturbing realizations, and frustrating dead ends. (That's my best guess, by the way, as to why Elihu seems partly right and partly wrong. In the midst of processing pain, some of our thoughts are correct and others aren't. The presence of Elihu embodies that dichotomy.)

That God "answers" Job with questions rather than answers is an appropriate climax to a book that processes more than it proclaims. God's is the monologue that trumps all previous dialogues. To be sure, that God holds the superior hand is frustrating. But the greatest need we have, when we insist upon God justifying Himself, is not an intellectual explanation. We need to be put in our place. So God graciously gives us questions—several of which could have been worded, "Who do you think you are?"

We've set a mental stopwatch, giving God a deadline by which to explain Himself. But on and on goes the inquisition, ticking off the seconds, ticking away at our demands. God persistently asks; we eventually kneel. Don't you feel that effect in your soul as He asks, "Where were you when I laid the earth's foundation? Tell me, if you understand. Who marked off its dimensions? Surely you know! Who stretched a measuring line across it?" (38:4–5). On and on He goes, asking more than seventy questions over the course of four chapters (38–41). Why? Because it takes that long for us to get off our high horse.

Apparently, God *doesn't* want us to know why bad things happen to good people because He doesn't tell us. Our expectations always rise when we get to the end of the book and we read that God appeared to Job in a whirlwind. Surely now He'll tell Job about that cosmic bargain that He struck with the devil back in the first two chapters. That glimpse into the heavenlies (a glimpse, it must be noted, that Job never sees!) makes the problem only more baffling. God was the one who suggested Job as a target for Satan's attacks. "Have you considered my servant Job?" he posed to the devil—not once, but twice (1:8 and 2:3). And God's repeated description of Job was that he was "blameless and upright" (1:1 and 1:8).

Perhaps that puzzling opening sequence is why the book is so long.

It has to be. God wants us to be strengthened to handle suffering, not informed so we can explain it. And that takes time. Given the complexity of the question of evil (which becomes more vexing, not less so, after reading Job), no wonder the book is as long as it is. Job finally declares, "My ears had heard of you but now my eyes have seen you" (42:5). His declaration confirms that, more than the answer to the ultimate *why* question, God wants us to know the answer to the ultimate *who* question.

In effect, then, the book offers us a choice. Will we choose to respond to life's trials and pains as Job's wife recommended: "Are you still maintaining your integrity? Curse God and die!" (2:9)? Or will we follow Job's example and proclaim, "Though he slay me, yet will I hope in him" (13:15)?

Partial Answers That Are Nonanswers

When I couldn't stand watching TV anymore after September 11, I read, instead, the book of Job. I sobbed with him, raged with him, put my hand over my mouth with him. Although frustrating, I learned there's wisdom in living without an answer. In addition, it's humbling. It brings our very finiteness to the surface of our souls. It reminds us we are *not* God! Although painful, we must repent of our insistence for an answer, seeing the very demand as a form of idolatry.

The difficulty of living without an answer can cause us to do what Job's friends did—offer a partial answer as if it were the whole answer. Consider, though, what the Bible does teach us about the problem of evil. It gives us slivers of a pie chart. One tiny sliver (and I'm convinced that it's no more than that) would be labeled, "We live in a fallen world." Another sliver would say, "There is a devil." Other tiny slivers would be labeled, "People have free will," "Sin has consequences," "Sometimes God disciplines His people," or "Good can come out of suffering."

Perhaps there are more slivers. I tire even writing them because they offer such little consolation. A large segment of the pie chart (if you could quantify such things) would be labeled in bold, bright letters, "WE DON'T KNOW." I have found tremendous strength in Tim Keller's insight:

We do not know the reason God allows evil and suffering to continue, or why it is so random, but now at least we know what the reason is not. It cannot be that he does not love us. It cannot be that he does not care. He is so committed to our ultimate happiness that he was willing to plunge into the greatest depths of suffering himself. He understands us, he has been there, and he assures us that he has a plan to eventually wipe away every tear. Someone might say, "But that's only half an answer to the question 'Why?'" Yes, but it is the half we need.[2]

However we choose to word our answer, we must not imply that one of the slivers is the whole pie. Our "answer" must sound and feel like it's 25 percent sliver, 75 percent "I don't know." If our words have no Job-like angst, we'll sound more like Job's friends and receive a similar response.

Other Nonanswers

Living without an answer can lead us to another mistake—stating things that are blatantly untrue. Insisting upon answers can lead us to wrong conclusions. Rabbi Harold Kushner's best-selling book *When Bad Things Happen to Good People* falls into this trap. Demanding an answer for why his son suffered and died so tragically, he concluded that "God can't do everything" and we need to "recognize his limitations . . . [and] forgive him for not making a better world." Rabbi Kushner concludes his book with this seemingly holy but actually self-righteous question: "Are you capable of forgiving and loving . . . God even when you have found out that He is not perfect?"[3]

Even Job didn't stray so far from orthodoxy. He concluded his search with the words, "I know that you can do all things" (Job 42:2). The rabbi's book has a sense of comfort in it—at first. But that

---

2. Timothy Keller, *Walking with God through Pain and Suffering* (New York: Dutton, 2013), 121.
3. Harold Kushner, *When Bad Things Happen to Good People* (New York: Schocken Books, 1981), 134, 148.

comfort soon wears off, and the pain of having such a pitiful God leads to insurmountable despair. No one should trust such an impotent deity. If God were so powerless, contrary to so many statements in Scripture, the better advice to follow would be that of Job's wife: "Curse God and die!" (2:9).

Living without an answer has led some people to even worse options than offering untruths—they offer utter nonsense. Well-meaning friends, desperate to say anything to people in pain, do more harm than good. To a mother who lost her son to a shark attack off the Virginia Beach shoreline, a "friend" said that God had taken her son because He needed another angel. This was supposed to bring consolation? Who would want to worship such a needy god!

But living without an answer should not lead us to silence.

A friend of mine related what happened in his church on the Sunday after a tragic event. After a time of singing hymns and offering prayers for the victims and their families, the pastor climbed the few steps to the pulpit for the sermon. He stood there in silence for a moment and then said, "I have nothing to say." He then sat down.

The effect was dramatic and powerful. But isn't that taking things too far? Such a response ends up in hopelessness, a place of non-Christians. Hasn't God indeed spoken to us in our pain? Although He didn't give us all of the answers we demanded at the end of Job, He is not silent. Hasn't He given us Psalm 23, Lamentations 3, a host of lament psalms, the assurances of Romans 8:28, and a litany of comforting Scriptures about our promise of heaven and eternal life? It would have been far more dramatic and truly helpful for that pastor to say, "I have nothing to say. But God has spoken. Hear the word of the Lord," and then read the Holy Scriptures for the rest of his sermon.

Although we live without an answer, our partial understanding is better than anything that any nonbiblical worldview has to offer.

Answering a Different Question

So when people ask us (or our own souls cry out within us), "How could a good God allow such a thing?" we need to ask a different question—one that points to the pain behind the question. Then we won't rush to utter things that we shouldn't—things that are incomplete, untrue, or foolish.

How much better it would be for us to respond with the words, "I wish we knew." After a pause to grieve, sigh, and even shed tears along with the questioner, we could ask, "Can you tell me what you're feeling right now?" By answering the question with a question, we would be showing the person that we care. Later, we could add, "There are some things I *do* know about God and life that help me at times like these. Would you be interested in hearing them?"

There are other questions that we might pose:

- "What have you found to be helpful in handling such difficult things?"
- "What has brought you hope during this trial?"
- "Do you have the kind of faith that has helped you deal with this?"
- "Some people have been comforted by praying during these times. Have you?"
- "I've been praying for you. Would you mind if I prayed with you right now?"

In the case of someone who's dealing with the death of a close friend or relative, we could ask the bereaved person to tell us about the deceased. Smiling over a funny story about the loved one, or asking the bereaved to relate a favorite memory, or just saying, "She sounds like a great person; I wish I had met her" could be a way to set the stage for the answers we really want to convey—later!

We would do well to follow Billy Graham's example. When he spoke to the grieving families after the Oklahoma City bombing, he found that elusive balance between the known and the unknown. After comforting people with the assurance of God's knowledge, power, and care, he plainly answered the ultimate *why* question with those three great words, "I don't know." But then he added:

Times like this will do one of two things: they will either

make us hard and bitter and angry at God, or they will make
us tender and open and help us reach out in trust and faith.
. . . I pray that you will not let bitterness and poison creep
into your souls, but you will turn in faith and trust in God
even if we cannot understand. It is better to face something
like this with God than without Him.[4]

That last statement suggests that living without an answer can be
liberating. Once we let go of our idolatrous demand for intellectual
satisfaction, we're set free to seek God for comfort, hope, healing,
peace, and, most importantly, salvation. When our friends ask us
the ultimate *why* question, that's what they really need. And that's
an answer we *can* give them.

Not everyone who asks the ultimate *why* question ("Why does a
good God allow evil and suffering?") wants an answer. Sometimes
their question is an attack. Often fueled by anger or by a need to justify
themselves, their question is not a real question.

My high school friend Ned poses these nonquestions to me regularly
via email. I hadn't heard from him in almost twenty years when the
wonders of the internet enabled him to find me. Our telephone reunion
went toward spiritual things after catching up about marriage (I am
married; he's living with a woman), children (we have three sons; he
"would never bring children into this world"), and careers (I'm in ministry; he's a New York City policeman). I told him the most significant
thing that happened in my life since we saw each other last was my
coming to faith in Christ. He responded, "As a New York City cop, I've
seen too much evil to ever believe in a god." He continues to send me
email, restating his unbelief. I continue to ask him how he explains
the horrors he sees. He never answers my questions.

I'm convinced that he doesn't want to answer them. His question is
really a smoke screen to hide his refusal to humble himself before God.
With the smoke screen in place, he feels shielded from conviction of

4. Robert Torricelli and Andrew Carroll, eds., "The Reverend Billy Graham, After the Okla-
    homa City Bombing, Offers a Sermon on the 'Mystery of Evil,'" in *In Our Own Words*
    (New York: Kodansha International, 1999), 414–15.

sin. Smoke screens work—for a while. As we seek to bring the gospel to questioners, we must be careful to treat their smoke screens as such rather than as real questions.

We are regularly tempted to answer the ultimate *why* question with evidence for the existence of God. After all, there's a lot of it. There's cosmological evidence, teleological evidence, ontological evidence, christological evidence, and just plain logical evidence. We'd love to jump into our dump truck full of apologetics, back it up, and bury someone with proof. Rarely, however, does that approach work.

In some cases, answering people's questions with content that they really don't want only solidifies their unbelief. Consider the pair of seemingly contradictory exhortations in Proverbs 26:4–5. The first one warns us, "Do not answer a fool according to his folly, or you yourself will be just like him." But the second one tells us, "Answer a fool according to his folly, or he will be wise in his own eyes." No wonder people have considered these two statements as evidence of a contradiction in the Bible. The fact that they occur one after the other, however, could argue for just the opposite conclusion. In rabbinic style, they show two sides of the same coin.

We should *not* answer fools according to their folly (i.e., using their style of expression) in a derogatory, argumentative tone, for example. The result would be a shouting match between two people who disrespect each other. Such a display of godlessness is fitting for a fool but not for a follower of a gracious God. Other types of foolish responses include reacting to sarcasm with more of the same, replying to ad hominem attacks with even worse slander, or employing any kind of flawed logic in our arguments simply because our opponent does so. Increasing the percentage of "fooldom" does little to advance the kingdom.

On the other side of the coin, we *should* respond to a fool's question "as his folly deserves" (v. 5 NASB1995). Failure to do so could make the fool feel good about his or her foolish position, reinforce it, and make the fool even less open to considering the truth that could set him or her free.

At times, it's best to lob the question—that is really an attack—back at the questioner so that he or she will see the true motive behind the question. Granted, that's difficult. Responding in kind with a lack of respect or worse is an easy trap to fall into. Nevertheless, when a person's choice of words or tone of voice tells you that he or she isn't looking for an answer, it's best not to give one.

Imagine, for example, that someone asks, "In light of the Holocaust, you don't honestly believe in a god, do you?" It might be best to say, "You mean you don't?" and let your tone of voice convey the despair to which atheism should lead someone in the shadow of the Holocaust.

Or imagine someone says, "I suppose that your God would just heal you if you got cancer!" It might be appropriate to say, "Well, what would *your* god do in that case?"

This kind of evangelism doesn't sound like the normal kind—the kind that's smooth and soft-spoken, like a well-oiled insurance policy sales pitch. But note how Jesus dealt with the Pharisees. I prefer His method over the sales pitch when dealing with people who are merely looking to justify their unbelief.

Jesus had good reason to warn us, "Do not give what is holy to dogs; and do not throw your pearls before swine, or they will trample them under their feet, and turn and tear you to pieces" (Matt. 7:6 NASB1995).

Better than answering skeptics' nonquestions would be putting them on the defensive, asking how they'd answer their own question. In other words, how do they, as atheists or agnostics or skeptics, explain the Holocaust, earthquakes, or terrorists' attacks?

Allen, president of the Atheist Student Association at a major university, was confronted with just such a question by Barry, leader of a Christian organization at the same school. Their two organizations were sponsoring a debate about the existence of God. Each side had booked a speaker to represent that side's perspective. The meeting between Allen and Barry had focused on logistics—room setup, publicity, ushers, audiovisual equipment, and so forth.

Then Barry asked Allen to share his atheist testimony.

"So how did you become an atheist?" he posed. "Were you raised in any kind of religious household?"

"Yes," Allen began. He was from Iran and was raised in a strict Muslim household. But then his uncle was diagnosed with cancer. As Allen watched his beloved uncle deteriorate before his eyes, his faith in Allah or any other god deteriorated as well.

Barry empathized before pursuing further discussion. "That must have been horrible for you. I'm so sorry. I guess you were very close to your uncle?"

"Yes, I was." Allen was still sad about the loss.

"So your uncle's sickness and death convinced you that the Muslim explanation for death was inadequate, is that right?" Barry clarified.

"Yes."

"And I guess that you ruled out other religious explanations as well—Christian, Jewish, and so forth."

"Yes."

"So what's your atheistic explanation for your uncle's death? How do you, as an atheist, cope with such a terrible thing?"

Allen was caught off guard. It was as if no one had ever posed that question to him. Had he even wrestled with it himself?

"Well, if you'll pardon the expression, it's like the bumper sticker says, 'Stuff happens.'" (His word choice was, of course, a bit different.)

Barry reflected a balance of respect and shock—respect for the person, shock at the shallowness of the answer. Allen was, after all, a philosophy major, and Barry expected his answer to be more substantive. But then again, maybe there's no substantive answer from an atheistic worldview.

"That's it? That's your answer for why your uncle died such a painful death? Does that really satisfy you? Does that give you any comfort?"

"There is no comfort; but yes, that's my best answer."

Barry was gracious but forceful.

"I know that the Christian answer isn't as satisfying as I'd like it to be—either intellectually or emotionally. But my answer is better than 'stuff happens.'"

Again, this kind of evangelism is different from what most Christian guidebooks suggest. But when folly is displayed, it's best to ensure that the fool is not left feeling "wise in his own eyes."

One must remember, too, some cautions. Francis Schaeffer—the great apologist, preacher, and founder of L'Abri in the 1960s—has much to teach us as we pursue evangelism in the days before us. His words are just as relevant today as when he wrote them:

> As I seek to do this, I need to remind myself constantly that this is not a game I am playing. If I begin to enjoy it as a kind of intellectual exercise, then I am cruel and can expect no real spiritual results. As I push the man off his false balance, he must be able to feel that I care for him. Otherwise I will only end up destroying him, and the cruelty and ugliness of it all will destroy me as well. Merely to be abstract and cold is to show that I do not really believe this person to be created in God's image and therefore one of my kind. Pushing him towards the logic of his presuppositions is going to cause him pain; therefore, I must not push any further than I need to.[5]

Yet the process of dialogue and questioning can help clarify the real issue. Often, when someone asks, "How can you believe in a god who allows evil?" the real question is something else. It could be, "Why should I *follow* a god who allows evil?" If asked to elaborate, the person might say, "You Christians talk a lot about worshipping this god, loving him, following him, serving him. Why? Why do you think it's a good idea to follow a god who doesn't answer your most difficult question? And, of all things, why do you let him call the shots about how you should behave, what morals you should adhere to, and who you should sleep with, for crying out loud?!" This is the real question behind some people's atheism, agnosticism, or skepticism.

Nonbelievers hear philosophical defenses for the existence of God and, after a while, they might offer a partial surrender: "Okay. So there is a god. So what? Who cares? Maybe there is a god; maybe

---

5. Francis A. Schaeffer, *The Complete Works of Francis A. Schaeffer: A Christian Worldview*, vol. 1, *A Christian View of Philosophy and Culture* (Westchester, IL: Crossway Books, 1982), 138–39.

there isn't. I don't know. I don't think anyone can know. It just seems so irrelevant to me."

Now what?

You've convinced them that their atheism/agnosticism is intellectually bankrupt, but they're no closer to saving faith than before the debate began. Is there something truly *compelling* that can draw them to Christ? I believe there is.

If we've correctly identified their true question, graciously shown them the logical end to their worldview, and humbly expressed to them that we don't have all the answers, then we're ready to say, "Here's what I *do* know that compels me to follow this God.

"I don't know why God allows evil things to happen, but I'm glad that He did allow one evil thing to happen—He allowed Jesus to die on the cross. That was, from the human perspective, an evil thing. He was an innocent man who died at the hands of angry, threatening people. This is fact. We know that it happened. And we also know that three days later, this Jesus rose from the dead. I could prove this to you with historical, archaeological, and other kinds of evidence, but I won't take the time to do so now. This one historical fact that we *do* know outweighs, for me at least, the many other things that I don't know about God.

"From God's perspective, this was a good thing. Because Jesus rose from the dead, I know there's life after death for those who follow Him. That guarantee of eternity makes the pains of this life seem a bit more bearable. As the New Testament says, 'I consider that our present sufferings are not worth comparing with the glory that will be revealed in us' [Rom. 8:18]. What I know outweighs what I don't know.

"As a result, I think that having hope makes more sense than having bitterness. I think that believing in God is better than cursing Him. I think that having Jesus's name on my lips as my Savior and Lord is better than having His name on my lips as a swear word. I think that joy fits reality better than despair does, and assurance of eternal life fits better than the fear of death. I think that basing that assurance on the historically factual events of the cross and the resurrection is better than any kind of false, psyched-up crossing of my fingers. I think that following and obeying Christ and His morals produces a much better life than following my desires, my hormones, or my sinful fantasies."

Would anyone listen to such a long tirade? Maybe not. But even if we deliver only a part of this message, we've given nonbelievers an answer better than the one they gave us. We've offered an answer to a different question than the one they posed, but it's the answer that they really need.

CHAPTER 6

What Do Christians Have Against Science?

The game of baseball changed forever on August 16, 1920. Before that date, pitchers ruled over hitters with numerous techniques of deception. In addition to varying the speed of pitches and putting a variety of spins on them, they had another trick up their sleeves: They "dirtied up" the baseball to make it harder to see. Using anything—dirt, licorice, tobacco juice—they made the ball darker and darker as the game wore on. Back then, baseballs were not replaced during a game as often as they are today. A single baseball might have lasted an entire game. As you can imagine, by the time of the later innings (when the sun was setting and shadows were growing), if a batter could even see the ball at all, he was lucky. Strikeouts increased as the ball's visibility decreased.

Until that day in August of 1920. That's when Ray Chapman, a shortstop for the Cleveland Indians, stepped into the batter's box and got hit in the head with a pitch he never saw coming. The sound of impact was so loud, it caused spectators to think the ball had struck his bat. The pitcher thought so as well, fielded the ball, and threw it to first. But Chapman took two steps toward first, then collapsed, "blood running from both ears, and died a few hours later."[1] From that day on, any ball that showed even the slightest amount of scuffing, dirt, or wear got tossed from the game and replaced with a bright, new, clean, easily seen, carefully inspected baseball. The game of baseball has never been the same.

---

1. Geoffrey C. Ward and Ken Burns, *Baseball: An Illustrated History* (New York: Alfred A. Knopf, 1994), 153.

In a similar way, the "game" of evangelism has changed dramatically since the start of the seemingly never-ending COVID-19 pandemic. Whether we like it or not, whether it's fair or not, or whether the facts support it, many (perhaps most) non-Christians assume evangelical Christians are anti-science, anti-vaccine, and have made a difficult situation worse. (White Evangelical Christians are less likely to get vaccinated than any other religious group.[2]) Some non-Christians assume that becoming a Christian requires them to also become a stupid Neanderthal (with heavy doses of climate-change denial thrown in).

Again, I want to stress that this may not be fair on their part. I'll leave that debate for other writers and researchers to sort out. And I certainly won't attempt a thorough treatment of the history and complexity of the tensions between science and religion.[3] But, for the sake of a chapter in a book on evangelism, I must offer some insight about how we can use conversations about science to point people to the gospel. I should add that this chapter may not be sufficient for Christians trained and employed in the sciences or at academic institutions. What I offer here is for nonscientists to engage with other nonscientists. Heavier lifting can easily be found elsewhere.[4] A little bit of reading can go a long way toward helpful, friendly conversations with scientifically minded non-Christians.

Evangelist and writer Glen Scrivener suggests that the three most frequent objections to the gospel today fall into the categories of sex, suffering, and science.[5] I believe his insight should help us prepare

2. Ian Lovett, "White Evangelicals Resist Covid-19 Vaccine Most Among Religious Groups," *The Wall Street Journal*, July 28, 2021, https://www.wsj.com/articles/white-evangelicals-resist-covid-19-vaccine-most-among-religious-groups-11627464601.

3. One helpful and balanced (in my opinion) resource is Lawrence M. Principe, *Science and Religion* (Chantilly, VA: The Teaching Company, 2006).

4. Some important contributors that I consult and trust are John Lennox, Alister McGrath, and Ian Hutchinson. I have also benefited from materials at The Veritas Forum's website: www.Veritas.org.

5. Glen Scrivener, "Help Them Imagine: The Need for Creativity in Evangelism," The Gospel Coalition Podcast, November 6, 2020, https://www.thegospelcoalition.org/podcasts/tgc-podcast/help-them-imagine-the-need-for-creativity-in-evangelism/, accessed September 20, 2021.

for these kinds of discussions and shed more light than heat onto already hot debates.

Our Firm Foundation

Let me begin with what some may consider a controversial claim. Christians should love science. How could we, who love the Maker of the heavens and the earth, not celebrate the systematic, diligent, communal investigation of the world God made?

To allow this wonder-filled truth—Christians should love science—to soak in, let's reflect on Psalm 19. The poetic beauty and theological depth of this masterpiece flows in three stanzas. The first rejoices in God's world where "the heavens declare the glory of God." The second stanza continues the doxology, marveling at God's Word which is "more precious than gold." Finally, a third stanza seeks to prompt an appropriate response.

Read the text slowly and allow it to enlighten both your heart and your mind. Feel the force of the notion that God's general revelation in the skies and his special revelation through the Scriptures[6] are worthy of deep inquiry and reflection.

The heavens declare the glory of God;
    the skies proclaim the work of his hands.
Day after day they pour forth speech;
    night after night they reveal knowledge
They have no speech, they use no words;
    no sound is heard from them.
Yet their voice goes out into all the earth,
    their words to the ends of the world.
In the heavens God has pitched a tent for the sun.
    It is like a bridegroom coming out of his chamber,
like a champion rejoicing to run his course.
    It rises at one end of the heavens

---

6. I am indebted to the poetic commentary of Derek Kidner on this Psalm, "The Skies, the Scriptures," in his brilliant *Psalms 1–72* (Downers Grove, IL: InterVarsity Press, 2008), 97, of the Kinder Classic Commentaries.

and makes its circuit to the other;
    nothing is deprived of its warmth.

The law of the LORD is perfect,
    refreshing the soul.
The statutes of the LORD are trustworthy,
    making wise the simple.
The precepts of the LORD are right,
    giving joy to the heart.
The commands of the LORD are radiant,
    giving light to the eyes.
The fear of the LORD is pure,
    enduring forever.
The decrees of the LORD are firm,
    and all of them are righteous.

They are more precious than gold,
    than much pure gold;
they are sweeter than honey,
    than honey from the honeycomb.
By them your servant is warned;
    in keeping them there is great reward.
But who can discern their own errors?
    Forgive my hidden faults.
Keep your servant also from willful sins;
    may they not rule over me.
Then I will be blameless,
    innocent of great transgression.

May these words of my mouth and this meditation of my heart
be pleasing in your sight,
    LORD, my Rock and my Redeemer.

The main point I want to drive home is that God's physical world—
something studied by the sciences—points to its Creator, should elicit

praise, and invites further investigation and appreciation. Science is one very important way of praising God and enjoying him forever. We must not miss the way this psalm comes to a close. You might expect, after such lofty praise for God's world and His Word, to hear the psalmist urge us to worship the Source of both revelations. We expect, "So, let us praise him all day long" or some other exultant admonition. But no! What comes next in the third stanza of the psalm is confession of sin! Staring at the stars in the sky and the sentences in the Scriptures should urge us to "put [our] hand over [our] mouth" (see Job 40:4), ask for God's forgiveness, and keep us from "willful sins."

Christians should love science. And science should lead us to worship. But science should also keep us in our place. Honest scientists, while celebrating their discoveries, should also humbly add, "But there's so much more we do not know. We have just scratched the surface."[7]

I remember hearing a noted astronomer who, together with a team of more than a hundred other brilliant researchers, tell of their excitement of "their" satellite orbiting Pluto. The spacecraft had been traveling for over a decade to get to that destination over three billion miles from earth. For years, they awaited the data that would come back to the Naval Research Laboratory in Washington, DC. Dozens of them camped out there for almost a month, with little sleep, to discover what they would discover. The accomplished astronomer told his audience how "surprised" they were—many times. They were wrong in many of their predictions and astonished by things they never anticipated. "Keep your servant from willful sins" indeed!

Science Grows from the Soil of the Scriptures

If we love science as much as I'm suggesting we should, we'll find we're not the first people of faith to do so. Philosopher Paul Copan summarizes, "The Christian faith is a knowledge tradition that once furnished a unifying vision that helped advance Western civilization,

---

7. For two enjoyable and informative explorations that include many refrains of "we just don't know," consider Bill Bryson's *The Body: A Guide for Occupants* (New York: Anchor, 2019) and *A Short History of Nearly Everything* (New York: Broadway Books, 2003).

education, and science."[8] We follow a long line of scientists who researched "to the glory of God."

Consider just a few.

Astronomer Johannes Kepler wrote, "Those laws [of nature] are within the grasp of the human mind; God wanted us to recognize them by creating us after his own image so that we could share in his own thoughts."[9]

Michael Faraday, groundbreaking researcher in the field of electromagnetics, wrote, "I cannot doubt that a glorious discovery in natural knowledge, and the wisdom and power of God in the creation, is awaiting our age, and that we may not only hope to see it, but even be honoured to help in obtaining the victory over present ignorance and future knowledge."[10]

Philosopher Del Ratzsch, whose work focuses on the relationship between science and religion, claims that "the literature is huge," that supports the notion that many scientists believed God was the one to aid them in their work, "involving Newton, Kepler, Boyle, Descartes, Maxwell, Faraday, Mersenne, Von Helmont, and others."[11]

These scientists and many others assumed scientific research could yield reliable results because the universe was created by an intelligent God who built everything through logically sound, verifiable principles and laws. This same God gave people, created in his image, the kinds of brains that could pursue such inquiry, understand findings, and build upon previous discoveries through rational thought. Science grows in the soil of Christianity. Systematic study fits with a worldview built upon the foundations of a personal, knowable, reasonable, revealing God.[12]

---

8. Paul Copan, "Science Is No Enemy of Christianity," The Gospel Coalition, January 28, 2019, https://www.thegospelcoalition.org/reviews/scientism-secularism, accessed September 27, 2021.

9. Carola Baumgardt, Johannes Kepler Life and Letters (New York: Philosophical Library, 2008), 50.

10. Bence Jones, The Life and Letters of Faraday, vol. 2. (London: Longmans, Green and Co., 1870), 385.

11. Del Ratzsch, "Science and Religion," in The Oxford Handbook of Philosophical Theology (Oxford: Oxford University Press, 2009), 74.

12. To explore this theme deeply, from a philosophical perspective, see Alvin Plantinga, Where the Conflict Really Lies: Science, Religion, and Naturalism (Oxford: Oxford University Press, 2011).

In discussions of science and religion, Galileo frequently gets mentioned as the best example of the church's abhorrence and rejection of science. Galileo disagreed with the Catholic Church's teaching that the sun revolved around the earth and argued for the opposite—that the earth revolved around the sun, as Copernicus had previously argued. Professor of History and Science Lawrence Principe warns, "Although often presented as a simple 'conflict' of religion against science, it is actually extremely complex, involving intellectual, philosophical, political, social, and personal clashes that far transcend in scope, interest, and importance any simplistic (and usually propagandistic) science-versus-religion readings."[13]

Here are just a few salient points to keep in mind if your conversation partner mentions Galileo.

- First, he wasn't imprisoned or tortured for his beliefs. If people have heard this, they should question their source of information.[14]
- Second, the Catholic Church at that time based their doctrine on a flawed interpretation of passages like Joshua 10:12. Poetic language such as this verse uses about the sun standing still should not be pressed to provide scientific explanations of the movements of the sun, stars, and planets. Even conservative interpreters of the Bible who employ a "literal" reading of the Bible allow for nonliteral readings of poetic parts of the Bible.
- Third, and to my mind, most significant, Galileo remained a Catholic for the rest of his life. While he disagreed with specific interpretations of a few passages of Scripture, he clung to his belief in God and love for the way God made his world.
- Fourth, Galileo wasn't right about everything. He argued strongly for how tides were formed and worked—and he was completely wrong![15]

13. Lawrence M. Principe, *Science and Religion* (Chantilly, VA: The Great Courses, 2006), 17.
14. Maurice A Finocchiaro, "That Galileo Was Imprisoned and Tortured for Advocating Copernicanism" in *Galileo Goes to Jail and Other Myths About Science and Religion*, Ronald L. Numbers, ed. (Cambridge, MA: Harvard University Press, 2009), 68–78.
15. See Principe's *Science and Religion* 17–24 and corresponding lectures.

One more important data point in the science-religion dialogue is that nonreligious people tend to see more of a conflict than religious people. According to recent research by the Pew Research Center, "Highly religious Americans are less likely than others to see conflict between faith and science." They found that the least religiously observant are most likely to say science and religion are often in conflict. Only 30 percent of people who attend religious services "at least weekly" think there's a conflict while 73 percent of people who "seldom or never" attend religious services say there is a conflict.[16]

It is important to remember that a common assumption does not necessarily line up with individuals you may know. Pew also found, while a majority of the public (59 percent) believe there is a conflict between science and religion, less than one-third say their personal religious beliefs conflict with science.

At the same time, we may need to look out for (and point out) that some pro-science people hold their views with an amazing amount of, dare we say, religious fervor. Thomas Nagel, an atheist and professor of law at New York University, wrote:

> I want atheism to be true and am made uneasy by the fact that some of the most intelligent and well-informed people I know are religious believers. It isn't just that I don't believe in God and, naturally, hope that I'm right in my belief. It's that I hope there is no God! I don't want there to be a God; I don't want the universe to be like that.[17]

Some Unwanted Discoveries

Scientific inquiry often yields mixed results. Some findings are good. Some are unwelcome. As we delve into this discussion of science and faith, we must acknowledge that Christians have not always behaved well. Despite the biblical and historical bases for Christian enthusiasm for science, some of our history isn't so pretty.

---

16. "Religion and Science," Pew Research Center, October 22, 2015. https://www.pewresearch .org/science/2015/10/22/science-and-religion, accessed September 27, 2021.
17. Thomas Nagel, *The Last Word* (Oxford: Oxford University Press, 1997), 130–31.

A great amount of Christian history followed a pattern of rigorous intellectual attacks against orthodox theology followed by equally rigorous intellectual defense. In the era of the church fathers, heretics denied the deity of Christ. The church responded with theologically rich statements like The Apostles' Creed and The Nicene Creed to separate orthodoxy from heterodoxy. In a later era, some questioned the way the church related to the world and proposed radical retreat into isolation. Augustine responded with careful, thorough, complex thought in his definitive *The City of God*. And challenges to the doctrine of salvation by faith alone (among other things!) were met with the intellectual, rigorous works of Martin Luther, John Calvin, and others during the Reformation. Intellectual attacks were responded to with intellectual defenses.

But another set of challenges, after the so-called Enlightenment, were not responded to with the same intellectual rigor as in previous struggles. In the early twentieth century, during what many have called "the fundamentalist-modernist controversy," the Christian church faced a barrage of attacks on numerous fronts. Humanistic psychology, philosophical skepticism, literary criticism of the Bible, and Darwinian evolution were met with more retreat than defense. Fundamentalist isolationists seemed to reply with a nonreply almost as strong as, "Your questions are not worthy of our answers." I admit I am painting with a broad brush and overstating my point for effect. But many church historians acknowledge that the early twentieth century spawned a kind of anti-intellectual Christianity that differed starkly from the previous nineteen centuries and sparked a distrust of science and other intellectual pursuits.

To be fair, I must add that the evangelical movement of the 1930s and 1940s, spearheaded by Carl F. H. Henry and others, reengaged intellectually rigorous faith and pushed for active dialogue with the best of contemporary scholarship. They reasoned, if God gave us such wonderful brains and revealed himself through general revelation, Christians could devote themselves to the best of intellectual inquiry, including the sciences. But we still have a long way to go to overcome the anti-intellectual brand of Christianity of the 1920s.

The Limits of Science

To prepare ourselves for helpful conversations about science, we need to understand two important terms: scientism and self-refuting. Scientism is an overstatement of the power of science and claims that science can explain everything. Sometimes it is stated as, "Science is the *only* way to know things" or, as a slightly less extreme version, "Science is the *best* way to know things."

A statement is self-refuting if it contradicts itself or states something that cannot possibly be true. As discussed in chapter 3, if I said to you, "I cannot speak or write a single word in English," that would be a self-refuting statement. How could I write or say that sentence in English if I cannot speak or write a single word in English! (By the way, didn't my explanation of why that statement was self-refuting seem unnecessary and possibly even annoying? And yet, when it comes to showing that scientism is self-refuting, the explanation is very necessary and may take several attempts before people admit their flawed thinking. Ask God for patience as you walk through this difficult territory.)

I will try to express that scientism is self-refuting numerous times and from numerous perspectives because it may be a difficult concept. Indeed, I find that when talking to friends who hold the view of scientism (whether they know that term or acknowledge its influence on their thinking), I need to say what I'm about to say several times in a variety of ways before people get it. Sometimes they claim, "I only believe things you can prove scientifically. You can't prove scientifically that God exists. That's why I don't believe in God."

Please hear me carefully. This is not because people are stupid. It is because our world has been immersed in scientism for so long, it is difficult to see its power to shape us. It's like asking a fish how it likes the water they're swimming in. The fish might very well reply (if fish could talk, of course), "What's water?"

So here are some attempts to show that scientism is self-refuting. You'll need to practice this and come up with your own wording. Don't be surprised if this takes a bit of back-and-forth conversation rather than a one-statement pronouncement.

- You say we cannot know anything unless we can prove it in a laboratory. But that statement cannot be proved in a laboratory.
- You say science is the best way to know things. That sounds like a philosophical assumption and not a scientific discovery.
- The belief that science is better than faith sounds like a faith belief.

Maybe asking some questions might be better than making statements. For example:

- You say that science is the only way to know things. How do you know that?
- Science is better than faith? Is that something you can prove in a laboratory?
- Isn't belief in science a kind of faith assumption? It sounds like you and I are both people of faith. You have faith in science and I have faith in the God who makes a world where science makes sense. Does that make sense?

Allow me to summarize what I've been saying so far. Christians should love science but Christians should reject scientism because it is self-refuting.

A Strategy for Science-Faith Conversations

Here is a suggested four-stage strategy for helpful conversations about science and faith.

First, do no harm.

Resist the temptation to start with condemnations of scientists who have overstated their case or made nasty, sarcastic comments about Christians. If ever there was a time to "turn the other cheek," it's now. Resist as well, during the early stages of the conversation, the temptations to point out the limits of science, its failures, and biggest blunders.

You may need to acknowledge that some Christians have said

foolish things about science, climate change, vaccines, evolution, the age of the earth, or some other hot-button issue. As much as possible (without compromising your own integrity and beliefs) try to distance yourself from the voices that have said anti-intellectual or foolish things about science. You may even want to say that some of that behavior does not fit with Christian teaching of humility, kindness, and thoughtfulness.

Tell your friend why you love science and are thankful for the amazing advances science has made. Try to express that, as a Christian, you love the way God made this world so that scientific exploration is possible. Find ways to sound enthusiastic and positive rather than critical and negative, so that you might surprise your nonreligious friend. The goal of this stage is to have your skeptical conversation partner think, "Hmm. Maybe I need to give this guy a chance. He doesn't sound like an idiot. Perhaps there are other ways to think about this."

Second, call for complexity.

Science, by its very nature, sees and explores complexity. Christian faith, which makes claims on all of life and is revealed through very rich Scriptures, also sees and explores complexity. Yet much of the interaction between science and faith has sounded remarkably simplistic—on both sides. We all have a tendency to see ourselves as complex, multifaceted, nuanced, unique individuals while pigeon-holing others into simplistic, monodimensional categories. If you're thinking, "Oh, he's a scientist. All those scientists are the same" and he's thinking, "Oh, she's a Christian. All those Christians are the same," you're both heading for an unproductive exchange.

In this early stage of interaction, allow the problem to become messier before offering ways to clean it up. Science explains much but still finds a lot of mystery and unknowns. Faith helps in many areas but still has some unanswered questions—even for the most devout. The goal at this stage of the conversation is for both sides to move toward listening and away from pontificating. Now may be the time to ask questions like, "What aspects of science do you find most intriguing?" or "Which fields do you think need the most exploring today?" or "If you could read more in a particular field of study, what would that be? Why is that?"

Third, strive for humility.

A fair reading of the past shows ample display of arrogance and overstatement on both sides of the science-religion debate. Both sides should acknowledge failures in the past as well as limits of their fields.

Science can tell us a lot. But it can't explain all. Religion can tell us a lot. But it can't explain all. A frequently quoted illustration for science's limits asks the question why the water in Mrs. Jones's teakettle is boiling. A scientific answer would be that the heat from the stove transfers through the metal of the teakettle, which then transfers to the water inside the kettle. Then, because the boiling point of water is 212 degrees Fahrenheit, when the water reaches that point, the water boils. Science could explain what happens to the water molecules when they reach that point, how water is made up of hydrogen and oxygen in the important 2:1 ratio, stated as H_2O, and could explain much more about the nature of water, etc.

But, from another perspective, the answer to the question, "Why is the water in Mrs. Jones's teakettle boiling?" might be, "Because Mrs. Jones wanted some tea." Science could never arrive at that answer. We need other methods of investigation than scientific ones.

We could also point out the limits of religion to explain all or help in some areas of life. In case you haven't picked it up by now, I'm a big fan of science and I have more than intellectual curiosity as the basis for my enthusiasm. When I was only fifty-one years old, I had a heart attack and needed a stent put into one of my coronary arteries. Science saved my life. Since then, I've had two other "procedures" (isn't that a nice euphemism for "life-saving emergency surgery"!) to alter my cardiac hardware. I am grateful that the surgeons consulted the best and most up-to-date scientific writings before applying their healing arts to my body. I would be encouraged if I heard that the medical staff all read their Bibles the morning of my surgery. But I hope they would have consulted more than God's Word for insight about cardiac care. The Bible could tell them *why* they should devote themselves to healing people (all people are made in the image of God and, therefore, to be treated with dignity and honor, all human life is precious, etc.). But the Bible could not tell them *why* to put the stent into my circumflex artery instead of into my left anterior descending artery.

Pro-science people need to admit we still don't know a lot of things. People of faith need to admit God hasn't told us all we'd like to know. (Meditate a bit on Deuteronomy 29:29: "The secret things belong to the LORD our God, but the things revealed belong to us and to our children forever, that we may follow all the words of this law.") The goal of this stage is to see a change in the temperature of the conversation. If both sides can consider that, perhaps, science and religion can work in complementary fashion, our knowledge of the world and our lives can expand. Don't be surprised if this takes time.

Fourth, bring in some experts.

As mentioned above, this chapter is geared more for nonscientifically trained Christians to interact with nonscientifically trained outsiders. Two people with PhDs in the sciences will need help from others with similar training. But the great news is that, in this day of easy access to immense resources on the internet, we have the greatest minds available to us at our fingertips (literally). When I am asked questions about science that I cannot answer (which is the vast majority of the time; I was a music major!), I ask people if they've ever heard of John Lennox. Most have not. I then point them to some of his YouTube videos about the nature of science and faith. As an Oxford professor of mathematics who has lectured and debated about science and faith for many years, he can address the topic far better than I can or ever will.

Part of "always be[ing] prepared to give an answer to everyone who asks you to give the reason for the hope that you have" (1 Peter 3:15), involves doing some homework on the internet to find articles, blogs, and videos by academically credible Christians who can join us as we reach out to people with more or different expertise than we have. The goal of this stage of the dialogue is to expose your friend to large quantities of information he or she may have never heard or seriously considered. Be careful not to use these resources as a club. The anti-religious, pro-science crowd have their favorite websites too.

A Conclusion and a Hypothesis

Not that long ago, a church in my area hosted an evening of exploration about science and faith. Three university professors in three different fields shared how their love of science and love of God fit together. An astronomer spoke of how "the heavens declare the glory of God." An oceanographer presented, "The depths declare the glory of God." A biologist shared how "our bodies declare the glory of God."

Listening to these three people of faith, one could sense a common route their lives took. One of them could have been speaking for all three when he recounted, "Science led me away from religion. But then science led me back to God." His path started in one of those anti-intellectual churches that told him he had to choose between science and God. "You can't be a scientist and a Christian," they insisted. So when he went off to college and fell in love with science, particularly the stars and planets, he assumed he needed to become an atheist. And that's how he lived through the rest of his undergraduate and master's degree years and well into his doctoral studies. But, during PhD-level research, he found the order, design, and wonder of the heavens too beautiful to attribute to the chaotic by-product of a random, impersonal, soulless universe. "Science brought me back to God," he said, with a delightful smile on his face.

I conclude this far-from-complete chapter on science and faith with a hypothesis. My hunch is that many intelligent, scientifically minded non-Christians could find, with a little help from their Christian friends, a coherent worldview and spiritually satisfying faith in the gospel of Jesus. If we can disrupt their preconceived notions that Christians are unintelligent or anti-science and point them to the God who gave them such great brains, perhaps they can find forgiveness as well as fascination, salvation as well as inspiration, eternal life as well as earthly blessings, and come to know the Wonderful Counselor while they wonder at His creation.

CHAPTER 7

Why Should We Believe an Ancient Book Written by Dead Jewish Males?

I hate spending money unnecessarily. So when my wife and I made our first major purchase—a washer and a dryer—I declined the salesperson's offer to add "installation" to our bill. (That would have been $25 more!) After all, how difficult could it be to plug in two machines and hook up a couple of hoses?

When the machines arrived, I immediately set out to justify my frugality. I plugged in the dryer and attached the plastic vent hose that I'd purchased on our way home. (The plastic one from the hardware store cost me several dollars less than the metal one at the appliance store.)

In less than five minutes, I finished "installing" our dryer, marveled that some people would pay $25 for such an easy chore, and proudly pushed the power button to admire my handiwork.

The next few minutes were scary. The dryer shook violently and actually crept toward me. The front door flapped open and shut, making the machine look like something out of a Stephen King novel. Before I could turn off the power switch, black smoke started billowing from the back of the dryer. The plastic exhaust hose had melted and was disintegrating. Somehow I reached through the smoke, pulled the plug, and saved my life.

That was when I reached for an important document—the manufacturer's installation instructions. The first page blared the following warning in big bold letters: **FAILURE TO FOLLOW THE MANU-FACTURER'S INSTRUCTIONS MAY RESULT IN SERIOUS IRREPARABLE DAMAGE!**

All twenty-two steps of the installation instructions proved to be very informative. Before turning the dryer on, I learned, you must ensure that the front door is closed firmly and that the four feet are adjusted so the machine does not move (or creep up on you, as the case may be). I also learned that this machine required a metal exhaust hose rather than a plastic one (which could "melt and start a fire"). I read every word of this fine piece of literature, followed the instructions carefully, and again bravely turned on the dryer. Thankfully, "serious irreparable damage" had not occurred, and our dryer worked flawlessly.

When it came time to install the washing machine, I did everything that the manufacturer's manual said. As a result, I reaped the blessed fruit of my labor—clean clothes, smoke-free air, and no Stephen King laundry monster.

It makes sense, doesn't it? Manufacturers know how their machines work—they made them! Manufacturers know what will make their machines perform at their best and what will harm them. People really should follow the manufacturer's instructions. Serious irreparable damage doesn't seem like an unreasonable consequence for failing to do so.

So it is with *our* Manufacturer's instructions. As God and Creator, He knows how our machinery works and what will cause us harm. His "thou shalt nots" are for our own good. Yet with ignorance, pride, and rebellious hearts, we seek shortcuts and thrills, following our own way of doing things. The results can be far worse than serious or irreparable.

This antiauthoritarian bent can add an obstacle to the evangelism process. Even if our gospel presentation is well crafted and biblically sound, we might face significant resistance because people often think, *Says who?* Instead of hearing biblical quotations as proof of the truthfulness of our message, people marvel at what simpletons we are to follow an ancient book written by dead white males.

Well ... dead *Jewish, Middle Eastern* males would be more accurate. But "dead white males" is the catchphrase of scholars who critique Western civilization's canon, and it has more sting to it. Through use of the catchphrase literary critics have undermined people's confidence in any written text. They contend that societies are shaped by a collection of diverse stories, none of which are more inspired, valid, or objective than any other. Thus, Bible believers are accused of arrogance, ethnocentricity, conceit, or worse when they fail to toe this multicultural line.

The Real Question

Many of our answers to accusations about the Bible fail to compel belief because they fail to address the real issue. When people ask, "How can you believe the Bible?" some Christians mistakenly respond with a history lesson. We display charts of manuscript statistics, quote little-known archaeologists, cite historical verification from obscure journals, and speak affectionately of the Dead Sea Scrolls.

Our questioners remain unmoved because historicity isn't the issue. Authority is. And despite the question that's posed (e.g., "Why do you believe the Bible?"), these are the real questions:

- "Why do you submit to the Bible?"
- "Why do you allow it to dictate how you live?"
- "Why should anyone give allegiance to a book that discourages looking out for number one?"
- "Isn't *your* Bible racist, sexist, and anti-science?"[1]

I once saw an advertisement for SpiritScrolls[2] that captured the sentiments behind these questions. Under the photo of a necklace, from which dangled a scroll-like charm, the ad read:

---

1. These questions are posed more frequently today than issues of historicity or anything that archaeology can address. A helpful research for equipping Christians to answer them is Rebecca McLaughlin, *Confronting Christianity: 12 Hard Questions for the World's Largest Religion* (Wheaton: Crossway, 2019).
2. At the time, the ad was in *The New Yorker* magazine, and the product ("available at boutiques worldwide") had its own website at www.spiritscrolls.com.

This is my SpiritScroll
I keep inside a reminder of what is important to me.
I walk down life's path with eyes wide open and senses
awake
to discover the unveiling of my spirit within.
My SpiritScroll is my compass.

Write your own scroll to keep next to your heart or
to place next to the heart of someone special.

A SpiritScroll embodies the philosophy that most people subconsciously hold: "I am my own authority. I write my own scripture. I play by my own rules. No god will tell me what to do or how to live." Although this particular product is no longer on the market, dozens of similar items exist that tell people they are their own authority and they create their own truth.

A cover story in *USA Today* signals where this philosophy takes us. The headline declared, "Scandals Lead Execs to 'Atlas Shrugged'—1957 Ayn Rand Novel Sanctions Self-Interest." The second paragraph read, "Executive headhunter Jeffrey Christian says many of his clients are re-reading the 1,075-page novel to remind themselves that self-interest is not only the right thing to do from an economic standpoint but is moral, as well. CEOs put the book down knowing in their hearts that they are not the greedy crooks they are portrayed to be in today's business headlines but are heroes like the characters in Rand's novel."[3]

The article quotes research that documents the Bible as the book that has influenced more people than any other; *Atlas Shrugged* is ranked second. It goes on to suggest that the gap might be narrowing, however, as is evidenced by the increase in hits to the website for The Atlas Society, an organization dedicated to promoting Rand's philosophy. One wonders what other books have influenced people the most in our day and age. I'm inclined to believe they would be

---

3. Del Jones, "Scandals Lead Execs to 'Atlas Shrugged'—1957 Ayn Rand Novel Sanctions Self-Interest," *USA Today*, Tuesday, September 24, 2002, 1–2.

similar to *Atlas Shrugged* in the way they promote self-autonomy. Increasingly, self-autonomy trumps submission to authority.

Different Answers for Different Questions

So why do we believe that the Bible deserves our allegiance? And what do we say when people attack it?

Considering the changes in our questioners' attitudes, we need a different approach to apologetics. This new approach offers factors (see the definition of *factor* below) rather than proofs. We want, of course, the ultimate response of "My Lord and my God! I accept the Bible." But the factor approach aims more for a preliminary response of "That's reasonable. I think I'll read the Bible." By presenting factors that lead someone to read the Bible, we let the Scriptures authenticate themselves rather than trust our extrabiblical arguments to seal the deal. We settle for a partial victory and let the Bible do the rest. In other words, in some cases, we might accomplish more by attempting less.

There may have been a time when most people already had read much of the Bible. If they were familiar with its message but did not believe it, apologetics persuaded them of the Bible's authenticity, historicity, reliability, and trustworthiness. But those days are gone. Today, most people don't even know the parts of the Bible that once were standard fare. Therefore, today's apologetics should encourage literacy before defending historicity. We must challenge people by asking, "Why don't you *read* it?" more than, "Why don't you *believe* it?"

The burden of proof, so to speak, then falls upon the Bible's shoulders, not ours. Considering such claims as "My word . . . will not return . . . empty" (Isa. 55:11), this is, indeed, good news.

Four Factors of Belief

According to *Webster's II New College Dictionary*, a *factor* is something that "actively contributes to an accomplishment, result, or process." No single apologetic factor makes for a watertight case of biblical authority. But taken together, acting like straws on a camel's back, the following four factors increase the likelihood that a hotel room's Gideon Bible will get opened, read, believed, and—yes—submitted to.

Factor 1: Plausibility

Plausibility is the first factor. Similar to what was presented in chapter 3, we propose to our inquisitive friends, "Isn't it reasonable to believe that a God who created us could, if He wanted to, communicate with us? And further, couldn't He do so through the vehicle of inspired writing?" That's not far-fetched. Getting someone to agree to this minimal proposal paves the way to fuller acceptance of the Bible's authority.

When I met with J.P., a twenty-year-old undergraduate student, he described himself as "not a Christian but definitely considering it." I was surprised to hear how open he was to the plausibility of inspiration. I asked him, "Do you think it's possible that a god could choose to communicate with us in verbal, written form?" He nodded his head in the affirmative and added, "I suppose it's best to treat the Bible as innocent [of fraud] until proven guilty rather than the other way around." Wouldn't it be great if more non-Christians were so open-minded?

Suppose, however, that someone isn't open to the plausibility factor. What if that person is an atheist? This isn't the place to restate the arguments against atheism.[4] But here's how my conversation went with an atheist friend named Art. Using the visual aid of a circle with a dot in the middle helped me get this atheist unstuck from his arrogant position.

RANDY: Isn't it possible God has communicated with us already?

ART: You're assuming that I believe in God.

RANDY: You're right. I guess I shouldn't assume that.

ART: No, you shouldn't. I don't believe in God.

RANDY: Why not?

---

4. Defenses for theism abound, but one of my favorites is in Ken Boa and Larry Moody, *I'm Glad You Asked* (Wheaton: Victor Books, 1994), 21–47.

ART: I just don't. I don't think there's any proof of His existence. People just believe in God by faith.

RANDY: Is it possible that there's evidence that you just don't know about?

ART: What kind of evidence?

RANDY: Well . . . could there be, for example, strong historical evidence that Jesus rose from the dead?

ART: How would that prove the existence of God?

RANDY: It would validate a lot of what Jesus taught, and He had a lot to say about God's existence.

ART: Okay. Yes, that would be some evidence that I haven't heard about. So what?

RANDY: It means that you might be wrong. Here. Let me draw something. [I drew a circle on a napkin and labeled it "All Knowledge."] This is all of the knowledge there is to know. How much of this circle would include all of the knowledge that you currently have? [I handed him the pen. He thought for a minute and did what most people have done when I've posed this question. He drew a small dot in the middle of the circle.]

RANDY: That's about what I'd say for me too. [I now shaded in the part of the circle that was not represented by his dot—in other words, about 99 percent of the circle.] Is it possible that there is some knowledge in this shaded portion that could be evidence for God's existence?

ART: Yes.

RANDY: Well, then, you should say that you're an agnostic, not an atheist, right?

ART: I don't like the term *agnostic*. I think an agnostic is an atheist with no guts.

RANDY: But *agnostic* means that you don't know. *Atheist* means that you *know* that God does not exist, and you can't say that, can you?

ART: I would say *atheist* means someone who doesn't believe in God. Who knows if He really exists?

RANDY: Okay. Let's not quibble about philosophical terms. I'll leave that for philosophers.

ART: Me too.

RANDY: My point is, it's possible, isn't it, that a god does exist?

ART: Yes, that's possible.

RANDY: Then wouldn't you be better off, intellectually speaking at least, to see what some people claim is evidence of God's existence?

ART: Like what?

RANDY: Like reading the Bible. Have you ever read it?

ART: No. I haven't.

RANDY: Even if you think that it's all baloney, if you read it, you'll know what all the fuss is about—firsthand! It's the greatest best seller of all time, and a lot of our society

has its roots in the Bible. Just for the sake of considering
yourself intellectually well-rounded, it's helpful to have
a knowledge of the Bible. Wouldn't you agree?

ART: Yes. "Intellectually well-rounded" is a good way to put
it. Do you know where I could get a Bible?

Factor 2: Messiness

Messiness is the second factor. The Bible is messy. At first glance, it
seems like a document that would discourage acceptance. The Bible
is long and repetitious; was written by forty different authors rather
than a single person; and contains a diversity of locations, languages,
genres, and literary styles. The Bible's hodgepodge construction seems
to detract from its credibility rather than build it. The multiplicity
of miracles (in both Testaments) seems hard to swallow. And some
of it's just plain confusing. Controversy over end-time events is only
one of the problems caused by the fantastic assertions of the Bible.
If it's plausible to believe that God is behind the Bible, one wonders
why He wasn't more clear in making His point.

But then again, couldn't these very qualities give credence to the
Bible's claims of inspiration and sacredness? Maybe the Bible's messiness corresponds to *our* messiness, making it the perfect revelation to
get us out of our mess. Perhaps its use of various genres corresponds
to our complex nature—the intellectual, emotional, volitional, social,
and physical components of our personhood. Maybe God inspired
the Bible to suit our total being.

Of course the messiest aspect of the Bible is that it challenges us.
Tim Keller has stated:

> If you don't trust the Bible enough to let it challenge and
> correct your thinking, how could you ever have a *personal*
> relationship with God? In any truly personal relationship, the
> other person has to be able to contradict you. For example,
> if a wife is not allowed to contradict her husband, they won't
> have an intimate relationship. Remember the (two!) movies

The Stepford Wives? The husbands of Stepford, Connecticut, decide to have their wives turned into robots who never cross the wills of their husbands. A Stepford wife was wonderfully compliant and beautiful, but no one would describe such a marriage as intimate or personal.

Now, what happens if you eliminate anything from the Bible that offends your sensibility and crosses your will? If you pick and choose what you want to believe and reject the rest, how will you ever have a God who can contradict you? You won't! You'll have a Stepford God! A God, essentially, of your own making, and not a God with whom you can have a relationship and genuine interaction. Only if your God can say things that outrage you and make you struggle (as in a real friendship or marriage!) will you know that you have gotten hold of a real God and not a figment of your imagination. So an authoritative Bible is not the enemy of a personal relationship with God. It is the precondition for it.[5]

Again, our goal in proposing these four factors is to get our friends to read the Bible, not to convince them to believe it. If it really is the inspired, powerful, untamed Word of a sovereign God, it can be trusted to do its own convicting, humbling, salvific, worship-inducing work.

A conversation around these first two factors might sound something like this:

NON-CHRISTIAN: It's great that you've found something that works for you. But I just don't believe the Bible.

CHRISTIAN: Why not?

NON-CHRISTIAN: It's just too far-fetched for me to believe.

---

5. Timothy Keller, *The Reason for God: Belief in an Age of Skepticism* (New York: Dutton, 2008), 113–14.

CHRISTIAN: What about it is far-fetched?

NON-CHRISTIAN: All of the miracles. I mean, parting the Red Sea, healing crippled people.

CHRISTIAN: How much of the Bible have you read?

NON-CHRISTIAN: Oh, hardly any of it. I just know a lot of the stories.

CHRISTIAN: But you haven't read it?

NON-CHRISTIAN: I've read some of it.

CHRISTIAN: But not a lot of it?

NON-CHRISTIAN: No.

CHRISTIAN: Well, do you think it's possible that, if there is a God, and He wanted to communicate with us, that He could inspire some kind of written revelation like the Bible?

NON-CHRISTIAN: Yeah. I think so.

CHRISTIAN: Then I'd encourage you to read it. It's a best seller, and many people say that it's helped them more than any other book.

NON-CHRISTIAN: But it's so weird. I've read enough of it to know that it's hard to get into.

CHRISTIAN: Maybe that's the way it's supposed to be.

NON-CHRISTIAN: What?

CHRISTIAN: Maybe it's supposed to be hard.

NON-CHRISTIAN: Why in the world would God make it hard?

CHRISTIAN: So that it challenges us. I mean, if it's a book about God, doesn't it make sense that it would be hard to grasp on the first go-around?

NON-CHRISTIAN: Could be.

CHRISTIAN: The more you get into it, the more you see how the hard parts fit into the whole thing.

NON-CHRISTIAN: It probably couldn't hurt.

CHRISTIAN: Do you have a modern translation of the Bible? If not, I could get you one.

Factor 3: Reality

Assume, then, that an inquirer has granted that an inspired, written revelation from Creator God is at least possible. And assume, too, that the inquirer perceives the Bible's messiness as an advantage. That inquirer is better prepared and could be ready for the kind of apologetic evidence that's usually presented without such preparation.

This evidence comprises the third factor—the reality factor. We can demonstrate that reality (verified by archaeology, history, eyewitness accounts, literary criticism, etc.) overwhelmingly supports the claims of the Bible. The multiplicity of manuscripts, the historical and archaeological support from without, and the presence of authenticating material from within point to accurately recorded history.[6]

These three preliminary factors do not, however, replace the substance of the Scriptures themselves. The sooner we declare *what* the Bible says rather than defend *how* the Bible says it, the more powerful our case will be.

---

6. The website for Stand to Reason (www.str.org) is an invaluable source of apologetic support of the Bible.

We should do so by telling a story—the Bible's story. Rather than listing disconnected propositions, we should show that the Bible's story connects with our story at our point of deepest need.

Factor 4: Need

The fourth factor is the need factor. Much has been made lately of the need to present the gospel as a story. In observing that more than 70 percent of the Bible is narrative, some people have advocated following its lead.

"Jesus told stories, and so should we," they maintain.

True enough. But is presenting the gospel as a story doing more than merely following our Master's model? Did Jesus use narrative to announce the coming of the kingdom simply because He was a good storyteller or because people had short attention spans?

Some people have argued for the story approach to evangelism because our postmodern, narrative-loving audience prefers stories and will more likely respond to them than to a philosophical treatise. Granted. But postmoderns prefer a host of other things to which we certainly shouldn't cater. Maybe there's a better reason to use story— one that promises a good response but for a deeper reason.

Could it be that stories communicate so well because we are, in essence, story creatures? Isn't it possible that being a person (a human being who exists in time) means having a narrative nature? Having a chronological beginning (birth) and end (death), we respond better to stories—which have a beginning and an end—than to ahistorical proclamations of dogma. Stories, then, connect with us at our very core.

Proclamations do have their place. The Bible's inclusion of epistles and prophecies validates their importance. But we should read Romans and other didactic material in the context of the larger story line of God's divine narrative. In evangelism, we should declare the doctrine of Romans—the gospel—as narrative so that our message appeals to the whole person. We want to convert, not merely convince. Narrative evangelism does both.

Propositional Melodies Embedded in Redemptive Drama

Talking to Lisa taught me to do narrative evangelism. I met her in a food court on a commuter campus and soon learned of her dramatic role in a local production of *Les Misérables*. I had been praying for a way to share the gospel naturally with someone that day. Hearing of her theatrical experience opened that door.

If you're not familiar with Victor Hugo's classic novel, you're missing one of the most powerful pictures of grace ever put into print. The story contrasts Jean Valjean's redemption with Inspector Javert's hard-heartedness. Valjean, as both a recipient and a granter of grace, puts flesh to that biblical concept. After being released from years in jail, a punishment that he didn't deserve, Valjean is transformed by a gracious act of kindness by a priest. This changes his entire approach to life, transforming him into an honest and generous businessperson and mayor. But the chief of police, Javert, pursues him relentlessly, believing the transformation to be impossible. The idea of "once a thief, always a thief" propels Javert in his relentless pursuit. I can think of no more dramatic portrayal of the contrast between grace and law.

In the musical adaptation of the book, the music never stops during the three-and-a-half-hour production. Yet through astounding creativity, the composers use the repetition and intertwining of a few simple melodies. Valjean, for instance, sings praise for incredible grace before leaving his life of crime. In haunting contrast, the same musical notes are used by Javert to curse his own existence before he jumps off a bridge. Numerous such subliminal parallels occur throughout the production. Thus, musical themes subconsciously reinforce the drama's message.

Les Mis reminds me of the Bible. Throughout the scriptural drama, themes of holiness, redemption, love, and a Messiah are woven like threads in a tapestry. In talking with Lisa, I compared the message of *Les Mis* with the message of the Bible. I retold the biblical plot as the ultimate redemption narrative—one that *Les Mis* imitated. Being a drama-enriched actress, she was poised to listen.

If we can share the gospel by retelling the biblical story, we might get more of a hearing than we're used to receiving. Our message draws people in, so they want to hear how the tension is resolved rather than hope we'll just finish as soon as possible.

The Bible's Story

How do we do this? In telling any story, we mark in our minds the high points or turning points of the action as well as recurring themes. The points propel the drama; the themes add emotional color. We keep these markers in the forefront of our minds while filling in the dramatic details with our spoken words.

If you were telling the story of the three little pigs, you might have in mind this outline of points and themes, the drama to be added through narrative:

    I.   Who the Pigs Are
    II. Who the Wolf Is
         Theme: "Who's afraid of the big bad wolf?"
   III. First House—Straw
         Theme: Huff/puff/blow the house down
    IV. Second House—Wood
         Theme: Huff/puff/blow the house down
    V. Third House—Brick
         Theme: Huff/puff/do not blow the house down
   VI. How the Wolf Dies
         Theme: "Who's afraid of the big bad wolf?"

The Bible's story might have this outline:

    I.   Creation
         Theme: Nature of God
         Theme: Nature of people

II. Rebellion
　　Theme: Tension between God and people
　　Theme: Messiah (predicted)
III. Redemption
　　Theme: Messiah (arrived)
IV. Consummation
　　Theme: Messiah (returned)

This concept might seem difficult, but too many people have *not* responded to our nonnarrative approaches to evangelism. In particular, artists, musicians, actors, and intellectuals have dismissed our simplistic ahistorical presentations as irrelevant simply because of the way they were packaged. Taking the effort to learn the narrative approach may well pay off. It's worth the experiment of telling the gospel *story* to these people to see if they respond more readily than to a gospel *outline*.

The section below shows a way to tell the story, but let's first ensure that we have a deep appreciation for it. The following is one way to think of the Bible's story line.

When everything began, there already existed an eternal God who created all that is. He created us—people—as the high point of His creation and fashioned us after Him. We were made to have an intimate relationship with this creative, communicative, loving, powerful, and sovereign God. Maintaining this intimacy was the most important thing for the first people—Adam and Eve. Today, it's still the most important thing for us. Something within us cries out for this kind of intimacy.

It is unfortunate, however, that something within the first man and woman rebelled against this relationship. Just as we still do today, they sought to be their own bosses, thinking that, on their own, they could provide what was best. The results were disastrous—and eternal. God is eternal and He created us as eternal beings, thus the consequence of their rebellion was eternal—eternal separation from Him and everything that is good and holy.

The recurring themes within the Bible's stories reflect this created-for-God/rebelling-against-God tension. The lives of Abraham, Isaac, Jacob, and the collective experience of the nation of Israel embody this tension. God's choosing of Israel and His giving of the law to them showed how a relationship between God and a group of people was supposed to be. It was to be a relationship characterized by holiness and graciousness on one side, obedience and worship on the other. The poetry of the Psalms and other Wisdom Literature paints pictures of how it feels to be close to God (worship) and the results of turning away from Him (lamentation, confession, and alienation). The Prophets and other didactic parts of the Bible taught the Israelites ways to draw close to God and warned them of the consequences of not doing so.

Another theme intertwines with these stories—the theme of an Anointed One, a Person who would someday rectify the alienation and eliminate the tension. He was introduced in the Bible right after the first rebellion and was identified as a human being (Gen. 3:15). As the best prophet of all time, He would someday be our teacher (Deut. 18:18).

Whenever this Anointed One was mentioned, unusual language was employed that caused the reader to slow down. Like rumble strips on a highway slow you down as you approach a toll booth, messianic prophecies slowed readers down and made them wonder, *Who will fulfill such things?*

He was described as a King who will someday reign (2 Sam. 7), a Servant who will someday suffer and die (Isa. 53), and a Judge who will someday return (Zech. 12–14), and He was actually declared to be God Himself in human form (Isa. 9:6).

The dramatic high point of the Bible occurs when this Anointed One arrives—as a baby who is born precisely when, where, and how it was predicted. He taught the most amazing lessons ever proclaimed and pointed to Himself as the One in whom people could find their redemption. His death paid for sin, and His resurrection validated the completion of that payment. He was the One to whom the Bible had been pointing and the One for whom our restless hearts have been crying. His name is Jesus, a name meaning "salvation."

The Bible ends with the consummation of the story—a picture of eternity when all the redeemed people relate to their God with perfect intimacy. Fulfilling the very reason that they were created, they worship this God the way He deserves and without the hindrances of sin, sickness, sadness, and death. If we respond to this story in the way it says we should, we will experience an abundant, eternal life—in quality and quantity—united with our creator-redeemer God.

Telling the Story

Sound too complicated? It doesn't have to be. I've shared the gospel in this storylike way as I've sat with people in coffee shops, simply by scribbling four words on a napkin:

- Creation
- Rebellion
- Redemption
- Consummation

I talk of the inherent human tension—being made for God while at the same time rebelling against Him. While explaining details about the Messiah's resolution of that tension, I watch my listener enjoy the unfolding story. After intertwining my own story with that of the Bible, I ask my listener to share his or her story.

To encourage that person to do so, I ask a few questions:

- "Have you ever wondered about such things?"
- "Who would you say Jesus was?"
- "Have you ever read the Christmas story and asked how it fulfilled prophecy?"
- "Have you ever read the Bible for yourself?"

I try to use the statement, "What I love about the Bible is that its story connects with our story at our point of deepest need."[7]

---

7. A recent tool that tells the gospel as narrative, retelling the Bible's story line and connecting it with the reader's, is "The Story" produced by Spread Truth at http://spreadtruth .com and http:thestoryfilm.com.

The Problem with Other Stories

Unlike the Bible's story, the narratives of other worldviews fail to connect with reality. They promise more than they can deliver. Some narratives deny the personal nature of God, calling Him a force or a concept. Other narratives reject the specialness of people, what Francis Schaeffer called "the mannishness of man." Still others suppress our fallenness. None of these narratives can save, and all of them will disappoint.

In reading the Scriptures, though, people find release from the burden of having to explain reality on their own. If they seek truth from God's revelation, they escape the despair, emptiness, falsehood, or arrogance that comes from believing their own revelations.

Consider, for example, the following. It's a submission to *The Washington Post* column "Autobiography as Haiku," which consists of one-hundred-word essays submitted by readers.

> My younger brother recently died unexpectedly. My daughter . . . comforted me one day when I was feeling especially sad. "Mommy," she said, "you just don't understand. Life is a process. You are born from your mother, you become a child, then you grow up, and then you are gone, you go to God. It's just a process." I was touched but wondered how she had derived such cosmic insight at age eight. So I asked. She sheepishly reported that her third-grade class had just learned about the "life cycle of a bug." I laughed and hugged her tight.[8]

I read this anecdote and wondered why it comforted the woman. How can she consider it a "cosmic insight"? Not to pick on an eight-year-old girl, but equating our existence to a bug's life cycle should insult us, not comfort us. I turned the page and I muttered, "This doesn't resolve the pain for this upset woman."

People *should* get upset about the death of a loved one! The explana-

---

8. Elaine Kaplan, "Autobiography as Haiku," *Washington Post*, September 29, 2002, C1.

tion that "it's just a process" degrades the dignity of personhood that God has built into us. When we share the good news of the Scripture as narrative, we offer a much better story than the "bug's life cycle" answer. (It is significant to note that *bugs* don't get upset about such things. There is a qualitative difference between creatures that are created in the image of God and those that are not.)

Retelling the Bible's story line (creation, rebellion, redemption, and consummation) as a way of presenting the gospel is the appropriate and best response to a question about the Bible. It gives people an answer, one that they need more than historical evidence, archaeological discoveries, or literary analyses.

The story line also connects people to their roots—regardless of whether they know it. It affirms a longing that we all have—a longing to know our Creator. By beginning the message with creation, we appeal to our listeners' image-bearing nature and tap into the "eternity in their hearts" (see Eccl. 3:11). We assure them that their desire for something other is not neurotic. Properly presented, the gospel sounds, indeed, like refreshingly good news.

The Bible story line also awakens a God-implanted desire for a happy ending. By presenting the gospel in a fuller dimension, one that points to a culmination, we reassure people that a dread of death, no matter how small, makes sense. We ascribe value to people, declaring that they have eternal significance. We validate the feeling of incompleteness that people feel in this life—because they were meant for something better, something eternal.

Martin Luther once said that the Bible is like a lion. If people criticize it, you don't defend it—you let it out of its cage. Even in these skeptical times, when the Bible is tossed into a pile of irrelevant books written by dead white males, the lion still roars and the cage still must be opened.

CHAPTER 8

Why Are Christians So Homophobic?

John 3:16 has been replaced.[9] Oh, if you open your Bible to the third chapter of the Gospel of John, the sixteenth verse still reads, "For God so loved the world . . ." But when it comes to the most frequently quoted verse on Twitter, Instagram, Facebook, and other popular venues, pride of place now goes to a popular paraphrase of the King James Version of Matthew 7:1: "Judge not, lest ye be judged."

These Bible quoters likely don't have evangelization as their goal. Rather, it's telling Christians to leave them alone—"Get out of my face" might be an accurate paraphrase.

A topic for which "judge not" is used with increasing frequency deals with issues relating to homosexuality. *Judge not, lest ye be judged is* shorthand for "How dare you Christians tell people who they should sleep with!"

How should we respond to this kind of Scripture quoting? What are we to think when a steady stream of voices, including the US Supreme Court, affirm gays while condemning homophobia as the worst sin? What can we say when a coworker leaves his wife of fifteen years to be with a man so he doesn't have to "live a lie" anymore?

At times, we seem to have only two bad options: either accept homosexuality as an innate condition to be embraced and supported, or view it as an abomination to be hated and condemned.

Do Jesus's oft-quoted words in Matthew 7:1–5 offer us another alternative? They do—but we must first understand what they do *not*

---

9. Portions of this chapter were published in the November/December 2003 issue of *Discipleship Journal*.

mean. We must ask, too, what do issues that relate to homosexuality have to do with sharing the good news? We must also look at all the words that Jesus spoke, not just the ones that fit on bumper stickers.

Jesus said:

> Do not judge, or you too will be judged. For in the same way you judge others, you will be judged, and with the measure you use, it will be measured to you.
>
> Why do you look at the speck of sawdust in your brother's eye and pay no attention to the plank in your own eye? How can you say to your brother, "Let me take the speck out of your eye," when all the time there is a plank in your own eye? You hypocrite, first take the plank out of your own eye, and then you will see clearly to remove the speck from your brother's eye.

My wife and I began to wrestle with this passage's relevance to homosexuality when our close friend Jim (not his real name) came out to us. We'd wondered. He hadn't dated a woman in more than ten years, and now that he was in his early thirties, we thought that we'd finally ask. His response was laughter. He'd wondered how long it would take us to figure it out. He'd decided that he wasn't going to tell us, but if we asked, he wouldn't lie.

What followed probably sounded like a standard coming-out conversation—with an unusual twist at the end.

"Jim," we asked, "when did you became gay?"

"I've always felt this way," he said.

"When did you first realize it?"

"When I was about eleven."

"Who else knows?"

He paused and looked us square in the face. "I've told only those who wouldn't judge me."

"Did you ever tell anyone at your college Christian fellowship?"

A look of pain crept into his face, as he recalled an unforgettable experience. As one of more than three hundred students involved in a campus ministry, Jim sat in horror as the director told the crowd at their weekly meeting how they *must* confront their homosexual friends.

"Someone had just stood up and asked for prayer," Jim related, "because his roommate had told him, 'I'm gay.'"

Rather than leading the group in prayer for this brother or his roommate, the director seized the moment and proclaimed (in a harsh tone that Jim will never forget) what must be done.

"You need to be uncompromising. You need to be scriptural. You need to be bold."

"Nothing," said Jim, "communicated that you need to be kind. I decided, then and there, that this was not a safe place to share the difficulties I'd faced."

After catching our breath, we told Jim some things that he didn't expect. We told him that we loved him, that we wanted to do everything we could to keep our friendship strong. And we asked him if he'd ever heard of Christian ministries that help people "who struggle with homosexuality."[1]

His face suggested amusement at our choice of the word *struggle*. "I've never heard of those kinds of ministries," Jim said. "But how does your suggestion that I seek their help jibe with your affirmations of love for me?"

"Because we love you," we said, "we want the very best for you. There's another side to the homosexual life that we think you should hear. We're convinced that the gay life, even if it seems natural, isn't good."

Jim listened politely, but we sensed that we were being dismissed. The fact that we stopped hearing from him for the next year confirmed our fear. If he had chosen a verse to quote to us during that time, it would have been, "Judge not, lest ye be judged."

---

1. Many new books address homosexuality from a solidly biblical perspective. Two recent ones are Kevin DeYoung, *What Does the Bible Really Teach About Homosexuality?* (Wheaton: Crossway, 2015); and Sam Allberry, *Is God Anti-gay?* (Purcellville, VA: The Good Book Company, 2013).

LGBTQ+ and Evangelism

Before looking at Matthew 7, consider first what this present chapter is doing in a book on evangelism. You might have been puzzled about this when you looked at the table of contents. Perhaps you decided to skip this chapter—or perhaps you jumped to this chapter first.

Issues of sexuality dominate today's society. Scanning any news source or spending any amount of time online supports that assertion. Most people have subconsciously absorbed the notion that sexuality is innate and unchangeable, like the color of one's skin. Hence, "homophobia" and "transphobia" equate with racism, intolerance, and bigotry. People who disapprove of anyone who identifies as LGBTQ+ are painted with the same brush as those who burned African American churches in Mississippi during the 1960s.

So if we condemn LGBTQ+ people, non-Christians want nothing of our religion—or at least our brand of it. They want to believe that "real" Christianity is "loving" and "tolerant" enough to accept gays. That's the sentiment reflected in advisor Carolyn Hax's response to the following letter that appeared in her *Washington Post* column, "Tell Me About It":

> Dear Carolyn:
>
> How do people come to terms with revelations about themselves that basically shatter who they've always thought themselves to be?
>
> I think I might be gay but I'm a Christian. These are diametrically opposed lifestyles, outlooks, behaviors, actions, thoughts! Is it silly to think that, because I am a Christian first, being gay is precluded? That in some twisted way, if I discovered I was gay before I came to know Jesus, then Christianity would fall by the wayside? Thoughts?

> Carolyn's response:

> How, exactly, is homosexuality "diametrically opposed" to being honest, patient, loving, kind, faithful, forgiving,

compassionate and just? For grins, go look up the word "catholic," small-c, in the dictionary. I think you need to extend several million apologies to all the gay and gay-friendly Christians out there in the world.

After several paragraphs of "just accept who you are," she concludes:

[This] might make more sense to you than the intolerant [ways] you've been taught. You're Christian. You're gay. Trust yourself.[2]

Carolyn articulates a limited understanding of what it means to be a Christian. And her perception is held by many people. Their brand of Christianity doesn't preclude homosexuality; it merely precludes homophobia.

Regardless of whether we realize it, the topic of sexuality might be lurking behind many evangelistic conversations. If the people we're talking to are not gay themselves, they know someone who is, or have a relative, coworker, or neighbor who is, and they refuse to be hateful toward them. They will not even consider our faith if it will turn them into bigots.

Sexuality and the Bible

We need to build the foundation of our beliefs about sexuality on the Bible, being sure to include 1 Corinthians 6:9–11. The church at Corinth was as messed up as a church can get—disunity of the most petty variety, sensuality of the most perverted kind, and misunderstandings about the gospel. Paul wrote to them:

Do you not know that wrongdoers will not inherit the kingdom of God? Do not be deceived: Neither the sexually immoral nor idolaters nor adulterers nor men who have sex with men nor thieves nor the greedy nor drunkards nor

2. Carolyn Hax, "Tell Me About It," *The Washington Post*, July 21, 2002, F1.

slanderers nor swindlers will inherit the kingdom of God. And that is what some of you were. But you were washed, you were sanctified, you were justified in the name of the Lord Jesus Christ and by the Spirit of our God.

Contrary to our relativistic culture's mantra of "whatever," this text declares that some things are, indeed, wrong. Although the incessant beer commercials make the alcohol-laden life seem fun and attractive, God still thinks that drunkenness is bad. Although sexual immorality is tolerated and even celebrated and lauded in popular media, God still thinks that sleeping around is bad. And, as Wall Street scandals make clear, swindling, theft, and greed are not without their tragic consequences.

Among the things that the Bible says are wrong are homosexual behaviors. The terms used in verse 9 (translated in the NIV as "men who have sex with men") are, in their original language, quite graphic. They describe the same sexual acts commonly practiced today. Dr. Jeffery Satinover, in his excellent book *Homosexuality and the Politics of Truth*, brings statistical and medical insight to the prevalence and health risks of homosexual activities.[3]

It should be noted that *activities* is a key term. The word choice in the 1 Corinthians passage above seems to emphasize a person's *behaviors* rather than his or her identity. In other words, these verses make the case that having an attraction to someone of the same sex is merely a temptation; acting upon it is the sin.

Because the interpretation of words is a weighty matter, leaders in the ex-gay movement (which continues despite the demise of the leading ministry, Exodus International, in 2013) stress the importance of terminology. One local director of an ex-gay ministry stopped using the word *homosexual* as a noun. He simply uses it as an adjective—describing behaviors or temptations, not the identity of people. Most people in the ex-gay movement also stay away from the word *gay*. They view it as a slick propaganda term that has served the pro-homosexual

3. Jeffrey Satinover, *Homosexuality and the Politics of Truth* (Grand Rapids: Baker, 1996), 49–70.

movement well. It sounds fun and harmless, having quite a different connotation than *homosexual*. More and more writers who address homosexuality talk of "people with same-sex attraction" (SSA) and avoid the term "gay Christian."[4] The term "same-sex attraction" is making its way into support groups and helping people "come out" from their homosexual behavior. We would do well to adopt this vocabulary.

We should also consider the term *homophobic*. Like *gay*, it serves the pro-gay movement well. It stigmatizes someone who refuses to get on the bandwagon and agree with the prevailing sentiment that "gay is okay." "You're not homophobic, are you?" has the same end-run punch as "Have you stopped kicking your dog?" Someone who has a phobia has a problem, something for which they need healing. So when someone asks us if we're homophobic, we might shake up their thinking by responding, "I'm not afraid *of* homosexual people, but I am afraid *for* them." Our explanation could bring some light to a topic that usually generates only heat.

Nor should the list of wicked behaviors in these verses be skimmed too quickly. Notice that homosexual behaviors are just part of a list—a list containing behaviors with which many of us, regardless of sexual orientation, struggle daily. Your name and mine are attached to almost every one of them. In one sense, homosexual behavior is no better or worse than greed.

The list of offenders in 1 Corinthians, for example, contains those who are "idolaters." What an odd term for us to apply in the twenty-first century! The notion of bowing down to a statue and offering our devotion to it seems so alien. But is it? Hasn't sexuality become a god to us? Don't we sacrifice for it, set our affections upon it, place it in high esteem (higher than we should!), and worship it?

Seeing the idolatry in our hearts brings to light its degenerative

---

4. The use of the term "gay Christian" has become quite controversial, but I side with those who see more problems with it than benefits. Two helpful resources are Ed Shaw, *Same-Sex Attraction and the Church: The Surprising Plausibility of the Celibate Life* (Downers Grove, IL: InterVarsity Press, 2015); and Rachel Gilson, *Born Again This Way: Coming Out, Coming to Faith, and What Comes Next* (Purcellville, VA: The Good Book Company, 2020).

nature. When we set our affections on something that cannot satisfy, demanding of it something that only God can provide, we lose the glory of being fully human. If this sounds overstated, consider the downward progression presented in Romans 1:21–32. The threefold repetitions of "they exchanged" and "God gave them over" draw a graphic of the relationship between idolatry and sexual sin (of which homosexuality is just a part).

Reasons for rejoicing, however, are abundant. Note that the most notable quality attributed to *all* the people mentioned in 1 Corinthians 6 is that *all* of them can be *washed, sanctified,* and *justified* "in the name of the Lord Jesus Christ and by the Spirit of our God." We should sing the words "and that is what some of *us* were" as a repeated chorus of praise whenever we gather to worship our gracious God. No other phrase in Scripture carries such hope and optimism—or more clearly proclaims the level ground at the foot of the cross.

Addressing issues of sexuality, then, requires a painfully honest look into our own hearts. The humility that should result could make us more attractive mouthpieces for our message of grace and healing.

Sexuality and Judging

Now we are armed. Knowing how sexuality relates to evangelism and how, in context, the Bible treats these issues, we can approach Matthew 7:1 with a proper perspective. Many people interpret the "judge not" verse to mean that no one should ever tell anyone that he or she is wrong. Judging, according to this interpretation, means any kind of negative evaluation. You shouldn't tell anyone that his or her lifestyle is sinful or harmful because Jesus told us to "judge not."

But is this what Jesus really meant?

Consider that in this very context He warned us not to be undiscerning: "Beware of false prophets, who come to you in sheep's clothing" (v. 15 NKJV). He used strong language, too, in warning us not to "cast [our] pearls before swine" (v. 6 NKJV). How could we be obedient to these commands, or how can we identify the "false prophets" or the "swine," without making some kind of negative evaluation? "Judge not" must mean something else. If not, Jesus Himself—who kicked people out of the temple, told an adulterous woman to "sin no more," and called others whitewashed tombs—would have been the biggest violator of His own admonition.

What, then, did Jesus mean? The answer lies in translation. The word that Jesus used, the one translated "judge," has in the original language the connotation of "condemn." It portrays a spirit of harshness that should never be expressed by one person to another. You can correct someone or express your concern and love for that person without judging, condemning, or demeaning that person. Jesus told us not to relate to people this way, because if we do, we'll receive the same kind of treatment.

Noted Welsh pastor Martyn Lloyd-Jones presented this interpretation in his commentary on the Sermon on the Mount. "What is this spirit that condemns?" he wrote. "It is a self-righteous spirit. Self is always at the back of it, and it is always a manifestation of self-righteousness, a feeling of superiority, and a feeling that we are all right while others are not."[5]

Therefore, it is not judging to tell your homosexual friend that you don't think his actions are good—even if they seem natural. It is not judging to tell your lesbian friend that you want the best for her—not just her finding the right woman. It is not hypocritical to hug your struggling friend while telling him or her about people who have come out of homosexuality.

It most certainly *is* judging for you to proclaim things such as "God hates fags," as the late Fred Phelps did on his website. (Not surprisingly, just as Matthew 7:2 predicts, some critics of the Baptist pastor used their websites to proclaim, "God hates Fred Phelps.")

Understanding the correct definition of the word *judge*, then, is the first key to unlocking this passage. A second key is to keep reading Jesus's words through the end of verse 5. Many people would have us quit after "You hypocrite, first take the plank out of your own eye."

---

5. D. Martyn Lloyd-Jones, *Studies in the Sermon on the Mount* (Grand Rapids: Eerdmans, 1960), 2:167.

Period. But Jesus fully intended for us to go further—"and then you will see clearly to remove the speck from your brother's eye."

Obstacles for Us to Overcome

It is crucial to note both halves of the task. First, remove *our* planks. Then help them remove *their* specks. We can do both if we identify the most common planks and specks.

Some of us have a plank of superiority. We think that LGBTQ+ sin is worse than any of the sins we struggle with. We use a different vocabulary and tone of voice when talking about homosexuality than for talking about "the tragedy of divorce," "the unfortunate circumstances of an unplanned pregnancy," or "the struggle with addiction to pornography."

Some of us have a plank of denial. We don't call our sins of greed, lust, or immorality what God calls them—"idolatry" (see Col. 3:5). We call them "slipups" or "only natural," or we excuse them as unavoidable.

Not long ago, a Christian friend and I were watching TV together when a commercial for some seductive lingerie came on. His enthusiasm for their products was embarrassing—especially since both of us had teenage sons in the room. I doubt that he'd have been so jovial if a gay man in the room responded with similarly lustful comments about the men in Calvin Klein jeans commercials. Some of us think that straight lust is entertainment whereas gay lust is an abomination. God, however, sees them both as idolatry.

Some of us have a plank of hatred. If we're honest, we'd admit that we have contempt for gays. We're angry they've won the culture war. Many of us who would never utter a racial slur become quite fluent in using terms such as *faggot, queer,* and *dyke.* We thoughtlessly utter the platitude, "Hate the sin but love the sinner," but a serious examination of our hearts might show that, in actuality, we hate both.

Some of us need to remove a plank of fear. We really don't trust that the kingdom of God can withstand the sin of LGBTQ+ behavior. We're scared because we doubt that "greater is He who is in [us] than he who is in the world" (1 John 4:4 NASB1995). So we panic and yell and hate because our trust in a sovereign God is faulty. Our homophobia (in the most literal sense of that term) is rooted in theological insecurity.

A plank of disbelief causes us to doubt that homosexual behavior can be changed. But *all* the sinners listed in 1 Corinthians 6:9–10 (the sexually immoral, idolaters, adulterers, homosexual offenders, thieves, the greedy, drunkards, slanderers, and swindlers) are included in Paul's reminder—"that is what some of you *were*" (v. 11, emphasis added).

It is certainly true that the change process is difficult. For some people, it is a lifelong struggle with little progress. Dr. Satinover reports that some ex-gay ministries report success rates of no higher than 50 percent. Yet he notes, too—and with documentation—that Alcoholics Anonymous has reported success rates as low as 30 percent.[6] Few, if any, people would say that AA should fold up shop because 70 percent of their people have fallen off the wagon.

Some of us have a plank of a cold heart. We feel no compassion for those with SSA. "The Bible is clear," we reason. "Homosexuality is a perversion, and that's all there is to it." But to tell a young man or woman that God's best for them is a lifetime of celibacy and denial of feelings that seem so natural, and to tell them so without the slightest sense of compassion, is terrible. Such coldness cries out for our own need of cleansing and change.

Likewise, to tell someone, "You chose this lifestyle" is not only untrue but cruel. I'm acquainted with a number of Christian men and women who struggle with SSA. Without exception, they've told me, with tears in their eyes, that they would have chosen anything other than homosexuality.

We should certainly encourage our friends who struggle with sexual sin to connect with ex-gay ministries. God has used these ministries in remarkable ways. But the healing process is never easy, and we dare not promise easy cures. Some people have been disappointed with their level of healing and have declared themselves to be "ex-ex-gay."

6. Jeffrey Satinover, *Homosexuality and the Politics of Truth* (Grand Rapids: Baker, 1996), 170, 186, 196–209.

For far too many people, the healing process is missing a crucial ingredient. They need friendship with heterosexual Christians who will pray with, accept, and hug those who struggle, even if they experience failings along the way. That takes a contrite heart that is aware of its own sexual brokenness, not a cold one that is poised and ready to cast the first stone.

The worst plank may well be a reluctance even to talk about LGBTQ+ issues. The topic is simply taboo in many churches. Whether it's because it's too repulsive to the people in the pews (see the plank of superiority mentioned earlier), too dangerous for pastors seeking church growth, or some other excuse, our silence is a failure to show the power of the gospel.

More than thirty years ago, Francis Schaeffer quoted the following words of Martin Luther. One wonders how these two men would respond to today's gay community.

> If I profess with the loudest voice and clearest exposition every portion of the truth of God except precisely that little point which the world and the Devil are at that moment attacking, I am not confessing Christ, however boldly I may be professing Christ. Where the battle rages, there the loyalty of the soldier is proved, and to be steady on all the battlefield besides, is mere flight and disgrace if he flinches at that point.[7]

The aforementioned last plank might be the worst because it creates an environment of silence and secrecy—two of the devil's favorite tools. How can people confess struggles that aren't even allowed to be mentioned? If the silence is to be broken, pastors must set the pace by preaching about sexual issues with compassion and concern. They could include this struggle with others as illustrations in sermons on other topics. If Paul included homosexuality and greed in the same illustration, so can we (see 1 Cor. 6:9).

---

7. Martin Luther, quoted in Francis A. Schaeffer, *The Complete Works of Francis A. Schaeffer: A Christian Worldview*, vol. 1, *A Christian View of Philosophy and Culture* (Westchester, IL: Crossway Books, 1982), 11.

Only after we have had planks removed can we be broken, humble, honest, and gracious enough to help our friend with his or her speck. Despite our society's acceptance and even celebration of homosexuality, the specks *do* need to be removed. If we really love our neighbors as ourselves, we can't just leave them alone.

Obstacles for Them to Overcome

It is, perhaps, best to learn about the gay life from people who either have counseled men and women out of it or have themselves been set free from it.

Psychologist Elizabeth Moberly is often quoted for the foundational insights she expressed in her book *Homosexuality: A New Christian Ethic*. She asserts that "the homosexual condition is one of same-sex ambivalence, not just same-sex love."[8] Coining the term *defensive detachment*, Moberly paved the way for therapists to help people get to the root of their problem.

People who have come out of the gay life and have found health, wholeness, and, in some cases, a sexually satisfying heterosexual marriage, provide powerful testimonies that must not be ignored. Their stories can be a source of hope for homosexual people as they seek healing.

Joe Dallas's book *A Strong Delusion* tells of his leadership in and his subsequent exiting from the Metropolitan Community Church (a pro-gay denomination). The elements inherent in homosexuality, he shows, include "deep problems with intimacy," a lack of "confidence before God, and the peace that comes with it," and an idolatry that puts "gratification" above truth and anything else.[9] His sample dialogues throughout the book answer pro-gay theology and bring to light the depth of its rationalizing and compromising.

To hear from those who have come out of homosexuality is to learn of a very different world than the one portrayed by gay characters

---

8. Elizabeth Moberly, *Homosexuality: A New Christian Ethic* (Cambridge: James Clarke and Co., 1983), 17.
9. Joe Dallas, *A Strong Delusion: Confronting the "Gay Christian" Movement* (Eugene, OR: Harvest House, 1996), 224–26.

on television. For some people, intertwined with homosexuality is anger (at God, parents, or those who sexually abused them), depression, addictions, and compulsive behaviors. They tell of difficulties with intimacy—difficulties that never improve until the root cause is addressed.

Mere "tolerance" is not what our homosexual friends and relatives need. They need love, compassion, and a listening ear. And they need to hear that we want a much better life for them than what the gay world can provide.

Underlying Principles

You might ask at this point, "What do I say?" or "What words do I use to communicate with my gay neighbor, my coworker with a gay brother, or anyone who thinks that I'm homophobic?"

Before practicing dialogue, we must grasp some underlying principles that might never get expressed, but that serve as a foundation to our words.

First, we should expect this to be extremely difficult. I anticipate far less "success" in this area of apologetics than with any other issue. Christians have always been "on the wrong side of history" when it comes to sexuality and have been hated and persecuted for it. One of the reasons John the Baptist got his head cut off was for daring to tell Herod he shouldn't be sleeping with his sister-in-law (Matt. 14:3–12).

Second, we must accept that God (and only God) has the right to declare what is right and what is wrong. He is our Creator and, as such, has the authority to tell us who to sleep with and what to do with our bodies.[10] Coming into relationship with God involves a bowing of our wills to His sovereign lordship. As long as we uphold our sexual autonomy as the highest value in our lives, we separate ourselves from God's majestic and redemptive reign. One of the tragedies of the LGBTQ+ mindset is its insistence that sexual identity be the unquestioned starting point of all discussion. For LGBTQ+ people,

---

10. A brilliant recent resource for thinking through and articulating this perspective is Sam Allberry, *Why Does God Care Who I Sleep With?* (Purcellville, VA: The Good Book Company, 2020).

the essence of their personhood is their sexuality, rather than what it means to be human—that is, God's image-bearer. Gay churches that insist no conflict exists between being gay and being Christian miss this primacy of "gayness" over "createdness." In doing so, they distort the gospel—or present something that is no gospel at all.

Third, we must realize why sex is such a big deal. Unlike any other aspect of life, sex is both pleasurable and profound. God has given us many pleasurable experiences—seeing the beauty of a field of flowers, feeling a cool breeze through our hair, tasting the spices in a well-prepared meal, hearing both the complexities and the simplicities of a symphony, or a million other pleasures—all of which are gracious gifts from a creative, loving, pleasure-giving God.

He has also prescribed things that have profound meaning for us. The celebration of the Lord's Supper translates a mystery that cannot be put into mere words. Baptism works similarly for us. Worship transforms us in unparalleled ways. Ceremonies such as weddings or funerals highlight the transcendent realities behind earthly experiences. But none of the pleasurable experiences that I've listed are as profound as sex, and none of the profound experiences are as pleasurable as sex.

In a unique way, sexuality may be God's greatest gift to us (apart from the gift of life, or the base upon which all other gifts are received; and the gift of salvation, or the base upon which all experiences are redeemed). Sex uniquely engages all of our being—physical, psychological, spiritual, emotional, and intellectual. It is unparalleled as both pleasurable and profound.

No wonder it so captivates our hearts.

No wonder the devil so wants to distort it! The act of sexual intercourse has the capability of uniting two people on the deepest level and occurs within the context of holy matrimony, an institution that incarnates Christ's love for the church. It's no surprise, then, that God's enemy (and ours!) wants to distort such a thing. His goals are to make it a mere physical act, with no profundity; a painful act of abuse; a comical act, reducing it to crude joking; or an enslaving act, transforming people into addicts or idolaters. His tactics are seemingly without number!

Fourth, we must remember that to disobey God's commandments brings bondage, not freedom. The Serpent in the garden said, "You will be like God" (Gen. 3:5 NKJV), but God says, "You will surely die" (Gen. 2:17 NASB1995). The poet of Proverbs 29:18 put it thus: "Where there is no revelation, people cast off restraint; but blessed is the one who heeds wisdom's instruction."

"Revelation" (a better translation than "vision," as states the NASB1995) is something communicated by God to be the plumb line or standard of truth, hence its coupling with "wisdom's instruction" in the second line of the verse. "People cast off restraint" (a better translation than "perish") happens when no standard of right and wrong exists. Casting off restraint is what the people did at the foot of Mount Sinai when they gave up hope of Moses ever returning from his encounter with God. Because God was not speaking to them, they abandoned all restraint and engaged in the limitless debauchery described in Exodus 32. (Words used in this chapter are identical to those in Proverbs 29:18.)

God's people must grasp that disobedience brings bondage, or we'll never understand why our culture continues to spiral downward. Without the boundaries of Scripture, our sinful hearts flee from the good things that God has for us, imagining that we'll find them on our own. Attempting to do so leads only to misery.

At one time I worked at the American University in Washington, DC. The school led the way for campus acceptance of sexual diversity. While other campuses were establishing groups with such titles as "Gay Student Alliance," American University had already moved on to "Gay-Lesbian-Bisexual Alliance." When other campuses caught up to "GLB," American University added *T* for "transgender." Finally, realizing that the list might grow indefinitely, they chose the very inclusive "Sexual Minorities Organization."

I approached the director of the Sexual Minorities Resource Center, which was housed in a large office with two full-time staff and funded by the university's central budget. "Would the center be inclusive enough," I asked, "ever to sponsor a student pedophile organization, should some students want one?" He paused and said, "Let me think about that. I'll have to get back to you."

He never did.

Contrary to how sin markets itself, abandonment of restraint is not pleasant. The Hebrew poetry of Proverbs 29:18, in fact, pits "cast off restraint" against "blessed." To choose to live within the confines of God's precepts is not confining; to free oneself from God's law is not freeing. In other words, a pillar in the Christian worldview on sexuality is that gay really isn't okay. Even if our culture fully embraces it and removes any social stigma from it, homosexuality will never be healthful or good for either the person who indulges in its behaviors or the society that promotes it.

The LGBTQ+ community has done a marvelous job of denying this truth by propagating two related fictions. The first minimizes the dysfunctional nature of homosexual relationships. The second exaggerates the dysfunctional nature of heterosexual ones.

Portraying all marriages and heterosexual relationships as dysfunctional works in tandem with the first distortion. If everyone has sick, emotionally dependent relationships, who has the right to declare one messed-up situation to be better than another? But this is simply inaccurate and unreasonable. Some things are bad and harmful and must be corrected and healed. As followers of Christ, we must reach out in love and say things that, although completely out of step with our culture, have the power to bring healing and hope.

Different Kinds of People—Different Kinds of Questions

No topic demands the twin qualities of wisdom and compassion as much as sexuality. Settling for partial victories is more necessary here than in most evangelistic conversations. Given the heat of emotions that sexuality invokes and the conditioning toward "tolerance" that our society has received, we would do well to ask questions that plant the seeds of doubt. Then, with prayer, we can wait to continue the conversation at other times. Still, the Christian perspective on sex has always been a minority view and subject to a great deal of ridicule. We need to have realistic expectations.

In conversing with heterosexual persons who sympathize with LGBTQ+ people, we can fend off the accusation that we're homophobic with questions like these:

- "Have you ever heard a perspective about homosexuality that was neither pro-gay nor homophobic?"
- "Have you ever met someone who left the gay life?"
- "Do you think that someone can change from being straight to gay? How about the other way?"
- "What does *homophobic* mean? Is it possible for someone to think that homosexuality isn't good but at the same time not be 'phobic'?"
- "Isn't it possible that homosexuality isn't as good as it's made out to be?"
- "Do you know why the American Psychiatric Association changed their views about homosexuality?"[11]

In anticipating questions from those with SSA, we may encounter four situations: non-Christians who are content with their sexuality, non-Christians who aren't content with it, Christians who see no conflict with being gay and Christian, and Christians who want to change.

To our non-Christian gay friends, we should steer our conversation toward the gospel and away from sex. The starting point of the conversation is the same as it is for anyone else:

- "Do you ever think much about spiritual things?"
- "Have you come to the point in your spiritual journey where you know for certain that you'll have eternal life?"
- "Do you ever wonder about life after death?"

---

11. Joe Dallas, *A Strong Delusion: Confronting the "Gay Christian" Movement* (Eugene, OR: Harvest House, 1996), 69–82, 121–25.

If and when the topic of their homosexuality arises, your questions could include the following:

- "Have you ever heard about people whose sexual orientation has changed?"
- "Are you open to hearing other perspectives about being gay?"
- "Can I tell you about someone who resolved her gayness and her Christianity in a way that you might find interesting?"
- "Do you think that some things might be more important than your sexual identity?"

For non-Christians who haven't yet embraced their homosexuality, we can say something like this:

- "There might be another way to deal with this."
- "I know that this might sound crazy, but some people have come out of homosexuality and found a much better way to relate to people of the same sex."
- "How do you feel about your sexual orientation?"
- "I've seen some amazing changes in my life because of my faith in Christ. There have even been changes in my sexuality. Would you be interested to hear about the changes in my life?"

For the Christian who identifies as a "gay Christian," the issue is much more complex. A tangled web of behavior, theology, and even politics is a tough opponent to approach. Joe Dallas's book *A Strong Delusion* contains sample dialogues that are more helpful than anything that can be presented here. A good starting point might be simply, "There might be another way to deal with these attractions" or "Are you sure you've given a fair hearing to both sides of this story?"

For the Christian with SSA, a long-committed friendship with someone who does not struggle with SSA has power far more potent than words. A hug is a transformational thing. Nevertheless, words such as these can be spoken:

- "I want to be your friend no matter what."
- "I'm not going to stop caring about you."
- "I really want the very best for you—not just what seems most natural."
- "Have you ever heard about other Christians who struggle in this way?"
- "Have you ever heard of ex-gay ministries?"
- "Would you be willing to pray with me about this struggle of yours?"

A full year after our coming-out conversation with our friend Jim, he returned one of our phone calls. He'd been watching a television show hosted by Oprah Winfrey that featured ex-gays and ex-ex-gays. The former group was gentle, secure, and relieved. The latter group was loud, angry, and defensive. The timing for Jim was significant— yet another relationship had ended badly, and his gay friends were struggling with depression, alcohol and drug addiction, and suicidal tendencies. He was ready to start reading a book that we'd sent him. He was confused and needed help.

The next ten years were difficult times that included relapses, doubts, support groups, individual therapy, conferences, a lot of books, and even more prayer. Not too long ago, he married a woman who also is a grateful recipient of and an amazing vessel for transformational grace. Their church has been an unusual place of refuge for not only them but also many others.

Jim's story is only one of many.[12] There are as many different situations as there are people who struggle. Knowing how to respond to each one takes understanding, prayer, sensitivity, and compassion. If we display these traits, perhaps we'll be able to point people toward John 3:16.

---

12. Two excellent examples are Becket Cook, *A Change of Affection: A Gay Man's Incredible Story of Redemption* (Nashville: Thomas Nelson, 2019); and Jackie Hill Perry, *Gay Girl, Good God: The Story of Who I Was, and Who God Has Always Been* (Nashville: B&H Books, 2018).

CHAPTER 9

What's So Good About Marriage?

It helps to know when you're sick. If you have plaque clogging your arteries, it's crucial to find out before you have a heart attack. If you know you are sick, you take medication or get treatment before something terrible happens. Many of us know people who, one day, felt "just fine" and the next day learned they had cancer. A few months later, they were gone. It helps to know when you're sick so you can do something about it before it's too late.

A convincing case could be made that our culture is sexually sick. You don't have to hold traditional moral convictions to see that something is terribly wrong. Sex, which is supposed to bring ineffable pleasure, often delivers horrific pain instead.

Consider some of the presenting symptoms.

An ever-increasing percentage of college students—both women and men—report being sexually assaulted at least once during their years of living on campus.

More than a few Catholic priests as well as Protestant ministers have resigned over allegations of sexual abuse. Some have gone to jail.

It's not just the odd horror stories of predatory monsters who routinely assault young men at football camps or young women in gymnastics programs. It's seemingly ubiquitous reports of people coming out of the shadows to say they've been raped, abused, or sexually harassed. In some cases, these abominations occurred countless times over many years.

In one very short year, over nineteen million people retweeted the hashtag "MeToo," indicating they had been sexually abused.[1]

By some estimates, there may be more people traded as sex slaves today than ever before in human history.[2]

If we could look at our culture as outside observers, we might detect an odd split-screen view of dramatically different scenes. On one side, we'd see multitudes of graphic sexual depictions in television, movies, and the internet with little or no personal consequences. On the other side, we'd note a painful avoidance of sex and confused disillusionment about it, with therapists and researchers scratching their heads.

After interviewing scores of college students about sex, researcher Donna Freitas reported her findings in a disturbingly titled book *The End of Sex: How Hookup Culture Is Leaving a Generation Unhappy, Sexually Unfulfilled, and Confused About Intimacy.* For her opening sentence of her well-documented study, she writes, "Amid the seemingly endless partying on America's college campuses lies a thick layer of melancholy, insecurity, and isolation that no one can seem to shake."[3]

What does all this have to do with evangelism?

Into this world of sexual sickness, we proclaim the gospel, a message that centers on forgiveness and reconciliation, but also includes biblical morality. That ethic has the audacity to declare, "You shall not commit adultery," "The marriage bed is to be undefiled," and "Flee also youthful lusts" (Exod. 20:14; Heb. 13:4 NASB1995; 2 Tim. 2:22 NKJV).

In the process of evangelism, we must answer not only the questions people ask with their mouths but also the ones they express in their hearts. If no one has actually asked us, "What's so good about

1. Dalvin Brown, "19 million tweets later: A look at #MeToo a year after the hashtag went viral," *USA Today*, October 13, 2018, https://www.usatoday.com/story/news/2018/10/13/metoo-impact-hashtag-made-online/1633570002/; and Monica Anderson and Skye Toor, "How social media users have discussed sexual harassment since #MeToo went viral," Pew Research Center, October 11, 2018, https://www.pewresearch.org/fact-tank/2018/10/11/how-social-media-users-have-discussed-sexual-harassment-since-metoo-went-viral/.
2. This information comes from the anti–human trafficking organization, International Justice Mission. You can read more at https://www.ijm.org, accessed September 11, 2021.
3. Donna Freitas, *The End of Sex: How Hookup Culture Is Leaving a Generation Unhappy, Sexually Unfulfilled, and Confused About Intimacy* (New York: Basic Books, 2013), 1.

marriage?," it's likely that some of them see monogamy as an obstacle to accepting Christianity.

If someone has already tasted the forbidden fruit of immorality, they might have been transformed by its seductive powers and might wonder why it ever was forbidden. Even if a person hasn't been promiscuous, committed adultery, or sat bleary-eyed in front of an internet porn site, many, if not most, people in our sex-saturated world have questioned the antiquated morals of the Bible. Merely quoting Bible verses to those people might not reverse their doubts. We need other answers besides "You'll catch a disease," or "You'll hurt your partner if you cheat on her or him."

If the underlying issue is one of personal autonomy ("How dare anyone tell me who to sleep with!"), we must build our case and not just point one finger at the Scriptures and another in their faces. We must ourselves have a solid grasp of *why* the Bible condemns sexual immorality, adultery, and divorce. Until we convey that truth, our proof-texting will fail to overcome the hardness that comes as a result of sexual sin.

Better still, we need the conviction that we have "a better story" about sex, marriage, and love than the alternatives flooding our culture. Those stories "promised more and better sex, but failed to deliver." Glynn Harrison, longtime professor of psychiatry, argues that "the Bible's teaching is still good news . . . its teaching is life for the world and the only true foundation of human flourishing." He says this is because "we flourish as human beings when we work with, rather than against, the grain of God's reality."[4]

What's So Bad About Adultery?

When we first read 1 Corinthians 6:12–17, we might wonder what these verses mean and how they fit into context.

> "I have the right to do anything," you say—but not everything is beneficial. "I have the right to do anything"—but I will not

---

4. Glynn Harrison, *A Better Story: God, Sex, and Human Flourishing* (London: Inter-Varsity Press, 2016), 91, xvii, 127.

be mastered by anything. You say, "Food for the stomach and the stomach for food, and God will destroy them both." The body, however, is not meant for sexual immorality but for the Lord, and the Lord for the body. By his power God raised the Lord from the dead, and he will raise us also. Do you not know that your bodies are members of Christ himself? Shall I then take the members of Christ and unite them with a prostitute? Never! Do you not know that he who unites himself with a prostitute is one with her in body? For it is said, "The two will become one flesh." But whoever is united with the Lord is one with him in spirit.

In regard to context, what Paul says before these verses is easy to grasp. Verses 9–11 tell us that certain things are wrong and will prohibit someone from inheriting the kingdom of God. Among these things are sexual sins of various kinds. What comes after this paragraph, verses 18–20, is also relatively easy to understand: get as far away as possible from sexual sin because it'll really mess you up. But the substance in the middle opens itself for misinterpretation, misapplication, or being ignored outright.

Paul seems to be quoting some common clichés that the Corinthians must have been hearing. That's why several Bible translations place these phrases within quotation marks.

Paul quotes the popular slogan, "I have the right to do anything," and then adds his commentary: "but not everything is beneficial." He repeats the quotation, "I have the right to do anything," and then adds his insight: "but I will not be mastered by anything" (v. 12).

In other words, sins are wasteful and enslaving, regardless of how forgivable they might be. (Paul had just said in verse 11, "And that is what some of you were [referring to a whole list of sinners]. But you were washed. . . .") He could well have added, "Sure, you'll be forgiven of this sin, but you won't walk away untarnished."

Paul's quoting of a second prevailing slogan is a bit more difficult to interpret but no less crucial. He counters the slogan "food for the stomach and the stomach for food" with "the body, however, is not meant for sexual immorality but for the Lord, and the Lord for the body. By his power God raised the Lord from the dead, and he will raise us also" (vv. 13–14). The naturalistic worldview denies any spiritual component to our lives. We are merely physical beings. We're just food-processing machines—mere stomachs. So, "food for the stomach and the stomach for food" is another way of saying, "There's nothing eternal about us." It follows, then, that sex is nothing more than a physical act without any moral, emotional, or spiritual significance.

Paul couldn't be stronger in arguing against such nonsense when he points to our ultimate, spiritual, eternal significance; we're made by and for the Lord (see v. 13). Our physical bodies and the food that we put into them will pass away, but our spiritual natures will be raised from the dead (i.e., will last forever) just as surely as God raised Jesus from the dead.

"If you Corinthians believe in the resurrection," he appeals, "you must also believe in the sacredness of sex."

Paul's next line of reasoning deserves our full appreciation. Having refuted the naturalist's view of humanity, he uses Genesis 2:24 ("they shall become one flesh" [NASB1995]) in a remarkable way. Not only does marital sex unite husband and wife inseparably, but *any* kind of sex has that same power. If casual sex, on the level of someone having sex with a prostitute, can be described as "one flesh" (as v. 16 terms it), then the transforming nature of sex cannot be overstated. Sexual intimacy has a bonding capacity beyond measure.

That's why adultery is called what it is. A person who has been united sexually with his or her spouse and then unites with someone else *adulterates* that sacred relationship. That act introduces an element of "disintegrity" to a relationship that was formerly integrated, whole, and pure.

Little wonder that Paul follows with the terse command, "Flee from sexual immorality" (v. 18). A qualitative and experiential difference exists between sexual sin and other transgressions. "All other sins a person commits are outside the body, but whoever sins sexually, sins against their own body" (v. 18).

Surely Paul does not mean that other sins have no physical consequences. Drunkenness rots your liver. Gluttony raises your cholesterol. Anxiety increases your blood pressure. Uncontrolled anger can cause ulcers and worse. He must have meant something other than, "Don't be promiscuous or you'll get some sexually transmitted disease."

With his Jewish frame of reference, Paul used *body* in the more biblical, holistic sense. To "sin against their own body" means to do damage to your whole personhood, at a deeper level than any physical disease can penetrate. Cirrhosis of the soul, if you will, destroys more essentially than does cirrhosis of the liver. How so? As noted in chapter 9, man and woman were created in the image of God. A quality of that image is intimacy. Involvement in sexual immorality debilitates that quality of God's image, leaving the person intimacy-impaired. That's what is so bad about adultery or any sex outside of marriage; it disintegrates people.

I tried to get this fact through to my friend Steve as we ate pizza one day. He had just confessed to me, "I'm not a very good Christian." His self-assessment was valid, as evidenced by his living with a woman but not being married to her.

I played devil's advocate and asked what was wrong with that.

"The Bible says that's wrong, doesn't it?" he ventured between bites.

"Yes," I said. "Why do you suppose it does?"

He was stumped. He honestly couldn't remember, figure out, surmise, or even imagine why sex outside the bonds of matrimony violates God's commands. When I explained the logic behind Paul's admonitions, he marveled that, although he'd heard the commandment "Thou shall not commit adultery," no one had ever told him the rationale behind it. I think he got it, because he nodded as I summarized: "We're built for intimacy. Sex either fosters it or spoils it."

Pro-Marriage Statements from Surprising Sources

Some positive endorsements for marriage have come recently from surprising sources.

From the world of academia, sociologists Linda J. Waite and Maggie Gallagher offered in *The Case for Marriage* (2000) researched evidence that, as the subtitle puts it, "married people are happier, healthier, and better off financially."

From successful media personalities Cokie and Steve Roberts came the book *From this Day Forward*. In it the authors confessed, "We do have a prejudice. We're big fans of marriage and don't apologize for that. . . . Marriage has enlarged our lives, not encircled them; it has opened new doors, not closed them. We are better people together than we were separately."[5]

Even from within feminist writings, marriage gets an affirmative nod now and then (although often surrounded by disclaimers). Novelist and journalist Anne Roiphe said in her cutely titled book *Married: A Fine Predicament*, "Marriage can answer one human problem better than any other solution yet divined. It can assuage our loneliness. It can give us a companion through the years. It can ease our self-centeredness and wear away at our faults by combining us with another who has other needs, other strengths."[6]

My favorite surprise endorsement came from Billy Crystal! In his 1991 hit movie *City Slickers*, Crystal's character, Mitch, and his two friends, Ed and Phil, embark on a midlife crisis/therapeutic cattle-drive vacation. Mitch defends his marital faithfulness against attacks by his playboy friend Ed. In a memorable scene, as the two are riding side by side on horseback, Ed presents this possible scenario:

> What if you could have great sex with someone very attractive and Barbara [Mitch's wife] would never find out?

Mitch reminds Ed that their friend Phil fell for that very trap. When Phil was caught by his wife, he lost his marriage and his job. Undaunted, Ed offers another scenario:

> Let's say a spaceship lands and the most beautiful woman you ever saw gets out.

5. Cokie and Steven V. Roberts, *From This Day Forward* (New York: William Morrow and Co., 2000), vi.
6. Anne Roiphe, *Married: A Fine Predicament* (New York: Basic Books, 2002), 277.

Mitch is so impressed by the "reality" of Ed's scenario, he says to his horse, "Are you listening to this!"

Ed continues:

> All she wants to do is have the greatest sex in the universe with you. And the second it's over, she flies away for eternity. No one will ever know. You're telling me you wouldn't do it?

Without a second's hesitation, Mitch responds:

> No. Because what you're describing actually happened to my cousin Ronald and his wife did find out about it at the beauty parlor. They know everything there.

Mitch concludes seriously:

> Look, Ed, what I'm saying is it wouldn't make it all right if Barbara didn't know. *I'd* know, and I wouldn't like myself.[7]

Out of the mouths of comedians flow wisdom and insight beyond all expectation.

What's So Destructive About Divorce?

As pro-marriage books appeared in bookstores and on Amazon, another round of ammunition also surfaced—books arguing against divorce. They refuted the prevailing notion that divorce would make things better for tormented children and unhappy spouses. Neither group, it turns out, benefited from split marriages.

Judith Wallerstein studied children from divorced homes over a longer period than any previous researcher had dared (twenty-five years!). She found some disturbing trends. Shorter term studies suggest that children would overcome the pain of their parents'

---

7. *City Slickers*, directed by Ron Underwood (Culver City, CA: Columbia Pictures, 1991).

separation. But Wallerstein found a reemergence of difficulties when those children reached young adulthood. She reports:

> A central finding to my research is that children identify not only with their mother and father as separate individuals but with the relationship between them. They carry the template of this relationship into adulthood and use it to seek the image of their new family. The absence of a good image negatively influences their search for love, intimacy, and commitment. Anxiety leads many into making bad choices in relationships, giving up hastily when problems arise, or avoiding relationships altogether.[8]

The Institute for American Values found that divorce didn't deliver for the adults either. "People who divorce are not, on average, more happy than spouses who stay in difficult marriages." In fact, "most spouses who stick with difficult marriages are *much* happier five years later."[9]

Barbara Defoe Whitehead's *The Divorce Culture* argued that divorce does harm far beyond the individual family. Society, in a larger sense, suffers a kind of degeneration.

The Case for Marriage (mentioned earlier) offers documented sociological, psychological, and historical support for the authors' hypothesis: married people are happier, healthier, and better off financially. But the book doesn't tell why.

That's a much tougher question. The answer might demand a look at the Bible's foundation for and description of matrimony. The proposition "the two will become one flesh"—introduced in Genesis 2, affirmed by Jesus, and elaborated on by Paul—entails far more than bodily connection (see Gen. 2:24; Matt. 19:5; Mark 10:8; 1 Cor. 6:16; Eph. 5:31). In a biblical union, becoming one flesh means

8. Judith Wallerstein, Julia Lewis, and Sandra Blakeslee, *The Unexpected Legacy of Divorce: A 25-Year Landmark Study* (New York: Hyperion, 2000), xxix.
9. Cheryl Wetzstein, "Divorce Not Needed to Cure Marital Misery," *The Washington Times*, July 23, 2002, 2.

that marriage, and sexual intimacy within marriage, transforms, binds, and sanctifies people supernaturally. The demands of such a marriage—service, sacrifice, humility, brokenness, contrition, and grace—make for an institution that requires at least fifty years to *begin* to get it right.

Consider this: Two friends met after a long separation. After greetings and pleasantries, one asked the other how his wife was.

"She's fine, I guess. We got divorced a year ago."

"Oh," the surprised friend responded. "I'm sorry to hear that. What happened?"

"I guess you could chalk it up to irreconcilable differences," the divorced man explained.

A long pause added awkwardness to the moment as the inquiring friend puzzled over the phrase, one that he'd apparently never heard. He broke the silence with, "Irreconcilable differences? I thought that was the whole point of marriage!"

The Wonders of Marriage

Another unlikely endorsement of marriage came in the film *Captain Correlli's Mandolin*. When a wise father noticed his daughter's symptoms of infatuation, he drew upon his years of satisfying marriage and offered this advice:

When you fall in love, it is a temporary madness. It erupts like an earthquake and then it subsides. And when it subsides, you have to make a decision. You have to work out whether your roots have become so entwined together that it is inconceivable that you should ever part. Because this is what love is!

Love is not breathlessness. Love is not excitement. Love is not the desire to mate every second of the day. Love is not lying awake at night imagining that he is kissing every part of your body.

No. Don't blush. I'm telling you some truths.

That is just being in love—which any of us can convince
ourselves that we are.
Love itself is what is left over, when being in love has
burned away.
Doesn't sound very exciting, does it? But it is![10]

Exciting? Something other than sexual heat is exciting? What is
this father talking about? And how can we articulate this truth to a
world that can't even imagine such a thing?

It would help if we stopped offering something that we shouldn't.
Somewhere along the line, the Christian world decided to compete
with our sexually charged culture. It was a competition that we never
should have entered. Christians writing about sex tried to counter
the sexual revolution of the sixties with claims of more excitement
in matrimony than in singles' bars. At best, we were comparing
apples with oranges. While numerous so-called sex experts measured
frequency, variety, and intensity of sexual performance, Christian
writers promoted integrity, oneness, and stability. By borrowing
the world's terminology, we sent a mixed message. Even if we could
document our claims, it was a setup for embarrassment, backtrack-
ing, and compromise.

If the truth could actually be measured (something that I doubt),
it might turn out that the most explosive sexual fireworks are not
experienced in marriage. The "winners" might be those who want
only sex without commitment. The same quality that makes cocaine
exciting is what many people want from sex. So what?

Here's what we should be offering: security, comfort, and sanctity.

Marriage Secures

What's so good about marriage is that it creates, fosters, and
strengthens security. When two people commit themselves to each
other for life, they build a secure foundation in a very insecure world.

---

10. *Captain Corelli's Mandolin*, directed by John Madden (Universal City, CA: Universal
    Studios, 2001).

By offering a constant partner in the midst of a lifetime of change, they might not always find ecstasy, but they do develop constancy— something more valuable, satisfying, and necessary.

Here's how someone might promote this benefit of matrimony in a dialogue with a friend:

LIVING-TOGETHER LUCY: Bob and I don't want to get married because we don't want to be hypocrites.

MARRIED MARY: Do you think Jim and I are hypocrites?

LIVING-TOGETHER LUCY: Oh no. I didn't mean to say that. It's that we think marriage confines people, and we don't want that for ourselves.

MARRIED MARY: How would it confine you?

LIVING-TOGETHER LUCY: I don't know if I'd want to stay with Bob for my whole life. I mean, I love him—for now. But how can anyone say that they'll always love someone? People change.

MARRIED MARY: They sure do. Jim is a completely different man than when I married him. And I would say that I'm a completely different woman than the one he married.

LIVING-TOGETHER LUCY: That's what I mean. I don't want to say I'll stay forever and then have to leave because Bob changed.

MARRIED MARY: *Have* to leave? Why couldn't you stay and see where the ride takes you? You're going to change too. What are you going to do, keep changing partners every time you change? That sounds pretty disruptive to me.

LIVING-TOGETHER LUCY: So you think we're wrong for not getting married?

MARRIED MARY: Well, yes. I think you're setting yourself up for trouble by not making a commitment.

LIVING-TOGETHER LUCY: Sounds like you disapprove of our living together.

MARRIED MARY: And it sounds like you disapprove of my disapproval!

LIVING-TOGETHER LUCY: What's that supposed to mean?

MARRIED MARY: It means that we both disapprove of each other in some way. Neither of us is as open-minded as you say you are. Look, Lucy, I don't want to condemn you or insult you. In fact, I really care a lot about you. You're my friend. That's why I don't want to see you get hurt.

LIVING-TOGETHER LUCY: How am I any more likely to get hurt than you are? Tons of people get married and then get divorced. I think it's like 50 percent, isn't it?

MARRIED MARY: I think so.

LIVING-TOGETHER LUCY: That's what I mean that we don't want to be hypocrites. We don't want to sign some stupid piece of paper and then get divorced.

MARRIED MARY: If you split up, do you think it'll hurt any less without the piece of paper?

LIVING-TOGETHER LUCY: I don't know.

MARRIED MARY: Lucy, I know you think this is old-fashioned, but I don't think it's just a piece of paper.

LIVING-TOGETHER LUCY: Why not?

MARRIED MARY: When Jim and I signed that piece of paper, we did so in connection with a ceremony before a whole bunch of people and before God. We made vows and told people to pray for us and to hold us accountable to stay together "until death do us part." That's no guarantee, but it did start things out on a different foot than you and Bob started on.

LIVING-TOGETHER LUCY: That sounds pretty judgmental!

MARRIED MARY: I'm sorry. I didn't mean it to be condemning. But I did intend it to show a contrast. We said we'd stick together for better *and* for worse, in sickness *and* in health—in other words, no matter what. We said we'd stay together even when the feelings of love fade for a while. And believe me, they do—quite regularly. But they also come back—in different ways. You guys only said that you'd stay together as long as it felt good.

LIVING-TOGETHER LUCY: That's not fair. Bob and I have a lot more than feelings.

MARRIED MARY: I know you do. But what happens when you change? Or the feelings go for a roller-coaster ride? Or someone else comes along who is more attractive? Are you committed to stay together no matter what? With your starting point, it's almost a guarantee that you will split up.

LIVING-TOGETHER LUCY: How can *anyone* make that kind of promise?

MARRIED MARY: They can only do it if there's something supernatural going on in their relationship. If we didn't have God in our lives, we would have quit our marriage a long time ago.

LIVING-TOGETHER LUCY: I see what you're saying, but I'm not so sure marriage is worth it.

MARRIED MARY: I guess we'd say it is. There's a kind of security and oneness that comes with marriage. It makes us different people, and I like what we're becoming. It's not always easy, but we don't want to short-circuit the process. That's all.

Marriage Soothes

What's also good about marriage is that it soothes our vulnerability. Being vulnerable is difficult because it's risky. When you open yourself up to someone, that person might reject or hurt you. Nevertheless, the case for marriage is a case for vulnerability—despite the risks. Unfortunately, taking the risk to be vulnerable is an all-or-nothing wager. Either you choose to open yourself up to someone—allowing that person to comfort, nurture, and love you—or you close yourself up, making intimacy nearly impossible.

One day, while stuck in traffic, I listened to a popular psychologist's call-in radio show. One female caller outlined a "better" plan than marriage—four different partners for four different stages of life.

You'd start out with your first spouse in a "starter marriage," in which you'd have a lot of fun while learning the tough lessons of sex, communication, and living together. It couldn't possibly last because the wounds incurred along the way would make the future too painful. So you'd progress to the next partner, one with whom you'd have children. This relationship would take the most effort in energy expended and would have the least amount of romance. Once the children were raised, it would be time to find your ultimate soul mate, with whom you'd enjoy your "mature" years. Finally, you'd enter your retirement years and find someone who would be a caretaker for you while you reciprocated. You wouldn't want to do this with your soul mate and "ruin a good thing."

I was grateful that the talk show host laughed! But I wondered if the caller was only verbalizing what many people use as a template for their marriages.

My wife's response to this caller's proposal was to ask, "What makes her think that someone *could* trust anyone after all that?" Indeed, a pattern of forging relationships followed by dismantling them only makes it difficult for the partners to trust and to become vulnerable.

The alternative, although even more difficult, can soothe a deep longing for acceptance and comfort—a process that probably takes an entire lifetime. A psychologist friend of mine told me that many of her patients are trying to sooth an ache from infancy. The ones who do so with affairs only make things worse. The ones who do so by working on their marriages find an incredible sense of calm—one that is actually better than what they could have found in the nursery. "We're hardwired for attachment," she told me.

Voluntary vulnerability leads to sexual intimacy and pleasure. That's what people are longing for. In sexual expression, marriage's most intense intercourse, couples allow each other to be "naked and unashamed." They remove fig leaves that hide imperfections, free themselves to be out of control, and find acceptance instead of ridicule. They display an aspect of their personhood that no one else sees or hears or feels, and they find themselves being captivated by the whole experience. Over time, a relaxing oneness emerges.

Or so it should be.

Part of the soothing process's power, though, comes from its very secretiveness. By protecting sex from outside pollutants, a married couple can heal each other at their deepest level of hurt. They can unify what has been fragmented. Sex loses that power if it is allowed to be dissipated or made public. It is no longer sacred.

How ironic (and tragic) that our current climate of sexual "openness" actually makes sex void of meaning rather than full of mystery. How unlike the most secretive book of the Bible, the Song of Songs. Poetic, mysterious, beautiful, sensual, and difficult to understand, Solomon's masterpiece reflects literarily what God wants us to experience sexually. You sense that the book, in fact, should be whispered.

No wonder the wise father of Proverbs tells his son to guard the exclusiveness of his sexual pleasure. He uses metaphor to symbolize the privacy of the matter.

> Drink water from your own cistern,
>   running water from your own well.
> Should your springs overflow in the streets,
>   your streams of water in the public squares?
> Let them be yours alone,
>   never to be shared with strangers.
> May your fountain be blessed,
>   and may you rejoice in the wife of your youth.
> A loving doe, a graceful deer—
>   may her breasts satisfy you always,
>   may you ever be intoxicated with her love.
> Why, my son, be intoxicated with another man's wife?
>   Why embrace the bosom of a wayward woman? (5:15–20)

One Sunday morning, after delivering a provocative sermon on the topic of marital fidelity, a pastor was approached by a regular attendee of his church. The conversation sounded something like this:

QUESTIONER: I don't see what's so bad about having multiple sex partners.

PASTOR: And never getting married?

QUESTIONER: I don't know. Maybe I'll get married when I find someone I want to settle down with.

PASTOR: Do you hope she's had a lot of partners before you?

QUESTIONER: Hmm.

PASTOR: Either way, you think that what I said in my sermon, having just one sexual partner, is a bad idea?

QUESTIONER: It seems so limiting. Why not experience variety?

PASTOR: Lifelong monogamy isn't my idea. It's God's.

QUESTIONER: You said that. I know. Why is that?

PASTOR: Do you think that God has the best in mind for you?

QUESTIONER: Probably.

PASTOR: So you tell me. The pros of multiple partners are variety, experience, and experimentation. What are the cons?

QUESTIONER: Well, there are a whole lot of sexually transmitted diseases.

PASTOR: That's pretty big. Any others?

QUESTIONER: I think it breeds mistrust.

PASTOR: That's also pretty big. I'm glad you see that.

QUESTIONER: I also think that kind of lifestyle, after a while, gets tiring.

PASTOR: Keep going.

QUESTIONER: It might make it harder to stay committed to someone once you do get married.

PASTOR: Bingo. Quite a few studies support your suspicion. When you see sex as something that's okay before marriage, you set yourself up for engaging in it outside of marriage. It's not a guarantee, but statistically it often leads to destroying a marriage.

QUESTIONER: I could see that.

PASTOR: What do you think are the pros of having just one partner?

QUESTIONER: Wow. That's a tough one.

PASTOR: You ought to think about that before you reject it as an option.

QUESTIONER: There *is* something special about reserving sex for just one person.

PASTOR: Your whole emphasis on variety and experience might be a bit overrated. My wife and I have plenty of variety and experience just within our exclusive relationship. And, so far, it hasn't gotten boring. I sometimes wonder what it would have been like to have had a lot of partners, but then I wouldn't know what exclusiveness would feel like. I guess for me, the pros of just one partner outweigh the cons. That's why I think God favors marriage.

Marriage Sanctifies

My wife drives me to the train station, taking Wakefield Drive. I never take Wakefield during rush hour. I take Guinea Road. I prefer Guinea. Pam prefers Wakefield. This will never change. On previous occasions, I've offered her my arguments for Guinea Road's superiority. She's argued back with her set of proofs of Wakefield's advantages. Yes, we've actually argued about things like this. Neither of us has ever changed the other's opinion. Sometimes we've not bickered out loud, but in our hearts we've festered and fumed, marveling how we could have ever married someone so stubborn, illogical, spiteful, or just plain sinful.

On one particular morning several years ago, we didn't argue. We weren't even upset. We simply remarked how different we are from each other, and relaxed in the realization that we don't have to change each other. (It took twenty-two years to figure this out!)

Hours later, after I'd arrived in New York, I sat across from my parents and filled them in on the morning's discussion about the superiority of routes. After fifty-four years of marriage, my mother and father knew exactly where this story was going—another tale of spousal differences. They laughed hysterically and remarked how great married life is.

Progress, so it seems, goes from anger ("Why are you driving on this stupid road?") to dominating ("Why don't you listen to me and go the way I want?") to self-righteousness ("Why can't you see the superiority of my way of doing things?") to acceptance ("It's okay for us to have differences.") to joy ("Isn't it great that we see things so differently!").

This is a silly example, but it differs only in degree, not in kind, from the countless ways a marriage transforms selfish people into sacrificial ones. Marriage promotes growth toward sanctification, making husbands and wives more like Christ and less like Adam and Eve.

To say the least, the process poses a number of challenges. But it also holds great promise. One marriage and family expert put it this way:

> The assumption is that there is someone right for us to marry and that if we look closely enough we will find the right person. This moral assumption overlooks [a] crucial [aspect] to marriage. . . . It fails to appreciate the fact that we always marry the wrong person. We never know whom we marry; we just think we do. Or even if we first marry the right person, just give it a while and he or she will change. For marriage, being what it is, means we are not the same person after we have entered it. The primary problem morally is learning how to love and care for this stranger to whom you find yourself married.[11]

When my wife and I were dating, I "checked her out" to see if she was the person I should marry. The problem was, I looked at Pam, the single woman, someone who was not married to me. Once she became Pam, Randy's wife, she changed. She had to—just as I had to change when I became her husband. And we, in fact, continue to change—so that today I'm married to a different person than the one I dated years ago, and years from now I'll be married to a different person from the one I'm married to today.

In *The Mystery of Marriage*, a wonderful, wisdom-packed book, Mike Mason shares his penetrating and insightful "meditations on the miracle." He sees that the intimacy we all crave comes with a price that we'd all rather avoid. But marriage is a package deal—exposing us, humbling us, breaking us, and perfecting us along the way.

> The process of discovering or finding another person is the process of losing oneself. This is certainly not a loss of identity, but only of the false identity that is founded upon self-will. Human beings are the presence of God in the world, and by

---

11. Stanley Hauerwas, *A Community of Character: Toward a Constructive Christian Social Ethic* (Notre Dame, IN: University of Notre Dame Press, 1981), 172.

drawing so close to one of them that we enter willingly into the fire of their judgment, it becomes possible for our own selfish will to be illuminated and cauterized. Intimacy is thus a fire of righteous purification, a fire we could never tolerate were it not for the assurance that we are loved.[12]

Loving cauterization—what a beautiful image! Marriage makes us better because it shows us how bad we are. Lifelong, unconditional commitment makes us more giving because it exposes how selfish we are. Loving someone who doesn't deserve love makes us more like the God who loved us "while we were still sinners" (Rom. 5:8). Unlike any other tool, then, marriage drives home the two-pronged message of the gospel: that we are "more wicked and sinful than we ever dared believe but, in Christ, we are more accepted and loved than we ever dared hope."[13]

As stated in chapter 3, proclaiming that gospel message often requires preparation—pushing in the clutch before shifting gears. That preparation—building, you will recall, a plausibility structure—sometimes involves a positive apologetic for God's design for marriage. In those instances, a dialogue promoting matrimony and salvation could be woven together as follows.

JERRY: Hey, so how'd your date go last night?

LUKE: Okay. I'm not sure how this relationship is going to work out.

JERRY: How come?

LUKE: Well, I asked her what she thought about spiritual things, and they're not that big a deal for her.

---

12. Mike Mason, *The Mystery of Marriage: Meditations on the Miracle* (Sisters, OR: Multnomah, 1985), 108.
13. From a visitor's information booklet from Redeemer Presbyterian Church in New York, 1999.

JERRY: So?

LUKE: So, they're a very big deal to me.

JERRY: As long as she's not hostile to your religion, what's the problem?

LUKE: I need someone who's more positive than just "not hostile."

JERRY: You make relationships too big a thing. I suppose you haven't slept with her yet either.

LUKE: Jerry, we've only known each other for two months. You mean you would have slept with someone after only going out a few times?

JERRY: Absolutely. If I'm not in the sack by the third date, it's goodbye for me.

LUKE: You know my stance on this. I think sex should be reserved for marriage.

JERRY: And you know what I think about that. Marriage just doesn't make any sense to me.

LUKE: Why not?

JERRY: Look. You go to a restaurant and you order a steak. And it's a great steak. Are you telling me that you're going to eat only steak for the rest of your life?

LUKE: Are you telling me that marriage is a steak?

JERRY: No, marriage is the restaurant. Sex is the steak.

LUKE: So you see nothing qualitatively different between having sex and eating a steak.

JERRY: None.

LUKE: Try telling some woman you think she's a steak, and see how quickly she jumps into bed with you.

JERRY: Okay. I can see your point. But staying with just one person throughout your whole life doesn't make any sense to me.

LUKE: In a way, I think you're right.

JERRY: What?

LUKE: Given what you've told me about your view of life—that there's no God, that there's no heaven or any kind of afterlife, and that there's nothing spiritual or eternal about us—then, yes, I guess marriage makes no sense.

JERRY: How does God fit into this?

LUKE: For me, my relationship with God affects everything I do. So it changes how I see women and marriage and sex. It tells me that sex is something sacred. It binds people together and changes them. I'm thinking that being married to someone will take a whole lifetime to get right.

JERRY: I guess.

LUKE: I really think that marriage and sex are more special than just eating a steak.

JERRY: Where'd you get these kinds of ideas?

LUKE: Do you really want to know?

JERRY: Yeah.

LUKE: The Bible.

JERRY: The Bible tells you about sex?

LUKE: Yes. And marriage, and commitment, and why I don't stand a chance at loving anyone the way I should unless I first get into a right relationship with God. Have you ever heard anyone explain that?

JERRY: Not the way you're doing.

LUKE: Wanna hear more?

JERRY: Maybe. Let me think about it.

LUKE: Fair enough. Let's go get some lunch—I'm in the mood for a steak.

CHAPTER 10

If Jesus Is So Great, Why Are Some of His Followers Such Jerks?

Someday, I'd like to meet Dr. Michael Newdow. If I do, I might want to apologize to him. Considering the messages left on his voice mail after the start of his extended legal challenges to the Pledge of Allegiance because of its inclusion of "one nation under God," he deserves an "I'm sorry" from somebody.

When the case gained considerable notoriety, the Sacramento physician, attorney, and ardent atheist had several voice-mail recordings left for him that were filled with invectives:

- "You need to fear for your life!"
- "You will be punished."
- "Mike, this is God. I'm really upset with you."
- "You're a dead man walking."

Some of the messages threatened such a level of violence that at one point Newdow arranged for his eight-year-old daughter to live away from her own house.

While Newdow brought the now-famous case in 2000 against his local school district and other officials for requiring his daughter to recite the Pledge of Allegiance, this and similar lawsuits spent the better part of two decades kicking around the court system. Though later overturned, in Newdow's first case, giving credence to the claim that the phrase "one nation under God" offended him as an atheist, a lower court ruled in his favor. This ruling sparked nationwide headlines, political outrage, atheists' celebrations, and volumes of voice-mail messages.

The responses from the legal, political, and atheist camps fit. The responses from "Christians" did not. True, it is questionable whether the people who left those caustic messages really are Christians. Most of the callers omitted their religious affiliation, but quite a few of them clearly articulated a pro-God stance. That a follower of Christ might do such a thing raises the age-old question: "Why are there so many hypocrites in the church?"

Some Christians say that this is the most common objection to Christianity they hear. This question is worded in a variety of ways:

- "Why is history littered with such hatred and oppression done by Christians?"
- "Why do some non-Christians I know live better lives than Christians?"
- "Why are Christians so full of hatred, insensitivity, and self-righteousness?"
- "I thought Christians are supposed to be humble, generous, morally pure, loving, or _____ [fill in the blank]."

However worded, the hypocrisy question poses the more substantive objection: "If this is what Christianity is all about, why should I want any part of it?"

The Objection Is Not to Mere Hypocrisy

A working definition for *hypocrisy* could be "saying one thing and doing another." James S. Spiegel, in his thorough treatment of the subject, calls it "a lie told with outward deeds."[1] He begins his book with the following recounting of his painful first encounter with the dreaded condition.

---

1. James S. Spiegel, *Hypocrisy: Moral Fraud and Other Vices* (Grand Rapids: Baker, 1999), 25.

When I was a young teenager I would often mow lawns for extra cash. On one occasion a friend and I approached a man who lived across the street from my house and asked him if he would allow us to cut his lawn. He agreed and offered to pay us twenty-five dollars for the job, noting that he would be gone for the weekend and would therefore pay us upon his return. That Saturday my friend and I worked for several hours, but because it was a rather large lawn, we had to finish it on Sunday. The next day we returned to obtain our wages from the man. In hopes that he would be impressed by our labor, we informed him that it took us two days to get the job done. "Two days?" he asked. "You mean to tell me that you mowed my lawn on Sunday?" We nodded. "Well, boys, I don't allow work to be done at my house on Sundays. I can't pay you." We watched him as he dug into his pocket and pulled out approximately two dollars in change. He handed it to us, saying, "I'm doing this out of the kindness of my heart."

In stunned silence my friend and I sauntered back into my house and informed my father as to what had just transpired. He was irate. "Hypocrites . . . lousy hypocrites!" he bellowed. "They smile so sweetly and look so righteous at church, but in the real world they're nothing but swindlers and cheats!"[2]

Swindling, cheating, lying, hating, running off with the church secretary—and these aren't the only hypocritical behaviors that bother people. Sometimes they're worse! People are rightly disturbed, for example, upon hearing reports of sexual abuse by clergy. Most sensible people cringe at the mention of the church's displays of hypocrisy throughout history—the Crusades, the Spanish Inquisition, countless episodes of anti-Semitism and racism, the Salem witch trials, and other moments of shame.

---

2. James S. Spiegel, *Hypocrisy: Moral Fraud and Other Vices* (Grand Rapids: Baker, 1999), 9.

Nonbelievers often express emotional heat behind the question, "Why are there so many hypocrites in the church?" Many go beyond, asking, "Why are some of Jesus's followers such jerks?" When we take on this common, painful, and—in some cases—complex hypocrisy question, we need to ensure that we answer the real question.

The Objection Is Not Really to Hypocrisy

Some people use the hypocrisy question as a weapon, similar to the way skeptics use the problem of evil. They have little interest in the reasons behind a lapse in righteous living. Nor do they feel any outrage or pain as a result of the church's hypocrisy. They merely use this question to attack, wanting to discredit the church and its messengers.

Their motivation might stem from attempts at self-justification. After all, the gospel message tells us we're not righteous—no, not one! If our hearers believe, though, that they *are* good enough, they need to shoot holes in our message to make themselves feel better. Just the mere smell of the gospel gets their guard up—and their attack comes in the form of, "Well, what about all the hypocrites in the church?" Paul's words to the Corinthians should help us anticipate this kind of reaction: "For we are to God the pleasing aroma of Christ among those who are being saved and those who are perishing. To the one we are an aroma that brings death; to the other, an aroma that brings life" (2 Cor. 2:15–16).

Jesus gives us insight as to why this is so. In His evangelistic dialogue with Nicodemus, He exposed the heart's condition behind the head's petition. After his account of the exchange between Jesus and Nicodemus, John wrote: "This is the verdict: Light has come into the world, but people loved darkness instead of light because their deeds were evil. Everyone who does evil hates the light, and will not come into the light for fear that their deeds will be exposed" (John 3:19–20).

Whether a question camouflages an angry attack, self-justification, or some other indirect assault, a straightforward answer should not follow. That would amount to, as discussed in chapter 5, answering fools according to their folly.

A case in point is Mohammed, whom I met at the University of Maryland. At the beginning of the school year, most student organizations set up a table to distribute information to boost membership. The atmosphere is rich. In addition to three dozen (!) religious organizations, students promote everything from animal rights to chess competition, hawk their wares, and hand out fliers advertising their first meetings.

Mohammed approached our table and announced, "I'm not a Christian. I'm from Saudi Arabia and a Muslim. I have just one question about American Christianity."

No one has just one question about anything, I thought. Sensing Mohammed's insincerity, I played along and asked what his question was.

"Why are you Christians so divided?" This is a popular form of the hypocrisy question. If we Christians are supposed to love one another in unity, our multitude of denominations evidences hypocrisy.

I answered his question with a question.

"Can you tell me why Muslims are so divided?"

Freeze this frame in your mind. You have to enjoy the irony and humor of the moment. The four or five young gentile Christian undergraduates standing behind me took a collective step backward. They felt the temperature rise. I, however, laughed inwardly at the thought of a New York Jew debating with a Middle Eastern Muslim about Christianity in front of a table marked "Campus *Crusade*"! If only I had had a camera.

Mohammed replied, "Oh no! Muslims are united. We're not divided."

"Oh, come on," I blurted out. "You must be kidding me. Muslims don't agree. Are you telling me the Sunnis and the Shiites agree on everything?"

"Well, they agree on the important things."

"Then why do they kill each other over unimportant things?"

By now the undergraduate crusaders had all left for their next classes. Suddenly, I was alone in this mini jihad. I pressed my Muslim acquaintance a little further.

"What's your point in asking this question?" I wanted him to get a glimpse of his own hypocrisy. "Are you saying that Christianity isn't valid because Christians don't get along? If so, then no one should be a Muslim either. And for that matter, no one should be Jewish, Hindu, Buddhist, or even an atheist."

"I just wanted to see why you thought there were so many different denominations of Christians."

"Really?" I said, letting him know I doubted his sincerity. I acknowledged his question with, "I don't know why there's so much division. I wish I did. It bothers me very much."

He left with a bit less swagger than when he approached our table. I hoped my "answers" defused some of his attack. I was sure that a detailed explanation of "why Christians are so divided" was not what the occasion demanded.

Pain Behind the Charge of Hypocrisy

Why is the question regarding hypocrisy so common? Are we really that bad? Is the church really *full* of hypocrites? Would a statistical analysis show the Christian world to have a higher percentage of failure than the rest of the world? Not likely. There must be more to the hypocrisy question than what meets the eye.

Yes, self-justification accounts for much, but not all, of the irrationality behind the question. Some people complain about hypocrisy, doing so from a significant amount of pain. For a variety of reasons, some of our neighbors and coworkers are angry at God. Because they can't punch Him in the eye, they take their potshots at us.

I believe that was the case with Bett. I wish I'd recognized it at the time. New to our campus fellowship, Bett was excited, having finally found a place to belong at the large, impersonal, urban university. She liked the spiritual as well as the social activities of our group, but never articulated a conversion testimony.

She attended every meeting, sang all of the songs, and even invited friends to join us—until someone suggested that we address the topic of abortion in one of our meetings. Suddenly, Bett turned cold.

"Why are we talking about that?" she complained. "Let's leave politics out of this. If we do this, I quit."

When I met with Bett to discuss her objections, I answered all sorts of questions—but none of the ones that she was asking.

I began with an arsenal of arguments—biblical, medical, sociological, pro-women, pro-child, pro-society—in favor of the pro-life position. I might just as well have been speaking in Martian.

She countered my blabbering with, "If Christians are so concerned about unborn babies, why don't they do something to help them? All they do is blow up abortion clinics. They're just a bunch of hypocrites."

I was well armed for this fight. I'd read many books about abortion. I had statistics and stories and evidence to show that Christians were doing plenty to help women with crisis pregnancies. I told stories of adoptions and gifts of maternity clothes and free ob-gyn care. It was all water off a duck's back. Nothing softened Bett's anger. In fact, my words fanned the flame of her indignation.

When I finished reciting some standard answers to the hypocrisy question, she politely excused herself and said goodbye. She never attended another fellowship meeting.

As I replay conversations with Bett, I hear evidence of what I later learned from others who knew her well—she had had an abortion a few years before coming to college. Like so many postabortion women, Bett harbored a tremendous amount of pain and unhealed anger behind her words.

Of all the books and articles about abortion, few offer the insight that Frederica Mathewes-Green shared in her book *Real Choices*. After interviewing hundreds of postabortion women around the country, she shared her findings with compassion and hope. I wish I'd read the following paragraph before meeting Bett:

> When I listened to women describe their situations in depth in small listening groups, a surprising theme emerged. In nearly every case, the abortion was undertaken to fulfill a felt obligation to another person, a parent or boyfriend. My assumption that abortion decisions were prompted by practical problems—food, shelter, poverty, clothing—was

not borne out. Instead, the woman felt bound to please or protect some other person, and abortion was the price she felt she had to pay.[3]

If Bett's situation was anything like these women's, I could understand why she harbored bitterness toward the people whom she felt had left her no choice—or the God who didn't stop them.

Many men and women, not just those who are connected to abortion, raise the hypocrisy question as an expression of anger and pain, rather than of curiosity or interest. We must discern the difference.

If I could turn back the clock, I'd pursue a very different kind of dialogue with Bett—one that might sound like this:

> RANDY: You're really opposed to our having that pro-life speaker, aren't you?

> BETT: Yes. I already told you that we shouldn't do it, and if we do, I'm quitting the fellowship.

> RANDY: Can you tell me why this is so upsetting to you?

> BETT: I'm not upset. I just think we should leave this issue alone. It's not what we're about.

> RANDY: But, Bett, you *are* upset.

> BETT: That's because no one's listening to me.

> RANDY: I'm trying to.

> BETT: You know, there are a lot of women on this campus who've had abortions. Some of them are my friends. They're strongly pro-choice and they'll hate us if we tell them they're wrong.

---

3. Frederica Mathewes-Green, *Real Choices* (Ben Lomond, CA: Conciliar Press, 1997), 22.

RANDY: Do you think abortion's wrong?

BETT: No, I don't. Well, maybe sometimes. At least, I don't think it's anyone's business except the woman's. And you've got no right telling me what I should do with my body.

RANDY: I think you're right that a lot of women on this campus have had abortions. Can you tell me how these women are feeling about their experience?

BETT: Some of them are fine about it. And some are just shut down about it. But some are really ticked off.

RANDY: Who are they mad at?

BETT: I don't know. Maybe their boyfriend for getting them pregnant. Or their parents for making them get an abortion. Or the church for making them feel like a slut. Why are you asking me all these questions? I told you I didn't want to talk about it.

RANDY: I'm sorry. It sounds like there's a whole lot of pain inside you about this.

BETT: You wouldn't understand.

RANDY: Do you believe me that I'm trying to understand?

BETT: Maybe. I don't know. Could we talk about something else? If you want to do this program about abortion, go ahead. It'll just mean that I'll have a lot more free time on Tuesday nights instead of going to the campus hypocrite meeting.

RANDY: I'm sorry to hear that. But I hope you'll believe me that I do care about your feelings. And I'm sorry to hear that this is so painful for you. Can I just say a few more words and then I'll shut up?

BETT: Sure.

RANDY: Some women I know have helped other women deal with the pain around abortion. They actually have support groups for what they call "postabortion stress." I really respect them a lot, and they're the exact opposite of hypocrites. They have an office on K Street downtown, and if you ever wanted to check them out, I think they could be helpful for some of these friends of yours who are angry. Here's one of their cards.

BETT: Okay.

RANDY: One last thing. It does sound to me like *you* might be angry at God.

BETT: Well, duh!

RANDY: I hope you won't stay that way for long. It's not a very fun way to live. If our fellowship can help you get over that, maybe just by listening, we'd like to try.

BETT: Thanks. I'll let you know.

I doubt that Bett asked the hypocrisy question as an attack to justify herself. The look in her eyes reflected disillusionment and pain.

When people complain about the moral failures of Christians—parents who made them get an abortion (or didn't stop them), pastors who had an affair, youth ministers who sexually abused teenagers—their bitterness could stem from crushed hopes. If they could verbalize all that's going on inside, they might say something like the following: "I knew it. I'd hoped there was such a thing as holiness and beauty and sexual fidelity, but there really isn't, is there? You got my hopes up, stirring up something within me—something that might have been planted by God—but then you dashed those hopes to pieces. You did more than just disappoint me. You impaired my ability to see God clearly. If He's holy and good and loving, the smear of your sin has tainted my lenses so I can't see it."

No wonder Jesus condemned religious hypocrisy so strongly—more so than the sin of nonreligious tax gatherers and prostitutes. Just as the prophets had done before Him, Jesus railed against those who claimed to be representatives of the divine. To punctuate His accusations against those who "do not practice what they preach," He used such terms as *blind fools*, *blind guides*, *whitewashed tombs*, *snakes*, and *brood of vipers* (see Matt. 23).

The Hypocrisy Question: An Opportunity to Clarify the Gospel

The good news about the hypocrisy question is that it can lead to sharing *the* good news. If questioners are sincere (and that's a very big *if*), we can show them some misconceptions behind their question—misconceptions about the gospel itself.

One common misconception is that profession equals possession. In reality, not everyone who claims to be a Christian *is* one. Unlike other religions into which a person can be born, Christianity is something into which a person must be *born again*. In other words, no one is born a Christian. Thus, people who never were authentic born-again followers of Christ have committed a great deal of evil and sin in the name of Christianity.

Lack of authenticity is important to remember when I converse with my Jewish friends. A great deal of anti-Semitism has been expressed through stained glass windows. When I was about ten years old, our family was asked to help guard our synagogue on Halloween night because during previous All Hallows' Eves the property had been defaced. One year someone delivered a message to our Jewish community using a lawnmower to carve a huge cross in our synagogue lawn. Far too many examples could be cited that demonstrate hatred "in the name of Jesus." Jesus Himself warned those who professed Him but never possessed Him that they would be greeted with, "I never knew you. Away from me, you evildoers!" (Matt. 7:23). Sharing that piece of the puzzle with those who raise the hypocrisy question could help clarify the need for each individual to receive the gospel's offer.

A second common misconception is that salvation means perfection. Somehow, people have gotten the impression that Christians claim to be perfect. They equate our condemnation of sin with a claim that we never sin. But the full picture of the gospel's work in our lives shows a multifaceted, progressive deliverance. We *have been* saved (past tense) from the *penalty* of sin. We *are* saved (present tense) from the *power* of sin. And someday we *will be* saved (future tense) from the *presence* of sin. Meanwhile, a mix of spiritual successes and failures remains more the norm than does total victory.

Portraying Christian experience as *a progressive journey toward* holiness rather than a present attaining of holiness can actually be liberating to questioners. That Christians are on a progressive journey is, perhaps, why some of the "church people" our questioning friends encounter *are* jerks—or just plain weird. Church is the one place where such people are welcomed. It could be said that the church is a haven for hypocrites—people who fail to perform according to the standards that they affirm.

So Why *Are* Hypocrites in the Church?

Even some Christians fail to realize the progressive nature of salvation. As a result, some of us boast a level of sanctification to which we're not even close. Or we fall prey to a hazard of finding the truth—we take credit for it. Even as redeemed children of God, our flesh occasionally rebels against the notion of grace—totally undeserved favor. We start to believe our own press releases and think that we are smart enough, good enough, or clever enough to deserve the cross. For others of us, our unwavering belief in absolutes (a good thing!) degenerates to an obnoxious display of haughtiness. Sometimes, then, the charge of hypocrisy is well deserved.

Yet something still feels unresolved, doesn't it? Even after dismissing some people's attacks, recognizing other people's pain, clarifying other questioners' misconceptions, or repenting of our own hypocrisy, the objection still lingers. Why *are* hypocrites in the church? Couldn't God have done a better job of establishing a PR firm on His behalf? If we're supposed to be His representatives, why didn't He put together a better team?

A sufficient answer can come only through theological reflection. If we think deeply about our place in God's redemptive plan, we'll be better equipped to respond to the hypocrisy question with both words to say and patience to listen.

Considering the dual nature of the kingdom of God can help us achieve perspective about hypocrisy. Jesus spoke often about the kingdom. Some people say that the kingdom was, in fact, His central message. His teaching built upon the Old Testament theme "The Lord is king," the Scriptures' declaring God's kingship both of Israel (see Exod. 15:18; Num. 23:21; Deut. 33:5; Isa. 43:15) and of all of the earth (see 2 Kings 19:15; Isa. 6:5; Jer. 46:18; Pss. 96:10; 99:1–4).

Although scriptural statements abound of the Lord's reigning *now*, many references also promise a later fuller reign (Isa. 24:23; Zeph. 3:15–17; Zech. 14:9). The late George Elden Ladd, a seminary professor and an influential writer about the kingdom, said of this twofold description, "This leads to the conclusion that while God is the King, he must also become King, i.e., he must manifest his kingship in the world of human beings and nations."[4]

Thus, Jesus announced, "the kingdom of God has come upon you" (Matt. 12:28), yet He also told us to pray, "Your kingdom *come*, Your will *be* done" (6:10 NKJV; emphasis added). The kingdom has already come—and people experience salvation, healing, forgiveness, and power in their daily lives. Yet it is not here in all of its fullness—some

---

4. George Elden Ladd, *A Theology of the New Testament*, rev. ed. (Grand Rapids: Eerdmans, 1993), 58.

diseases are not healed, some people do not bow the knee to the Lord's anointed, and lions do not lie down with lambs.

This already/not-yet perspective helps us understand why Jesus stopped reading Scripture, mid-sentence, in that synagogue in Nazareth (see Luke 4:16–21). The passage prescribed for that Sabbath, Isaiah 61:1–2, reads:

> The Spirit of the Sovereign LORD is on me,
>   because the LORD has anointed me
>   to proclaim good news to the poor.
> He has sent me to bind up the brokenhearted,
>   to proclaim freedom for the captives
>   and release from darkness for the prisoners,
> to proclaim the year of the LORD's favor
>   and the day of vengeance of our God,
> to comfort all who mourn.

Jesus stopped after "to proclaim the year of the Lord's favor" and did not announce "the day of vengeance of our God." This stopping point is significant. When He went on to declare, "Today this scripture is fulfilled in your hearing" (Luke 4:21), He was careful not to claim more than He should. His first coming, the "already," was fulfilled in their hearing. Good news (the message of salvation) was proclaimed to the poor, broken hearts were bound up, and captives and prisoners (to the slavery of sin) were set free.

But "the day of vengeance of our God" has not yet come. That part of the prophecy will not be fulfilled until the second coming, when final judgment and vengeance will be poured out.

The implications of living during what some have called "the time between the times" include a number of disappointments. Some people are delivered from crippling sins whereas others learn to live with that thorn in their flesh. Some believers are miraculously cured of cancer whereas others gracefully enter eternity and claim a new body there. Some political hot spots are cooled off by peace treaties whereas others fester and even erupt in violent war. Our swords have not been turned into plowshares—yet.

But living in the already/not-yet kingdom also results in a bitter-sweet longing for consummation. C. S. Lewis called it "joy" and described it as "an unsatisfied desire which is itself more desirable than any other satisfaction."[5]

That the kingdom is still unfulfilled, that final judgment has not been rendered, that our longing for the consummate kingdom is disappointed—all result in unsatisfied desire. Our dissatisfaction is why we sometimes behave as hypocrites, even while we hate doing so. The eternity that is planted in our hearts finds its initial fulfillment in our Savior's cross, yet it longs for total fulfillment in the very presence of that Savior. The church's being earthbound bothers us because we're destined for heaven, not for earth. Simply put, then, hypocrites are in the church because the church is still on earth, not in heaven.

Questions for Answering the Hypocrisy Charge

So what do we say when people raise the hypocrisy question? If they're just attacking us, we would be wise to deflect their barb and point out their own hypocrisy. If they're in pain, we must empathize and show that we care. If they're legitimately outraged, we should join them.

In cases where people really want to dialogue about the inconsistencies between what we practice and what we preach, we should use a variety of questions to guide them to the grace of the gospel.

First, our asking a negatively worded question can help diffuse the emotional heat and put their question into perspective.

- "You don't think that all Christians are hypocrites, do you?"
- "You wouldn't say that the church is full of hypocrites, would you?"
- "You wouldn't say that hypocritical behavior is the norm for Christians, would you?"

---

5. C. S. Lewis, *Surprised by Joy* (San Diego: Harvest Books, 1955), 17–18.

- "You don't think that hypocrisy is the kind of behavior that Christianity teaches, do you?"

A second kind of response, agreeing with them, is not a question at all. But it paves the way for questions that can bring insight. When people are right, we should take advantage of the platform that they've built for our message and offer statements of affirmation. We should agree wholeheartedly because some amount of anger over hypocrisy is God-given. When people recount a particular episode of hypocritical behavior, we can respond with affirming statements.

- "Wow. That is hypocritical."
- "Ouch. I can see why that's so painful for you."
- "I don't blame you for being upset."

A third kind of response that paves the way for probing questions involves surprising admissions.

- "Yeah, you're right. The church is full of hypocrites."
- "Well, you know, I'm a hypocrite too."
- "Actually, we're all hypocrites, if you think about it."

A fourth kind of response, appropriate for some people, turns the table on them.

- "Aren't you a hypocrite some of the time?"
- "Don't you fail to live up to your own standards?"
- "Don't you, on occasion, say one thing and do another?"

Finally, some questions, particularly for some of our more thoughtful interlocutors, bring to the surface deep dissatisfaction with the not-yet nature of our world. (In the questions below, note the use of *us* instead of *you*. We want our friends to know that we join them in their hatred of hypocrisy.)

- "Why do you suppose this hypocrisy bothers us so much?"
- "What is it about hypocrisy that makes us want to scream?"
- "The fact that this bothers you so much makes me want to ask why. What would you say to that?"

Somewhere in the dialogue, we should say something like this:

- "I think the fact that hypocrisy bothers us so much points to some sense of right and wrong, doesn't it?"
- "I wonder, is the fact that we hate hypocrisy so much a sign that there's some other way that things should be? What do you think?"

Sooner or later, we can admit our own hypocrisy as being the basis for our need for the cross. Such a pleasant surprise could help the questioners find relief for their hypocrisy as well. Here are a few ways we might say it:

- "One of the reasons I'm a Christian is because it solves my own hypocrisy problem. When Jesus died on the cross, He showed that there really are such things as righteousness and sin."
- "My problems include things that are even worse than hypocrisy. The Bible calls them sin. And although I've tried, I've never been able to rid myself of all hypocrisy. So Jesus's payment for sin seems like very good news to me. It resolves my hypocrisy."
- "I really deal with my own hypocrisy all the time. I guess that if I were really in touch with all that's going on in my heart, I'd see that I'm an even bigger hypocrite than I realize. I say that people shouldn't be rude, but boy, am I a jerk sometimes (especially when I'm behind the wheel of my car). I say that men should be faithful to their wives, but sometimes I look at women in ways that I shouldn't. The best thing about being a Christian, in my opinion, is that I'm forgiven for *all* my failings—not just my hypocrisy."

- "I guess that one of the reasons why the church has so many jerks in it is because it's the one place that acknowledges that we're *all* jerks! But the church helps us find forgiveness for being a jerk as well as the power to stop being one."

Would I leave any of these messages on Michael Newdow's voice mail? I doubt it. Should we try them out when a friend complains about Christian hypocrites he or she knows? I think so. Until we enter the next stage of redemptive history, we'll probably hear this question a lot. We might as well prepare an answer that displays wisdom, compassion, and agreement rather than the alternatives. How we respond to "Why are some of Jesus's followers such jerks?" shouldn't add fuel to the fire.

PART 3
WHY AREN'T QUESTIONS AND ANSWERS ENOUGH?

CHAPTER 11

The Question of Compassion: "What If I Don't Care That My Neighbor Is Going to Hell?"

Not too long ago, I received two emails with subject lines containing the word, "Taliban." Since I don't often see news from or about that terrorist group in my inbox, I opened both with fear and trepidation. One was a news report of how Afghanistan had quickly fallen into the Taliban's control after the rebels had been held at bay for twenty years. The other was a request to pray for the Taliban.[6]

"Pray for the Taliban?" I wondered. Why? They're scoundrels (and worse!) and may very well be plotting America's demise. I had heard people say they were praying for numerous terrorist group members to experience God's salvation. I think I was praying for another one of God's attributes to become real for them—his wrath!

Instead of praying for the Taliban, I prayed for myself.

This wasn't the first such confession. Months before, I had come to the painful realization that I just didn't care about my lost neighbors' souls as much as I should. And I don't think that I'm alone. As I rub shoulders with fellow believers, I hear a coldness and, in some cases, a contempt toward the lost world around us.

Consider the *tone* of some popular Christian bumper stickers:

- "Next time you think you're perfect, try walking on water."

---

6. Joe Carter, "How to Pray for Afghanistan—and the Taliban," The Gospel Coalition, August 16, 2021, https://www.thegospelcoalition.org/article/how-to-pray-for-the-taliban/.

- "Make your reservations for eternity now—smoking or non-smoking."
- "I'm a fool for Christ. Whose fool are you?"

My all-time favorite, complete with red flames coming from the bottom of the sticker, is, "If you're living like there is no God, you'd better be right!"

Do these sentiments sound like the One who appealed, "Come to me, all you who are weary and burdened, and I will give you rest" (Matt. 11:28)? Or are they the frustrated exclamations of an angry, contemptuous heart?

For a variety of valid reasons, some Christians are angry at the world around them (see chapter 12). But in some cases, we hold something worse—contempt. Dallas Willard, in his thoughtful examination of the Sermon on the Mount, was helpful in distinguishing between anger and contempt:

> In anger I want to hurt you. In contempt, I don't care whether you are hurt or not. Or at least so I say. You are not worth consideration one way or the other. We can be angry at someone without denying their worth. But contempt makes it easier for us to hurt them or see them further degraded.[7]

Somewhere along the line of the Lord's hearing and answering my I-just-don't-care-for-the-lost prayer, I met Nathaniel. My response to him has given me hope that God can defrost and heal a cold, hardened heart—if we ask Him.

I'd just finished speaking to a gathering of college students who were spending their summers as interns in Washington, DC. "Evangelism as a Way of Life" had been requested as the topic for my talk. These were Christians who wanted to share their faith with fellow

---

7. Dallas Willard, *The Divine Conspiracy* (New York: HarperCollins, 1998), 151.

interns and other coworkers. Nathaniel approached me after my message with a disturbed look on his face.

"Can we talk?" he asked.

I was more than glad to talk with him. Given the description of my audience, I assumed that he was a believer. I was wrong. A few introductory probes showed me that Nathaniel had been invited by a Christian coworker to taste some authentic Christlike community. He liked what he felt but couldn't reconcile it with his intellectual questions.

"My dad's a Christian," he began, "and he's given me every book you can think of to convince me that Christianity's the right way. I've read C. S. Lewis, Francis Schaeffer, Josh McDowell, you name it. I just can't seem to make sense of it all." Nathaniel's tone of voice betrayed a vulnerability that I had rarely heard from an inquirer.

"What, specifically, is confusing to you?" I asked.

"That's the problem. I can't even say for sure what bothers me. I just feel like my father doesn't make any sense to me. My past doesn't fit with my present, and I don't know what I'm going to do after I graduate." (He later told me that he had less than a year of college left, and he was terrified about what followed.)

Nathaniel spoke with only one voice, but I responded to two stimuli. One response was to the content of his question: What books could I recommend to him? What passages of the Bible would cut through his confusion? Who should he meet to see Christian graciousness incarnated?

The other response was much deeper. I felt a pain and a sadness for him that I hadn't often felt. I almost started to cry. How tragic that this young guy felt so much alienation—from God, from his father, even from himself. Confusion, I realized at that moment, is not simply an intellectual puzzle to be sorted out; it's an emotional knot to be untied.

What struck me even more was what I *didn't* feel. In similar conversations, I've felt, I'm ashamed to say, contempt for the questioner. If I'd put words to my caustic emotions, they might have sounded as bad as this: "Well, what do you expect from turning your back on

God? Peace and happiness? Your pride won't let you accept answers even though they're logical and reasonable. Your unbelief has caused you to be irrational. Professing to become wise, you've become a fool! Sooner or later, you'll pay for this pride. And if you wait too long, it'll be too late. Then what?"

I'm sad to say that I could go on. But remarkably, for me, as I sat next to Nathaniel, I didn't! God was answering my prayers for compassion in far greater ways than I could have imagined.

Examples to Follow

If we're to incarnate the gospel with our lives as well as communicate it with our words, we must be liberated from contempt and anger, and be transformed by grace and love. For that transformation to occur, asking God to bring it about is crucial. But we can also contribute to the process by reflecting on some great examples.

The supreme role model, of course, is our Lord Himself. "When he saw the crowds, he had compassion on them, because they were harassed and helpless, like sheep without a shepherd" (Matt. 9:36). This was a strong emotional response. Some people would say that the text implies a physical reaction as well.

Do we see people as Jesus does? Do we get beyond their veneer of success, wealth, laughter, confidence, or positive mental attitude? Imagine what it must be like to face death without the assurance of salvation, to handle sickness without the comfort of prayer, or to deal with uncertainty without the fellowship of the Holy Spirit. Imagining such despair can help us be more like Jesus.

Paul's emotional experience in Athens should also challenge us to adjust our perspective. Acts tell us that "he was greatly distressed to see that the city was full of idols" (17:16). Like Jesus's compassion, Paul's response had a physical dimension to it, but it also included indignation, sadness, and grief. He wrestled with a holy anger toward idolatry and a deep burden to see people delivered from it.

His impassioned response stands in stark contrast to the shallow ways of the Epicureans and Stoics who heard Paul on Mars Hill. These two competing worldviews continue to shape the souls of people today. Epicureans "held that pleasure was the chief goal of life, with the pleasure most worth enjoying being a life of tranquility free from pain, disturbing passions, superstitious fears, and anxiety about death."[8] We can easily see Epicurean influence in our if-it-feels-good-do-it culture.

It's disturbing that some Christians reflect more Epicurean sentiments than Pauline sentiments. With a high premium placed on "joy," or "fellowship," and a distorted view of "the abundant life," some people steer clear of any uncomfortable burdens connected with seeing a world in need. Sadness and burden, by definition, are excluded from a life that is supposed to be happy and full.

Similarly, some followers of Jesus have mistaken Stoicism for Christian maturity. They think that the healthy Christian is unflappable. They read the newspaper, listen to their neighbors, or watch television and remain emotionally unmoved. Their trust in God's sovereignty and their confidence in Christ's return put everything neatly in place for them. They don't get upset or angry (at least, not in a righteous way). They just "praise the Lord," knowing that they won't get left behind.

Neither Paul nor Jesus made such mistakes. They saw idolatry and lostness around them and were moved to distress—even tears. Without such anguish, we fail to reflect godliness and wholeness to a godless, fractured world. If Jesus wept and Paul groaned, we should do more than sigh or sneer.

Paul's distress might have stemmed from his deep understanding of idolatry. He knew what idols can and cannot do. They cannot save or satisfy, but they can enslave and dehumanize.

When people esteem anything as higher in value or with greater affection than the true God, they set their hopes for satisfaction in that revered thing. They offer "worth-ship." That's idolatry. Forget about the images of people bowing before statues. To be sure, they portray idolatry in its most simplistic form. But anything (a sports

---

8. Richard N. Longenecker, *The Acts of the Apostles, The Expositor's Bible Commentary*, vol. 9 (Grand Rapids: Zondervan, 1981), 473–74.

team, a car, a possession, a career, a relationship, a dream, an intellect, an accomplishment, pleasure, pain, the past, the future, an experience, approval, revenge, desire, or even a regret!) can be an idol. Such religiosity is so subtle and so prevalent in our world that it fails to elicit any response, let alone a distressing or compassionate one. And, if we're honest, we, too, might find a few of those things claiming primary allegiance in our hearts.

Paul and Jesus also grasped the real nature of unbelief. People do not reject the gospel primarily because they're too thickheaded to get it. Unbelief grows out of other soils besides intellectual confusion. Instead, people reject the good news because they're enslaved to other kinds of news. They're in love with something unworthy of such devotion, and it won't let them go.

An Example *Not* to Follow

When we see people as Jesus and Paul did—as sheep without a shepherd, or as misguided idol worshippers—we are more likely to feel compassion than contempt. In addition to appreciating these good examples, we can further adjust our compassion thermostats by examining a bad example—Jonah.

Many people are quick to condemn Jonah. We marvel at how silly he was to think that he could run from God. And with little compassion for him, we chide his lack of compassion for Nineveh. But a closer look at this short book should temper our dismissal of the so-called reluctant prophet. How loving would *we* be toward an invading enemy with a well-deserved reputation as heartless rapists and unrelenting murderers? The similarity between Nineveh and the Taliban might be closer than we think.

Given Nineveh's reputation, it is remarkable that God called Nineveh a "great city" three times: when He commanded Jonah to go preach there (1:2); when He issued the call a second time (3:2); and when He appealed with these words, "Should I not have concern for the great city of Nineveh?" (4:11).

Nineveh is described as "great" one other time. In chapter 3, at the onset of Jonah's obedience, the narrator identifies it in an unusual way, using a play on words to describe both Nineveh's large geographic proportions ("a three-day journey," as 3:3 [NKJV] puts it) and its special place in God's heart.

The Hebrew grammar of that phrase, usually translated something like "an exceedingly great city," is unique. Footnotes in many Bibles tell us that it could also be translated "a city important to God," or most literally, "a city great to God." I think that the evidence tilts the scales toward the footnoted rendition.[9]

God saw Nineveh as an object of his concern, a place that was filled with people who did not know their right hand from their left, and a place that owed its very existence, like the vine that sheltered Jonah's head, to God's sustaining hand (see 4:10). The narrator reminds us that Nineveh was "great to God" because God is the one who deemed it so—three times!

God could just as easily call our neighbors "great" or "important" because He created them in His image, lets the sun shine down on them—the wicked and the righteous—and grieves that they do not know their right hand from their left. If we do not share His concern for those around us, we need the same medication as Jonah: repentance.

Nothing short of contrition can transform us toward that end. Like Jonah, who cared deeply for a vine that he had no role in creating or sustaining, we have more compassion for pets, cars, golf clubs, or other inanimate objects than we do for people—image-bearers of eternal significance. It will not do for us to naively condemn Jonah with, "Oh, I'd never be so coldhearted," or simply resolve to be more compassionate. It took the salvific vehicle of a big fish to turn Jonah's heart around. (Read his prayer in chapter 2.) It takes another salvific vehicle, a cross, to get us into a similar posture.

But beware. The transformation must be complete, not just temporary. When the curtain falls on the drama of Jonah, we are left with uncertainty. Did the angry prophet ever respond to God's grace as

---

9. T. Desmond Alexander, *Jonah, Tyndale Old Testament Commentaries*, vol. 23a (Downers Grove, IL: InterVarsity, 1988), 119n3.

Nineveh did? They "turned from their evil ways" (3:10). Or did he continue to wallow in self-pity and get the answer to his prayer, "Take away my life, for it is better for me to die than to live" (4:3)?

A Transformation for Which to Ask

Looking to good and bad examples, grasping the full ramification of idolatry, and remembering the real nature of unbelief take us only so far in our quest for compassion. We must also marvel at the scandal of grace.

Scandal seems like the wrong word, doesn't it? It brings to mind something that causes (or ought to cause) disgrace—a politician's involvement in organized crime, for example, or a CEO's dishonest accounting practices.

But perhaps another dimension of the word *scandal* does point us toward Calvary. The New Testament terms *skandalon* and *skandalizo* are sources of our English word *scandalize*, meaning "that which gives offense or causes revulsion or arouses opposition."[10]

Scandal perfectly conveys the nature of Jesus, which He foresaw as a stumbling block. In distinction from "causing someone to sin" (a common meaning of the word, as in Matt. 5:29–30), Jesus caused people to be taken aback. His failure to fulfill their expectations gave offense and aroused opposition. He scandalized John the Baptist because He revealed Himself as an unexpected kind of Messiah (Matt. 11:6). The people in Jesus's hometown were scandalized by His ordinariness (Matt. 13:57). The Pharisees were scandalized by Jesus's insight—that their uncleanness flowed from what came out of their mouths rather than what went into them (Matt. 15:10–12).

Paul understood the cross as a scandal because it showed us how incapable we are of attaining kingdom righteousness by self-effort. Israel pursued righteousness "not by faith but as if it were by works" and thus did not attain it. They stumbled over the "scandal rock" (see Rom. 9:31–33; Isa. 8:14). In fact, Paul insisted that if we *could* become

---

10. W. F. Bauer, F. W. Danker, W. F. Arndt, and F. W. Gingrich, "Skandalon," in *A Greek-English Lexicon of the New Testament and Other Early Christian Literature* (Chicago: University of Chicago Press, 1979), 753.

righteous by mere works (symbolized by circumcision), the scandal of the cross would be abolished (Gal. 5:11). Peter concurred (1 Peter 2:8), citing the same verse from Isaiah.

In other words, grace should be both amazing and alarming to us. Although something in our bent toward self-sufficiency hates it, the wonder of it should overwhelm us with joy, gratitude, humility, and an urge to share it.

Yet grace can become mundane. We've read the ending of the story below so many times, it fails to startle us. But we can be sure that a smile was not the response for which Jesus strove when He told this scandalous parable. Try to read it as if for the first time, and see if you feel the intended surprising force.

> For the kingdom of heaven is like a landowner who went out early in the morning to hire workers for his vineyard. He agreed to pay them a denarius for the day and sent them into his vineyard.
>
> About nine in the morning he went out and saw others standing in the marketplace doing nothing. He told them, "You also go and work in my vineyard, and I will pay you whatever is right." So they went.
>
> He went out again about noon and about three in the afternoon and did the same thing. About five in the afternoon he went out and found still others standing around. He asked them, "Why have you been standing here all day long doing nothing?"
>
> "Because no one has hired us," they answered.
>
> He said to them, "You also go and work in my vineyard."
>
> When evening came, the owner of the vineyard said to his foreman, "Call the workers and pay them their wages, beginning with the last ones hired and going on to the first."
>
> The workers who were hired about five in the afternoon came and each received a denarius. So when those came who were hired first, they expected to receive more. But each one of them also received a denarius. When they received it, they

began to grumble against the landowner. "These who were hired last worked only one hour," they said, "and you have made them equal to us who have borne the burden of the work and the heat of the day."

But he answered one of them, "I am not being unfair to you, friend. Didn't you agree to work for a denarius? Take your pay and go. I want to give the one who was hired last the same as I gave you. Don't I have the right to do what I want with my own money? Or are you envious because I am generous?"

So the last will be first, and the first will be last. (Matt. 20:1–16)

Doesn't this parable bother you? Isn't something inside crying out for our kind of "fairness"? Many interpreters betray their discomfort with this parable by minimizing the scandal of it, and thus its potential to create stumbling. One such effort sees the five o'clock worker as so industrious that his output matched that of the workers who toiled all day. Another interpreter evens out the "willingness" of the workers at the beginning and the end of the day. Still another person, with an appeal to equality but little attention to the text, argues that all people and their efforts for the kingdom are equal before God. Each of these views, however, requires information from outside the parable. None does justice to the punch line, "So the last will be first, and the first will be last" (Matt. 20:16).

Doesn't this parable, too, infuse us with a sense of stunned humility when we hear, "Don't I have the right to do what I want with my own money?" One commentator explains, "If God's generosity was to be represented by a man, such a man would be different than any man ever encountered."[11]

Reflecting on the stumbling block of the cross and the counterintuitive nature of grace should drive us to a humbling yet beautiful

---

11. For a summary of these interpretations and Norman A. Huffmann's words, see D. A. Carson, *Matthew, The Expositor's Bible Commentary*, vol. 8 (Grand Rapids: Zondervan, 1984), 427.

intersection—that of God's awesome holiness and our utter unwor-
thiness. We should marvel that the God who reveals Himself as fire
(a frequent image of white-hot holiness) does not simply consume us
sinners. God did not consume even Moses, who whined and argued
on that holy ground. And like him (as well as the burning bush!), we
are not consumed. (See Lam. 3:22 for the reason.)

This humility, then, should extend outward, as noted evangelism
leader D. T. Niles would quip, like "one beggar telling another beggar
where to find bread." There ought to be, though, a far more adequate
analogy. The label of "beggar" doesn't quite encompass the extent
of our despair, and salvation is far greater than bread. Nevertheless,
the cliché does steer us 180 degrees from arrogance and haughtiness.

Steps Toward Compassion

So how do we become more compassionate? The first steps occur
on our knees. We must confess our lack of concern. The great promise
of 1 John 1:9 involves both forgiveness and cleansing: "If we confess
our sins, he is faithful and just and will forgive us our sins." When
we invoke the familiar words, however, we must press on to the rest
of the verse, "and purify us from all unrighteousness." God not only
declares us forgiven and justified but also furthers the cleansing
work that He began in us. When we confess that we don't care if our
neighbor is going to hell, God pardons and also perfects. He makes
us less stained, wrinkled, angry, contemptuous, or self-absorbed.

We might need to tell our heavenly Father, "I don't care about
people the way I should. I have a cold heart. Please make me more
like You—caring, compassionate, gracious, and abounding in mercy.
Give me as great a longing to see Your work in people around me as
I long for it within me. I need You to work because I cannot manu-
facture this kind of compassion by myself."

In offering such a prayer, we can be certain that God will work
to "de-Jonahize," giving us a heart for lost neighbors and friends.
Praying thus might make us feel as though we were learning a foreign
language. Contrition has fallen out of vogue, and weekly times of

corporate confession are almost extinct. This prayer from the Book of Common Prayer sounds, in fact, almost alien:

> ALMIGHTY and most merciful Father; We have erred, and strayed from thy ways like lost sheep. We have followed too much the devices and desires of our own hearts. We have offended against thy holy laws. We have left undone those things which we ought to have done; And we have done those things which we ought not to have done; And there is no health in us. But thou, O Lord, have mercy upon us, miserable offenders. Spare thou those, O God, who confess their faults. Restore thou those who are penitent; According to thy promises declared unto mankind in Christ Jesus our Lord. And grant, O most merciful Father, for his sake; That we may hereafter live a godly, righteous, and sober life, to the glory of thy holy Name. Amen.[12]

Becoming fluent in this language, as the church once was, could help us draw nearer to God and reflect His heart to those around us. We needn't fear that confessing will minimize grace. Nor do we offer confessions as atonement for sin, but rather out of gratitude for the work already done to pardon sin.

For individual confession, the following list, from John Baillie's classic *A Diary of Private Prayer*, provides a valuable template.

> O Father in heaven, who didst fashion my limbs to serve Thee and my soul to follow hard after Thee, with sorrow and contrition of heart I acknowledge before Thee the faults and failures of the day that is now past. . . .
> My failure to be true even to my own accepted standards:
> My self-deception in face of temptation:
> My choosing of the worse when I know the better:
> O Lord, forgive.

---

12. *Book of Common Prayer and Administration of the Sacraments and Other Rites and Ceremonies of the Church* (New York: Seabury Press, 1953), 6.

My failure to apply to myself the standards of conduct I demand of others:

My blindness to the suffering of others and my slowness to be taught by my own:

My complacence towards wrongs that do not touch my own case and my over-sensitiveness to those that do:

My slowness to see the good in my fellows and to see the evil in myself:

My hardness of heart towards my neighbors' faults and my readiness to make allowance of my own:

My unwillingness to believe that Thou hast called me to a small work and my brother to a great one:

O Lord, forgive.[13]

A second step toward compassion, still from a kneeling posture, involves praying for those who do not know Christ. When we plead for God to draw people to Him, we ourselves are drawn to those people. Making lists of those who are our "ten most wanted" and keeping them in our Bibles can prompt prayers as well as soften hearts. To do so in no way demonstrates a lack of belief in the sovereignty of a predestinating God. Even Paul prayed for lost people—whether it was the entire nation of Israel (Rom. 10:1) or the individual soul of King Agrippa (Acts 26:29).

To be sure, most people do not have the gift of evangelism and will never gush with the gospel as freely as those who have that calling. So we shouldn't expect the levels of burden for the lost, the free flow of speech, or the same kind of responses given to the likes of a Billy Graham or other evangelists. Nevertheless, we can ask and expect answers for increased levels of compassion and desire to tell others the good news that has transformed us.

A third step toward compassion involves empathy—seeing things from our neighbors' perspective. We usually zero in on the second part of Proverbs 14:12: "There is a way that appears to be right, but

---

13. John Baillie, *A Diary of Private Prayer: A Devotional Classic* (New York: Scribner, 1949), 15.

in the end it leads to death." We simply see people as lost and headed for hell. But the first half of the proverb is worth equal reflection. We should ask, "*Why* does this way seem right to them?" Even if we fail to accurately identify their motivation, compassion for them is bound to be stirred.

Buddhism seems right to many inquirers because it acknowledges an oft-neglected spiritual dimension of life. It also minimizes the difficulty of dealing with evil and pain, and appeals to people who are hassled by the noise and chaos of modern society. Sitting in silence for half an hour of meditation after fighting traffic and technology seems right to a lot of people.

Islam seems right to many people because it calls for an uncompromising moral purity in a world that has become nauseatingly immoral. New Age beliefs seem right to some people because they satisfy a longing for transcendence without the pain of contrition.

We could go on and on, citing valid attractions of each competing worldview. And indeed, we should, if we are ever to display respect for our hearers as we declare the superiority of the gospel.

The "way" might seem right, however, for less cognitive reasons. She might be pro-choice because she once felt trapped by an unplanned pregnancy and found acceptance only at an abortion clinic. He might be sympathetic toward homosexual people because a close friend was beaten and ridiculed for his sexual orientation. She might be an atheist because her overzealous Christian parents were harsh in her upbringing. He might be addicted to money because of a deep-seated fear of never having enough. She might be promiscuous because she never felt accepted by her father, who abandoned her at an early age. Their anger might have more substance than yours!

My encounter with Nathaniel encourages me to keep asking God to break my heart for people. As Nathaniel and I met over lunch several times that summer, I sought to see things from his perspective. I felt his fear of the future and confusion over ideas. We had some enjoyable times of debate about the gospel, and evangelism was both a delight and a burden for me. I think that's as it should be. It still is, as we exchange emails and phone calls.

I continue to pray for Nathaniel. I ask that God may open his eyes and his heart to the truth and the grace of the cross. I also pray for myself, that the circle of people I have this kind of compassion for will enlarge. God must be answering those prayers; I'm even beginning to pray for the Taliban.

CHAPTER 12

The Question of Anger: "What If I Really *Want* My Neighbor to Go to Hell?"

Is there such a thing as noise pollution? There certainly was on a beautiful April afternoon several years ago at George Mason University in Northern Virginia. As I walked out the door of the Johnson Student Center, I immediately felt two conflicting sensations. The first was a wave of relaxation. The sky was bright blue and the temperature was perfect for sitting on the lawn. The second sensation was tension, caused by some noise pollution. It was too loud to ignore but too vague to understand. So, out of curiosity, I moved closer to see what all the noise was about.

A crowd of about a hundred students had gathered around a man. He held a large ten-foot-tall wooden cross. He yelled. He called women in the crowd "sluts." He called the guys "fornicators." Anyone wearing a sweatshirt with Greek letters, indicating membership in a fraternity or sorority, became the target of particularly harsh condemnation. He held a Bible. He yelled angrily but had an expressionless face, making eye contact with no one.

This crowd was ever-changing. The net amount of about one hundred people stayed the same, but the perimeter was like a revolving door, with few staying for more than a minute. People would gather, listen for a few moments, and then turn away in disgust. Many of them were laughing. If anyone asked a question, it was more of a mocking accusation than a sincere inquiry. I would have left, too, but felt compelled to assess the situation. *What are people thinking of this guy?* I wondered.

This scenario was not new. Every spring someone showed up at Mason with this same shtick. It was a different guy each year, but the same presentation—and with, I'm inclined to guess, the same effect. It gave people a topic to rant and laugh about for the rest of the day. You could hear scoffing conversations all over campus: "Hey, did you see the Jesus freak out on the quad? What an idiot! I can't believe anyone would listen to him."

I can't believe it either. Yet these guys come every year, thinking that they're doing "the Lord's work." And George Mason is not an anomaly. On many campuses all around the country, loud campus preachers show up and yell. Religious noise pollution on campus has become a perennial problem.

I should inject here a qualifier. Some street preachers are excellent. Their presentations are powerful and respectful. They draw out sincere questions from the crowd and answer them concisely and in a way that satisfies both mind and heart. I've met people who've come to faith in Christ as a result of such bold preaching. But these good evangelists are rare exceptions. Most campus/street preachers I've seen produce more noise pollution than religious converts.

For several years I hoped that the yellers would stop showing up. Then I gave up that hope and decided to use the event as a springboard for evangelistic conversations. I, too, would ask someone, "Did you see that guy preaching outside?" If he or she said yes, I'd ask, "What do you think about that guy?" I'd be careful to distance myself from the preacher's approach, saying that I wondered how the yeller was so informed about people's moral lives without knowing them. But then I'd ask, "What do you think of his message?" Without aligning myself to him, the question gave me the chance to say what I thought about how a person gets to know God and goes to heaven.

It's interesting that most people I talked to expressed a similar interpretation about the preacher. Although their opinions varied about his message, they were unanimous about his delivery: "He sure sounds angry."

I have to agree. I have, in fact, come to hear that tone of anger in a lot of preaching and evangelizing. Even some everyday conversations between Christians and nonbelievers sound harsh and angry. If we're honest, we'd say that a great deal of our words sound angry for one very good reason: we *are* angry.

Social media has only exacerbated the expression of our anger. It's amazing how much "witnessing" goes on via social media. This is a good thing. But social media is dangerous because of its easiness. Without prayerful reflection or time to cool down or ask someone else to edit our words, the "post" button gets clicked far too quickly. The spread of anger across cyberspace is not helping the spread of the gospel.

It's worth asking, though: Is all this expression of anger a bad thing? Maybe God wants us to be angry. Although most people at George Mason were embarrassed by the campus preacher, several Christian students I talked with really liked him. "Didn't Jesus throw the money changers out of the temple?" they asked. "Weren't the Old Testament prophets angry a lot of the time? Shouldn't we be angry about sin?" They thought that the cross-carrying campus visitor displayed a righteous kind of anger.

To be sure, if our motivation for expressing anger is pure, unadulterated, righteous indignation—as it surely was for Jesus and Jeremiah—then we've got every right to yell. The problem is, what stands behind our ranting is often something else. Too many of our evangelistic efforts bear little fruit because our motivation, rather than being based on righteous anger, is tainted by sinful anger. Our words, then, have more sinful anger than truth in them.

Proverbs and Anger

A lot has been written—by both Christians and others—about anger.[1] The relationship between anger and evangelism, however, has not been deeply explored. Identifying the difference between righteous anger and sinful anger might be an important first step in understanding that relationship.

---

1. See, for example, Neil Clark Warren, *Make Anger Your Ally* (Wheaton: Tyndale House, 1993).

Proverbs warns us about the harm that anger can do. Perhaps some of the proverbs were on the forefront of James's mind when he wrote, "My dear brothers and sisters, take note of this: Everyone should be quick to listen, slow to speak and slow to become angry, because human anger does not produce the righteousness that God desires" (James 1:19–20).

That last phrase echoes two warnings in Proverbs: "An angry person stirs up conflict, and a hot-tempered person commits many sins" (29:22). And: "A quick-tempered person does foolish things, and the one who devises evil schemes is hated" (14:17). I wish that I didn't understand what Solomon was referring to in the latter proverb. Foolish things? Like putting a hole in the wall with a fist? Like saying words that insult and hurt one's spouse? Like yelling at a child? Like speeding and getting a $75 ticket? Like making a sarcastic remark to a non-Christian neighbor so that the gospel appears even less attractive to him? Proverbs sees where this kind of behavior leads: "A hot-tempered person must pay the penalty; rescue them, and you will have to do it again" (19:19).

As a young Christian, I spent one summer participating in a number of evangelistic outreaches at a beach resort. The premise was that people were there to relax and get away from the pressures of their day-to-day lives. Hence, we figured, they'd be more open to chatting with new acquaintances and more willing to discuss spiritual matters—things for which they had neither the time nor the energy in the normal course of life. The premise was right much of the time. But we still had our fair share of conversations that went as follows.

"Hi, my name is Randy and this is my friend Bob, and we're out on the beach today talking with people about spiritual issues. Do you ever think much about these things?"

"Get lost, Randy, and take your friend Bob with you."

On one particular Saturday afternoon, I met quite a few from the "get lost" crowd. I was frustrated (a common trigger of anger). As I approached one young man, I was determined that I was not going to "get lost" anymore. In fact, I was ready to tell him just how lost *he* was! I wouldn't be surprised if, as a result of our conversation, this guy now heads up some local atheist society. He didn't want to talk; I didn't want to get lost. He said no several times. I asked why the same number of times. He didn't want to give an answer; I didn't want to give in. As I think about the exchange, the whole episode could have been recorded and used to illustrate the proverb, "For as churning cream produces butter, and as twisting the nose produces blood, so stirring up anger produces strife" (30:33).

Even if we're on the "right side" of an evangelistic conversation, some kinds of anger might be terribly destructive. It's truly foolish to give "full vent to [your] rage," and it is truly godly to "bring calm in the end" (Prov. 29:11). Even being around others who are angry is something the Lord would have us avoid. "Do not make friends with a hot-tempered person, do not associate with one easily angered" (22:24). Apparently, this disease is contagious.

Proverbs also has some advice for handling other people's anger. The gospel message, because it touches upon the issue of people's sinfulness, often brings their anger to the surface. Even when we express ourselves in the most anger-free ways, some people respond in anger-filled ways. In many cases, it's best to overlook the offense. As Proverbs 12:16 puts it, "Fools show their annoyance at once, but the prudent overlook an insult." Proverbs 19:11 shows us what this takes: "A person's wisdom yields patience; it is to one's glory to overlook an offense."

When overlooking someone's anger doesn't work, we must employ tactics to turn it away; hence, the insight of Proverbs 29:8 that "mockers stir up a city, but the wise turn away anger," and the specific suggestion of Proverbs 15:1 that "a gentle answer turns away wrath, but a harsh word stirs up anger."

Having some of the following phrases on the tip of our tongues might be just what it takes to turn away anger and turn someone's heart toward the Savior:

- "Wow! You sound really upset about this. Is this a painful topic for you?"

- "I guess I touched a nerve. I'm really sorry. Should I change the subject?"
- "I hope I didn't offend you. What is it about spiritual things that seems so upsetting to you?"

Of course, this kind of coolheadedness when faced with anger—either someone else's or our own—requires our understanding anger. It also takes a spiritual maturity that has overcome the damage done by unresolved anger. That requires some work.

Getting at What's Behind Anger

Much of the literature on the subject of anger agrees that it's a secondary emotion, not a primary one. In many cases, something behind the anger triggers it into action. The three most common triggers are hurt, fear, and frustration. Thus, by finding out what's behind it, a great deal of destructive anger can be channeled into constructive behavior.

You might yell at your kids, for example, because you didn't get the recognition you thought you deserved at work that day—*hurt*. Or you might drive like a maniac because somebody just cut you off and you almost ended up in a ditch—*fear*. Or your spouse gets an earful that he or she doesn't deserve because that important package that you needed yesterday didn't come in the mail today—*frustration*.

Identifying the underlying stimulator can help diffuse the resulting anger. It can also free us up to address the real issue. If we fail to identify the primary cause, a residue of anger can develop. With such anger lurking below the surface, it doesn't take much to ignite it.

Recently, my wife and I had a lively interaction about a new light fixture I'd just installed in our hallway. (We used to refer to these conversations as "marital adjustment discussions." Then one day we realized that the first letters of the words in "marital adjustment discussions" spell out "MAD." We didn't think this was such a good title to use anymore. Now we just call them "fights.") I thought that the light fixture looked pretty good, thank you very much. My wife seemed annoyed by it. I asked what she thought. She didn't like it.

Her tone was harsher than you'd expect for an evaluation of hallway lighting. It seemed to me that something else was going on.

I asked if she was upset with me for picking out the fixture without her input. She was not. I wondered if I was supposed to be doing something else instead of this repair job. I was not. I probed. I wondered. She probed. She wondered. We both agreed that something else besides the hallway light was causing friction between us.

In our minds, we replayed the tape of what had happened before I worked on the light. We'd been discussing our sons' consumption of soda. They had asked me if they could have a soda, knowing—crafty fellows that they are—that their mother had already told them that they couldn't. I said yes. Soda was consumed. Our anger wasn't. In our discussion about the soda episode, I was frustrated with my wife for not having a better system for soda distribution, and I let her know that in some pretty insulting ways. She was frustrated with me because I didn't check with her first before giving the boys an answer. And she was hurt by the way I spoke to her about it.

Behind our discussion of the light fixture was a residue of anger that tainted our ability to connect. Finding the original seedbed for our anger helped us to focus on our present emotions. That freed us to confess our sin to each other (harsh, insulting speech), ask for forgiveness, and then deal accurately with the matter of the light fixture. It also helped us arrive at a solution to our boys' soda consumption problem—from then on it was H_2O, not 7UP!

The problem of residual anger affects us more than we realize. Specifically, it hurts our efforts at evangelism far too much. A lot of residual anger in the Christian community stems from the three triggers—hurt, fear, and frustration—and that anger comes out when we interact with non-Christians.

We're hurt that people don't respond to our outreaches as we think they should. If, for example, our non-Christian neighbors say no when we invite them to our church's Easter service, we might feel hurt. So we remind ourselves that Jesus told us that Christians would be rejected. We tell ourselves that we shouldn't take it personally. We try to drown the insult with a self-affirmation: "They're really rejecting the Lord, not me." But if we're honest with ourselves and with God, some hurt turns to anger, and it comes out when we tell them what a great service they missed.

My friend Troy now smiles when he talks about some of his early evangelistic efforts. There wasn't much smiling, though, the day he called for fire and brimstone to rain down on some people he'd just met in Memphis.

He'd decided to hand out tracts on the street corner. *Why wait for some organized campaign?* he thought. *God can use me all by myself, even if I just hand out a few.* So he took out his bag of tracts and started handing them out on the street corner. He had only a few minutes, but he encouraged himself with the truism that "it only takes a spark."

He smiled and handed out some good booklets about the gospel. Some people took them. Most people ignored him. Even when he made eye contact and said, "Hello," or "Have a nice day," some took the opportunity to stare at their feet. He didn't acknowledge it, but his feelings were being hurt, and an undercurrent of anger was percolating. Some of the people actually took the tracts, saw what they were, and threw them on the ground. Not wanting to contribute to some people's prejudice that Christians don't care about the environment, he picked up the discarded leaflets. People started laughing, and Troy's neck grew red. He was hurt and embarrassed. When he found himself picking up some tracts at the feet of some mockers, he couldn't resist.

"You'll all burn in hell," he told them, feeling more like Jeremiah than ever.

Was his theology right? Perhaps. Was his anger righteous? Hardly.

We Christians get hurt a lot, and we must be aware that it will happen. We also must be aware of our fear. We're fearful about all sorts of things. We're afraid we've lost the culture war and the horrors of sin will destroy the lives of people we love.

We're fearful because our marriages are threatened more than ever. We're worried that our kids might get sucked into pornography on the internet. We're afraid because of the rise of violence in our streets, the increase in drug usage . . . and I could go on indefinitely.

We tell ourselves that God is in control, but if we're honest with ourselves—and with God—fear has a certain hold on us every time we get news updates. This fear, like hurt, can be fertile ground for residual anger, which then spreads into our discussions of sin with our neighbor. He wants to play golf on Sunday morning instead of joining us at church. *If everyone were like him, what would become of society?* we wonder. That fear creeps into our conversations with him. The tone of anger that he detects in us only makes him long all the more for the first tee.

As with hurt and fear, a number of things cause frustration. Admit it. The kingdom of God isn't advancing as fast and as thoroughly as we'd like. The gospel isn't spreading through neighborhoods as rampantly as they say it is in Korea. The salt of the earth isn't as salty as it should be. More and more people are embracing (or at least tolerating) lifestyles that Christians find offensive. We see far too much evidence of our lack of influence on society rather than trophies of our efforts to transform it. So we're frustrated.

The point is, such situations are frustrating to Christians. And frustration is producing a significant amount of residual anger that we must acknowledge if we are to deal appropriately with it.

Other Roots of Frustration

Frustration stems from other emotions too. Feelings of helplessness, embarrassment, or sadness can cause frustration, intensifying expressions of anger and harming our attempts to tell people the good news.

After several years of being a volunteer with the pro-life movement, Hannah felt increasingly helpless to stem the momentum of the pro-choice machine. Several crucial elections had gone "the wrong way," and public opinion had swayed against the pro-life side. Just the night before, she'd watched an episode of a popular television series. The show painted yet another picture of pro-life people as crazed abortion clinic bombers. In contrast, the pro-choice position was portrayed as much more reasonable. Hannah was close to despair because so many babies were being slaughtered, but no one seemed to care.

When her coworker, Nancy, asked her if she'd seen the show, Hannah's tone of voice said much more than the words, "Yes, I did." Hannah had been praying for Nancy for months, ever since they were assigned to adjacent desks in the new office. She had been asking God to open a door for witness, and perhaps this was the open door. But because of Hannah's pent-up frustration, she drove a Mack truck through the open door.

"Yes, I saw it," she began, "and I thought it was a one-sided, condescending, slick piece of propaganda against the pro-life movement. You know, not everyone who's pro-life blows up abortion clinics. And not everyone who's pro-choice is as compassionate as that woman on the show last night. I wish they'd show both sides once in a while. I wish they'd show the love of Jesus in the pro-life movement sometime."

Nancy's "Oh" said it all. An open door had just been shut. Although Hannah's anger at abortion was righteous, her feeling of helplessness overshadowed her concern for Nancy's soul.

How might the conversation have gone if Hannah had responded as follows? "Yes, I did see it. I thought it raised a lot of issues in a short amount of time. What did you think of it?"

Barry, an astronomy professor, faced a similar situation. But his anger stemmed from embarrassment. As a strongly committed Christian on a very secular campus, he was embarrassed by the anti-intellectual things that Christians said on television and in the press. When he saw bumper stickers that read, "God said it. I believe it. That settles it," he was tempted to ram into the car. Some of his colleagues had been told that they were going to hell because they were too intelligent. Some of them had abandoned the faith because of a lack of satisfying answers. Barry was embarrassed by a Christian subculture that failed to answer sincere inquiries by intelligent people. He felt frustrated because his attempts to witness were thwarted when other Christians made statements that pushed his colleagues away.

The irony is, his embarrassment prompted expressions of anger that hurt, rather than helped, his attempts at evangelism. One day a colleague asked Barry what he thought about an interview of an anti-intellectual pastor in the local newspaper. Barry let it rip.

"It's unfair to hold up that idiot as a spokesperson for Christianity. He thinks that faith is just something of the heart, not the head. I hate that guy. I wish he'd just shut up already. Why anybody goes to his church is beyond me."

His efforts to distance himself from the preacher also distanced himself from Christ. Such a display of anger was unattractive to the colleague. If that's what Christian faith does to you, who wants it?

How much better would Barry's conversation have gone if he'd acknowledged and dealt with his embarrassment and anger before connecting with his colleague. Then, when he was asked about the foolish pastor's interview, he could have said, "Oh, that guy. Well, there sure are a lot of different expressions of faith, aren't there? I wouldn't say he represents my perspective very well. But that's okay. Some of us see our ability to think as a gift from God, rather than a curse from somewhere else. What did you think of the interview?"

Debbie's source of anger was much more subtle. Her disappointing marriage caused her a sadness and grief that permeated many of her conversations. Sadness and grief actually can be a healthy response to life's disappointments. But in Debbie's case that response led to another, unhealthy step—frustration. Her frustration was then expressed in anger and sarcasm. Her attitude toward men in general was antagonistic and caustic. It's easy to see that Debbie's antagonism wouldn't be the best advertisement for the gospel message—a message that proclaimed that God, our heavenly Father, loves us.

At the grocery store, Debbie ran into Barbara, her non-Christian neighbor. It was the perfect opportunity for Debbie to invite Barbara to the community Bible study. The leader of the study made it clear that providing a place for outsiders to investigate the Christian faith was a major goal of the group. Debbie had even thought of Barbara as someone to invite. Debbie's conversation in the produce section, though, was filled with complaints about her husband and men in general. When Debbie finally got around to the invitation, Barbara just wasn't interested.

The focus of Debbie's anger was her husband—and God, for not fixing him. Unchecked, however, her anger settled into a permanent undercurrent in her tone of voice that made her sound angry at just about everyone.

How much better if Debbie had poured her energy into the hard work of improving her marriage. Although her situation wasn't easy, a different sort of invitation might have been better received: "Hey, Barbara, I'm wondering if you'd like to join me at a community Bible study I attend. I'm really benefiting from what I'm learning, and I'm trying to apply some of those lessons to my marriage. We meet at my place on Thursday mornings. Have you ever been part of something like that?"

Recognizing frustration and its roots could have helped Hannah, Barry, and Debbie. Their having a good understanding of the ways anger arises, how it works, and why it's so prevalent could make them overcomers of frustration and anger rather than becoming consumed by it.

A case could be made that frustration over the lack of progress of the kingdom of God is unavoidable. Such frustration is the inevitable occupational hazard of a Christian who lives between the two comings of the Messiah. It's the reality of being part of a kingdom that is an already/not-yet kingdom. Helplessness, embarrassment, sadness, and grief are found here. If not handled properly, they likely lead to frustration, then to anger.

What Do We Do About Our Anger?

In a few brief but complex verses, the New Testament offers some insight on handling anger. Admitting that anger, in some cases, is real and natural and inevitable, the apostle Paul tells the Ephesians, "In your anger do not sin" (Eph. 4:26). By starting with "in your anger," he tells us that the mere *presence* of anger is not sinful; what we do with it can become sin. In other words, it's possible to be angry and not sin. We can experience the emotion of anger—prompted by hurt or fear or frustration—and express it in unharmful, unsinful ways.

It's not sin to say to someone, "I'm really angry at you. I wish you wouldn't have said what you did to me. That really hurt my feelings." It would be sin to add, "You stupid jerk!"

It's not sin to say to someone, "I am frustrated right now. I asked you to send me that package, but you still have not done so. That's caused me some problems, and I am angry at you right now." It would be sin to add, "The next time I see you, I'm going to punch your lights out."

This same passage in Ephesians sheds light also on how to handle anger. Before and after the admonition in verse 26, "In your anger do not sin," Paul gives the conditions under which anger management is more likely.

In verse 25, he gives a general admonition to be truthful: "Each of you must put off falsehood and speak truthfully to your neighbor." A firm commitment to truthfulness in *all* of our relationships (not just the ones inside the body of Christ) will prevent us from saying things that deny the reality of our anger:

- "I'm fine."
- "I'm not angry. I'm just concerned for you."
- "I'm not hurt. You're really just hurting yourself."

A strong commitment to deal truthfully and thoroughly with anger is what flows from the two statements that Paul gives in verses 26 and 27: "Do not let the sun go down while you are still angry" and "Do not give the devil a foothold." Saying nothing, in this instance, is not being truthful. When anger is present and conflicts must be resolved, silence is not golden. Anger must be acknowledged and handled (before the sun goes down), or we give a foothold to the devil that he will use to create further havoc. He can reverse the effects of our witnessing, turning it into angry and condemning noise pollution rather than loving and life-giving good news.

Neil Clarke Warren's excellent book *Make Anger Your Ally* offers encouraging words. After years of success in helping clients manage their anger, Dr. Warren assures us that "there are few experiences in life quite so exciting as knowing that you have become an expert in handling your own anger."[2] It might also be that such experiences, in addition to being exciting, can help change lives and expand the kingdom of God.

2. Neil Clark Warren, *Make Anger Your Ally* (Wheaton: Tyndale House, 1993), 135.

CHAPTER 13

The Question of Silence: "When Is It Time to Shut Up?"

My dentist drives me crazy. He asks the most thought-provoking, debate-inducing questions right as he puts sharp, pointed objects into my mouth. "So, what do you think about the upcoming election?" Or, "What's the real solution for the Israeli-Palestinian problem?" Or, "Aren't all religions basically the same?"

I want to respond every time. But my attempts have always been muffled by his hands in my mouth and that noisy suction thing he uses to remove excess saliva. The sign in his waiting room serves as his motto—as well as a warning to his patients: "Blessed are those who engage in lively conversation with the helplessly mute, for they shall be called dentists."

I sometimes wonder if some of our evangelistic conversations sound like interactions between my dentist and me. One side posits a question, not really expecting an answer or listening for a response. The other side sits frustrated, not really getting to answer or expecting to be heard.

Listening, though, might be the most useful tool we have in sharing the good news. It might also be the most neglected. The very skill that could prime the pump of thoughtful dialogue, open hearts to accept conviction of sin, establish common ground for further dialogue, or give insight to felt needs remains an untapped resource for a lot of Christians.

Why We Don't Listen

Why is this? It's certainly not for lack of endorsement from the Scriptures. Proverbs repeatedly encourages us to minimize our words and, by implication, replace them with listening ears. Consider the following example: "Sin is not ended by multiplying words, but the prudent hold their tongues" (10:19). Or, more strongly, "Even fools are thought wise if they keep silent, and discerning if they hold their tongues" (17:28). Or, more to the point, "To answer before listening— that is folly and shame" (18:13).

Perhaps we don't listen well because we don't think we must. After all, we have the truth! We follow the One who is the Way, the Truth, and the Life. What can some unsaved, unregenerate, unenlightened target for conversion have to say? To be sure, I've grossly overstated the case. But, because there's some degree of truth in my caricature, we might be less open to listening.

How We Can Start Listening

Our failure to practice good listening hurts our attempts to convey the good news. While it's true that 1 Peter 3:15 admonishes, "Always be prepared to give an answer to everyone who asks you to give the reason for the hope that you have," doing so requires listening in order to know when and what we're being asked.

Not all such inquiries have a question mark after them. Some people who "ask [us] to give the reason for [our] hope" do so with less direct methods. They wonder aloud why certain tragedies happen, or how someone who is convicted of a terrible crime could do such a thing, or how anyone can get through life with a certain disability, or whether life has any purpose. These comments, along with a host of other "Gee, I wonder" statements, can open a door for our answer—if we're listening.

Some people ask us for "the reason for the hope that you have" only after we've asked them a question and listened carefully to their answer.

Here are some good starter questions:

- "Do you ever think about spiritual things?"
- "At what point are you in your spiritual journey?"
- "Along the way, what part, if any, has God played in your life?"

- "How do you feel about your standing before God?"
- "Do you ever wonder about life after death?"

Not all questions are equally suitable for starting the dialogue. Some questions are a little more pointed. These questions might serve well after the relationship has been established or some of the walls of resistance have come down:

- "Has anyone ever taken the time to explain to you how a personal relationship with Christ is possible?"
- "What do you think it means to be a Christian?"
- "At times like this, what inner resources do you draw on?"
- "Have I ever told you what a difference my relationship with God has made in my life?" [Or some other introduction to your prepared short testimony. Remember, a testimony that emphasizes the daily differences that result from your faith in Christ is more valuable than the how-I-became-a-Christian variety.]

Still other questions have an even sharper edge to them. These should be reserved for the deep scalpel work, when people have shown a significant interest in the heart of the gospel:

- "If you were to die tonight, how sure are you that you'd go to heaven?"
- "If you were to die tonight, and God were to ask you, 'Why should I let you into heaven?' what would you say?"
- "I get the idea that you're ready to make this decision. Is that right?"
- "Are there any lingering questions that would prevent you from trusting in Christ right now?"

A wise baseball manager uses certain starting pitchers at the beginning of a game; middle relievers in the fifth, sixth, or seventh innings; and closers in the eighth or ninth innings. In a similar way, we should choose our questions carefully, depending upon where our friends stand on the path toward the cross. Listening to their answers can help us determine this point and move them further along.

How Not to Listen

Several years ago, my son Jon and I used an airport shuttle service. Returning from a retreat, we were tired after a long weekend, a delayed flight, and an interminable wait for our luggage. Our car was parked in the remote long-term parking lot, and we longed for a quick, quiet ride in the shuttle van to our own car for the short drive home.

Instead, we were treated to a barrage of Islamic propaganda on the radio station that our shuttle driver had strategically selected for his captive audience. For almost thirty minutes, while jostling around the parking lot, we listened to highlights from speeches by Malcolm X, Louis Farrakhan, and Elijah Mohammed. I wondered if I was feeling what some non-Christians do when we assault them with our evangelistic tirades.

Similar to what I sensed in my dentist's chair, I felt frustrated by the one-way conversation. I was particularly bothered by the misrepresentations of my beliefs, the misunderstandings of my feelings, and the dismissal of my concerns.

Since that bothersome ride, I've listened with more discernment to my own dialogues with people of other faiths. I've also done a fair amount of eavesdropping on interfaith exchanges and have identified some common pitfalls that tend to shut down dialogue rather than stimulate it.

"Me Too!"

When someone tells us a problem or a concern, our immediate response is often an uncomfortable one. So when we hear about a car accident, an illness, the breakup of a relationship, or something similar, we react with a knee-jerk response: "Me too!" We don't always use that expression but we're tempted to match their pain with a story of our own. So we tell about our car accident, or our brush with illness, or our similar trial. Rather than sensing empathy, our friend might feel dismissed or uncared for.

It would be far better to identify what the person is saying behind his or her words. Consider the following two short conversations—one bad, one good.

CONVERSATION 1

CHRISTIAN: I'm just wondering. Do you ever think much about spiritual things?

NON-CHRISTIAN: Not in a while. I used to think about God and religion and stuff like that a lot. But that was all before my cousin died. Once he passed away, I just gave up on religion.

CHRISTIAN: I once had a cousin die too. He died of cancer, and I remember it being really upsetting to me. But, I'm just so thankful to God that he had assurance of his salvation. Did your cousin?

NON-CHRISTIAN: Get me out of here.

CONVERSATION 2

CHRISTIAN: I'm just wondering. Do you ever think much about spiritual things?

NON-CHRISTIAN: Not in a while. I used to think about God and religion and stuff like that a lot. But that was all before my cousin died. Once he passed away, I just gave up on religion.

CHRISTIAN: Wow. It sounds like you were really close to your cousin.

NON-CHRISTIAN: Yeah, I was.

CHRISTIAN: How did he die?

Non-Christian: Cancer. It really took a long time too. It was so horrible to watch him waste away. I just can't figure out how anyone can believe in a good God after seeing something like that.

Christian: I can see why you'd think that. Have you ever met anyone who found hope after losing a loved one?

Non-Christian: Not really.

Christian: What's helped you get through this loss?

Non-Christian: I don't really know. Have you ever had anyone close to you die?

Resisting the "Me too" response can free you to focus on the feelings behind the words of the other person and keep the attention on that person.

"Oh Yeah?"

One step beyond the "Me too" response is coming back with an "Oh yeah?" Again, we might not use those words, but if we try to top someone's story by telling of a more severe experience, we dismiss that person and his or her issues. "Nobody Knows the Trouble I've Seen" might be a fine spiritual, but it's a lousy witnessing tool. When someone tells you of his two-car accident, don't recount your four-car disaster. When she shares about a C she got on her midterm, don't tell her about your D. Let people tell their stories and ask them for more details and color than they offered initially. Dig to reach the levels of emotions behind the facts. If you do, people may later be more accepting of your story.

Hot Buttons

A friend of mine confessed his embarrassment and regret after he had blown a witnessing opportunity. A colleague of his was trying to find common ground with him. The colleague, knowing that my friend was a Christian, asked if my friend had met one of their new coworkers—someone the colleague thought shared the Christian's point of view.

"You two would have a lot in common," the colleague said. "He's just returned from some kind of mission thing; he's very humanistic." *Humanistic* was the wrong word to use for several reasons. First, the colleague likely meant *humanitarian*. Second, the mission on which the guy had gone was a genuine evangelistic Christian mission, not a humanitarian trip. But such a distinction was alien to this non-Christian's frame of reference, so he tried to find a category that he understood. To his way of thinking, *humanistic* was a positive term. Unfortunately, it's a hot button for a lot of Christians. Usually linked with *secular*, the mere mention of the word *humanistic* is tantamount to starting a fight.

Before the well-meaning non-Christian could search his thesaurus for a better term, he got a mouthful from the would-be evangelist about the horrors of secular humanism, the dangers of leaving God out of a worldview, and a series of other topics unrelated to the original statement. What could have been a bridge-building effort turned instead into a bridge-burning encounter.

A better response could have gone along the following lines. "Wow. I'd love to hear about his mission trip. Thanks for thinking of me. It would be great if you could introduce us sometime. What did he tell you about this mission?"

A lot of topics today are hot buttons for Christians. We're ready with arguments, Scripture, quotations, and stories, and we lay them on anyone who happens to mention abortion, LGBTQ+ rights, transgenderism, or just about any other politically charged issue. Listening to what's behind the mention of these hot topics, however, could help us avoid wandering down rabbit trails.

"Yeah, Right!"

The potential for damage wrought by sarcasm makes it something to be avoided at all costs. We must resist the temptation to roll our eyes or blurt out a sarcastic "Yeah, right!" or "Oh sure!" when people offer outlandish theories about God and life. Given how far our society has strayed from biblical foundations, we shouldn't be surprised when people advocate the power of crystals, belief in aliens, or other such nonsense. Rather than scoffing, however, we should listen—and seek any principle that they might happen to get right. When they tell of their crystals, we can ask, "Do you believe there are some sources of power beyond the natural world?" Or when they talk about an animal's soul, we can respond, "There does seem to be a difference between an animal and a rock, doesn't there? Do you think there's a difference between an animal and a person?"

Resorting to sarcasm might feel good at the time, but it alienates and insults. It almost guarantees that your friend will seek serious conversation elsewhere.

Too Many Words

Our world hates silence. Background noise, elevator music, and constant sound effects permeate our environment. At Disney World music blares out of even the bushes! Somehow we think that lack of sound is lack of substance. More often than not, though, just the opposite may be the case.

Real conversations, the ones that connect hearts and transfer understanding, need breathing spaces. We don't have to jump in with words as soon as the other person pauses. In fact, we need time to hear and digest what has been just said before we jump in with the next thought that comes to mind. Training our hearts to be silent precedes our mouths doing the same. By doing so, we can develop the self-control we need for sharing the good news—both with and without words.

Dallas Willard offers insight about the discipline of silence:

> Practice in not speaking can at least give us enough control over what we say that our tongues do not "go off" automatically. This discipline provides us with a certain inner distance

that gives us time to consider our words fully and the presence of mind to control what we say and when we say it.[1]

Willard offers, too, specific application of the discipline of silence to the task of evangelism:

> In witnessing, the role of talking is frequently overemphasized. Does that sound strange? It's true. Silence and especially true listening are often the strongest testimony of our faith. A major problem for Christian evangelism is not getting people to talk, but to silence those who through their continuous chatter reveal a loveless heart devoid of confidence in God.[2]

Not only silence, but also other disciplines of abstinence—solitude, fasting, and sacrifice—can bring about an inner stillness that is unavailable to the untrained or undisciplined soul.

Too Few Words

Christians sometimes make another mistake in evangelistic conversations with others—we let *them* do too much talking. Just because the evangelistic conversation lasts a long time doesn't mean that it's moving cross-ward. A point comes when more words means less thought.

I realized this after listening to Bob for more than two hours. At first, I thought this was a good approach. His friend Darlene told me that he was "very open" to spiritual things. She arranged for us to meet over coffee because, as she told me, "He has so many questions that I can't answer." So we met. And he talked. And talked. And talked. It's a good thing the coffee shop offered free refills. Then again, it would have been wise if I could have switched his to decaf.

After a while, I realized that he had no interest in anything that

---

1. Dallas Willard, *The Spirit of the Disciplines* (New York: HarperCollins, 1998), 164.
2. Willard, *Spirit of the Disciplines*, 164–65.

Darlene or I had to say (whenever we could sneak a word in edgewise). He asked no questions. He left no room for disagreement. He did seem bent on impressing us with all of the things that he'd read, all of the evil that he'd seen (convincing him that "there just couldn't be a God"), and all of the nice people he'd met who had no religion at all. It occurred to me that we were doing him a disservice by letting him talk. We were enabling him to convince himself of his own folly.

I finally said something that seemed out of left field: "Bob, I need to go. I don't mean to be rude, but I need to be somewhere else right now. But let me ask you a question. If I sent you a short book, would you be open enough to read it and tell me what you think?"

He said he would. In fact, he started to tell us again how much he likes reading, how much he's read, and the names of some of his favorite books, and—

I interrupted. "Great. I'll mail it to you. Why don't you jot your address down on this napkin for me."

When Darlene and I got out to the car, she asked where I had to be.

"Anywhere else," I answered.

She looked puzzled.

"The more we let Bob talk, the more he'll convince himself of his own nonsensical beliefs. I had to shut him up before he became impervious to any amount of truth. He wouldn't let us speak at all, so I said, 'I need to be somewhere else.' I really do—for his sake as well as mine."

Before driving off, we stopped to pray. Those words were the most important words uttered all afternoon.

I mailed him a copy of C. S. Lewis's *The Case for Christianity,* a short fifty-six-page book. I attached a Post-it note with my phone number and an offer to get together whenever he'd finished reading the book. The note said, "When we get together, I'd love to hear your thoughts about this book. I'd also like to tell you some of my ideas."

I never heard from him. I don't think he was open. If we had let him talk even longer, he would have only hardened in his unbelief. Sometimes saying goodbye is the best evangelistic move.

How to Listen

It would be easy to read the suggestions that follow as a list of techniques that produce evangelistic converts. It would also be wrong. To the contrary, gracious listening flows from a heart that has been humbled, stilled, and transformed by the power of grace. Listening is simply a form of serving, of putting the other person first, as Philippians 2 implores us. It requires an inner concern for the person more than an outward practice of techniques. The words and skills are important, but only if they are outward expressions of an inward concern.

Failing to listen smacks of "selfish ambition or vain conceit" (Phil. 2:3). We can *develop* the humility necessary to perform these skills by practicing spiritual disciplines. Following are some ways that humility might be *expressed*.

Reflective Listening

Correctly receiving both the content and the tone of people's words sets the stage for your responding appropriately. Reflective listening thus lets them know that you value what they say and who they are. It also ensures that you'll not pursue needless distractions or irrelevant topics.

The tried-and-true reflective listening phrases still build bridges and convey friendship:

- "Let me see if I'm hearing you correctly. You're saying . . ."
- "So, are you saying that . . .?"
- "It sounds to me like you believe . . ."
- "If I'm hearing you right, the point you're making is . . ."

By making these statements, you're asking them to clarify what they've already told you or to correct any misperceptions you might have. Don't feel pressure to get their point exactly right the first time. Few communications are that flawless—from either side. Just getting close is good enough. The positive of showing that you truly want to understand them outweighs any negative of missing the bull's-eye on the first try.

A dialogue with reflective listening could sound something like this:

CHRISTIAN: Do you ever think much about spiritual things?

NON-CHRISTIAN: A little. I think religion is a private thing, though.

CHRISTIAN: Are you saying that people shouldn't discuss religion with others?

NON-CHRISTIAN: No, I wouldn't say that. I just don't like it when people blab on about it all the time.

CHRISTIAN: So you think that some talk about God is okay.

NON-CHRISTIAN: Sure. I just don't like it when total strangers talk to you about God the way they talk about the weather.

CHRISTIAN: Oh, I see why you say it's a private thing. You don't talk about private things with just anyone standing next to you somewhere.

NON-CHRISTIAN: Exactly. I think your religion is something you should reserve for only certain situations.

CHRISTIAN: It sounds like you believe religion is very important.

NON-CHRISTIAN: Yeah, although I can't say for sure what I believe about God.

CHRISTIAN: Is that something you'd like to find out more about?

NON-CHRISTIAN: I think so. But how do you even begin? Where do you look for answers?

CHRISTIAN: I think I've found some good answers. Would you be interested in what I've found?

Emotional Mirroring

Correctly sounding the content of someone's words represents only part of the story. Identifying and empathizing with the person's emotions might count for even more. Selecting terms that capture a feeling as well as gauge its level of intensity is a skill that might need developing. Emotional mirroring statements might sound like the following:

- "It sounds like this is something you feel very strongly about."
- "You sound upset as you tell me your thoughts."
- "Wow. This is something that touches a nerve, isn't it?"
- "As you tell me your thoughts, I'm sensing some anger in there. Am I right?"
- "I noticed you laughed when you answered my question. Does this topic make you uneasy?"
- "I sense there's more going on inside you than just telling me your thoughts. Am I right?"
- "It sounds like you've been through some hard times."

These kinds of probes, especially when the conversation touches the problem of suffering, can show you if people are engaged in merely an intellectual exercise or are speaking from personal pain. If the person is upset about a dying relative, a philosophical treatise on evil terribly misses the point.

A rule of thumb is to respond to feelings with feelings and to facts with facts. You won't get very far responding to feelings with evidence and diagrams. It's amazing how far you *will* get with empathy and validation.

Finding Common Ground

Many non-Christians likely think that they have little or nothing in common with Christian coworkers, neighbors, or acquaintances—at least nothing desirable. The more they develop impressions of religious people from popular media, the more they fear them or shun them. One of my favorite cartoons illustrates this cultural tension: A man is walking by a house, where a sign on the lawn reads, "Beware of dog!" Just behind that sign, standing on the porch of the house, is a dog—holding a sign that reads, "Jesus loves you!"

Finding common cultural ground, therefore, might be difficult when it comes to skeptics, agnostics, or people who are unaware of a spiritual realm. Some of the following phrases might help along the way:

- "I see how you could believe that."
- "I used to believe something along those lines." (Only say this if it's true!)
- "That makes sense to me. I'm not sure it takes everything into account, though."
- "I think you're right that life has a lot of puzzles to it. What have you found that makes sense out of it all?"
- "I don't blame you for thinking there are no answers. There are more questions than answers, that's for sure. But I think I know *some* of the answers."

Finding emotional common ground is also helpful. If we're not upset with some of the things that bother our neighbors—things that truly *are* upsetting—why would they want to believe what we believe? Doing so will just make them cold and uncaring—like us! So words that sow common emotional capital are worth their weight in gold.

- "Those kinds of things bother me, too" (i.e., disasters, crimes, evil).
- "I'm right there with you. I get angry when I hear that kind of stuff too."

- "That's horrible!"
- "What have you found to help you handle these kinds of things?"

Cool (Not Bebop) Listening

This heading needs a little explanation. Miles Davis revolutionized the jazz scene when he pioneered the "cool school" of jazz. After years of the bebop played by Charlie "Bird" Parker, Dizzy Gillespie, and others, Miles dared to use fewer notes rather than more. Dizzy is an appropriate name for the sounds of that brilliant trumpet player-composer-magician of sound, but his frenetic pace was wearing people out. They hungered for a few well-selected tones rather than the avalanche of notes that poured from Bird's saxophone and Dizzy's funny-shaped trumpet. The cool musicians Miles, Stan Getz, Bill Evans, and others overwhelmed people with how much they could "say" by playing less.

We could use a dose of cool jazz and less bebop in our apologetics and evangelism, that is, accomplish more by saying less. When people say things that seem to invite tons of evidence, facts, answers, quotations, and sermons, resisting the temptation to deliver all the goods might be a better path. It'll be hard to resist this temptation, particularly if you've read a lot of apologetics books (which we all should!). The amount of evidence is so heavily in our favor, we want to show just how good our case is. But a few well-chosen words that prompt our listeners to ask for more would be much better.

When people tell us that there's so much evidence for evolution, rather than nuking Darwin with all of our resources, a simple "Well, I guess that's one way to explain how we got here" might be better.

When people complain about all the evil in the world and say, "That's got to make you think there's no God," we might try, "Could be."

When friends who are into alternative religions go on and on about their beliefs, rather than tearing their faulty thinking to shreds, we might use a pause to simply say, "Hmm. That's interesting." If they ever turn things back over to us to respond more thoroughly, we could add, "That's one way to see things. I think there are other ways to consider." Waiting until they ask, "What other ways do you have in mind?" might increase the likelihood of their hearing us.

Other Miles Davisisms that could serve to prompt further thought include "Maybe," "I'm not so sure," "Don't be too sure," "I wonder," and "I doubt it."

Any phrase that leaves them wondering what else we're thinking, rather than wishing that we'd just shut up, is worth a try. It could get them to listen to us—which is what we were hoping for when we started listening to them.

EPILOGUE

Unanswered Questions

What happens when someone asks you a question? Do you start formulating an answer? Do you wonder why they asked such a question? Do you suspect this might be a trap? What happens inside you as you start to answer?

Did you see what I just did? Did you catch that I asked a series of questions? What do questions do that statements don't?

Much of the motivation for writing this book flowed from the fact that Jesus asked questions.

Observe what goes on in your mind and heart as you hear these questions from Jesus's Sermon on the Mount in the book of Matthew:

- "You are the salt of the earth. But if the salt loses its saltiness, how can it be made salty again?" (5:13)
- "If you love those who love you, what reward will you get? Are not even the tax collectors doing that?" (5:46)
- "Is not life more than food, and the body more than clothes?" (6:25)
- "Can any one of you by worrying add a single hour to your life?" (6:27)
- "Why do you look at the speck of sawdust in your brother's eye and pay no attention to the plank in your own eye?" (7:3)
- "Which of you, if your son asks for bread, will give him a stone?" (7:9)
- "Do people pick grapes from thornbushes, or figs from thistles?" (7:16)

Sometimes, Jesus's most powerful questions were ones that were merely implied but not stated. His parable of the two houses poses the penetrating question, "Upon what will you build your house?" See if you don't feel the force of that as you read these words:

> Therefore everyone who hears these words of mine and puts them into practice is like a wise man who built his house on the rock. The rain came down, the streams rose, and the winds blew and beat against that house; yet it did not fall, because it had its foundation on the rock. But everyone who hears these words of mine and does not put them into practice is like a foolish man who built his house on sand. The rain came down, the streams rose, and the winds blew and beat against that house, and it fell with a great crash. (Matt. 7:24–27)

I hope by now you have become convinced that asking questions can be used effectively in evangelism. But the wisdom of using questions has more to it than mere imitation of Jesus's style. Responding to the gospel involves more than agreement with theological propositions. Becoming a Christian takes total surrender of one's entire being. As C. S. Lewis put it: "Fallen man is not simply an imperfect creature who needs improvement: he is a rebel who must lay down his arms."[1] Thus, engaging people's whole being through penetrating questions may help them lay down their arms. They can be made into whole new creatures because questions do so much more than statements.

At some point, though, we need to shift from our pre-evangelistic conversations, plausibility-building questions, and common-ground explorations to posing *the* question Jesus asked Peter: "Who do you say that I am?" (Matt. 16:15 NASB1995).

The stakes are too high for us to never make this decisive turn. We must "cross the painline"[2] and ask people to respond. For most

---

1. C. S. Lewis, *Mere Christianity* (New York: Touchstone, 1996), 59.
2. Rico Tice, *Honest Evangelism: How to Talk About Jesus Even When It's Tough* (Purcellville, VA: The Good Book Company, 2015), 17.

of us, this will never feel comfortable. But comfort should never be our highest priority. We may need to repent of our worship of the idols of ease, others' acceptance, hassle-free living, and not rocking the boat. Then we can urge people to seriously consider the offer God has made to them—one of forgiveness of sin, adoption into God's family, and eternal life.

I recently attended a funeral for a friend who had lived a long, beautiful, faith-filled life that ended after a horrific year of dementia and several other body-destroying diseases. His homegoing brought an ironic sense of relief to his wife and adult children. One by one his sons told stories of how their Dad loved them, raised them to worship and adore God, and reminded them of just how good the gospel was. Several of them wanted us to know their father was not perfect. "Dad would be upset if you came away from this service thinking he never sinned and didn't need a Savior." One of them recounted how his father needed to apologize to him for losing his temper. Amid all the fun and pleasant stories, that one—certainly neither fun nor pleasant—stood out as indicative of the ways Jesus had shaped their father.

One son's remarks have stuck with me. He began by saying, "It's hard to overstate the cruelty of dementia. The systematic dismantling of cognition and memories causes loved ones to fade into strangers. One of its mercies, however, is that family and friends are invited to begin grieving before death occurs. But nothing prepares you for the finality of death."

For the next ten minutes he recounted the pain of the past year as he watched his father slip away from remembering one thing after another, *one person after another*, until, finally, no interpersonal connections remained. He stopped several times to wipe away tears and recompose himself. The sanctuary in which hundreds of us sat was filled with audible, palpable sorrow.

But then he said, "I opened by saying nothing can prepare you for the finality of death. Well, that's not entirely true. You see, in this case, death does not get the last word. We grieve *our* loss. But we celebrate *his* gain. Dad's was a life submitted to the lordship of Christ, and now he's with his Savior in glory with a regenerated resurrection body that yawns in the face of dementia. And one day we who are in Christ will be reunited with him before the Lamb of Glory, together with the angels declaring, 'Holy, holy, holy is the Lord God Almighty.'"

I wanted to stand and applaud. I'm confident I was not alone. The good news of the gospel is *so* good in *so* many ways but none greater than the way it defeats death and dares to shout, "Where, O death, is your victory? Where, O death, is your sting?" (1 Cor. 15:55).

Thus, we come to the end of a book about questions and ponder some unanswered ones:

- Given the emptiness of the sand on which people build their lives, might we be on the verge of a revival of interest in the gospel, the only source of satisfying life and joy?
- In a world filled with the spiritual equivalents of damaging rains, rising streams, and blowing winds, will we tell people about the rock that can protect them against such troubles?
- As we see decay in nihilistic culture, will we withdraw from it to try to protect ourselves, or will we engage with it and seek renewal for it? Will we apply the grace of the gospel to lives damaged by the world, their flesh, and the devil?
- Will we assume that people are not interested in faith because that's what the polls seem to indicate? Or will we trust more in the self-authenticating nature of God's truth and offer it boldly to friends? Might they show more interest than we anticipated?
- Will we devote ourselves to apologetic rigor so we can make defenses for new sets of questions? Or will we rest on our previous "successes" (which may not have been as victorious as we thought)?
- Will we harshly condemn people who have embraced lifestyles we find reprehensible (as if our sinful behaviors are less abhorrent to a holy God)? Or will we treat refugees from the sexual revolution as damaged image-bearers in need of redemption, cleansing, renewal, and power to overcome crippling sin?

- Will we love God with all our minds and study His world in ways that offer solutions instead of slogans? Will we reach out to thoughtful skeptics so that the fullness of all of God's revelation—in His world and in His Word—challenges them to consider the author of life?
- Will we keep responding to questions with answers, or will we answer them with questions?
- Will we announce our message the way Jesus the rabbi would? Or will we continue to follow the model of Murray the used-car salesperson?

Study Guide

These questions are designed for small-group discussion and application.

Chapter 1: Why Are Questions Better Than Answers?

1. Who are the "Artyums" in your life? In other words, who are you praying will come to a saving knowledge of Christ? Make a list of these people, and share with the group what your relationship with one of them is like.
2. What questions do people ask you about your faith?
3. Which stories from this chapter remind you of situations or relationships you've been in?
4. What training have you already had to prepare you for evangelism? What specifically did you learn? Of the three tasks related to evangelism that were mentioned in this chapter (declaring, defending, and dialoguing), which do you feel most adept at?
5. What books about evangelism or apologetics have you read? How did they help you?
6. Read Jesus's interaction with the woman at the well (John 4:1–26). What principles from this chapter (or other reading you have done) apply to this text? Discuss the relevancy of these principles to your world.
7. Spend time in prayer as a group, asking for boldness and wisdom to begin conversations with the people on your list.

Chapter 2: Solomonic Soulwinning

1. What are your hot buttons? In other words, which topics are you most likely to argue about? With whom?
2. When you see an argument coming, what can you tell yourself that will help you avoid "casting your pearls before swine"?

3. Can you remember any conversations that you've had about the Lord that actually should have been avoided? Why? How could you have handled it differently?
4. Which of Dale Carnegie's nine guidelines is most pertinent to you? Which ones are you most likely to forget?
5. Which of the proverbs mentioned in this chapter are most applicable to your life? Why? Where are you most likely to use that wisdom—at home, at work, with children, with neighbors, at sporting events, or elsewhere?

Chapter 3: How Do Questions Pave the Way for Answers?

1. Read Acts 17:1–4. What picture comes to mind when you read, "He [Paul] reasoned from the Scriptures"? What points do you think prompted the liveliest discussions? Which issues today need the most debate?
2. Brainstorm a list of common questions that people ask today. Which of the five principles would best apply to each? Which one-word response ("really," "so," etc.) would be most effective with each question?
3. Practice role-playing a dialogue about one of the questions. Have one person play the part of a non-Christian. (Don't be too tough on the Christian.) Have the other person try the suggested questions in the dialogue from this chapter. (Resist the temptation to be sarcastic or too strong.)
4. Recount any conversations that you've had in which the other person seems to think that the gospel was as likely as the plug theory. How could you have responded differently?
5. What did you think of this chapter's critique of "The Blind Men and the Elephant"? What else could be said for or against it?

Chapter 4 :Why Are Christians So Intolerant?

1. Have you ever found yourself confronted with the charge of intolerance (even if not in as extreme a situation as the author described in this chapter)? How have you responded?
2. What other exclusive claims made by Jesus or other New Tes-

tament writers can you recall? What do these claims tell you about Jesus?

3. What is your "so-what testimony"? (See chapter 1.) How does Jesus's claim to be the only way to God shape your so-what testimony?

4. This chapter suggests saying surprising things to counter the charge of intolerance. What other surprising things could you say?

5. Did the dialogues regarding the people who've never heard of Jesus make sense to you? What else can you say about this issue if it ever comes up?

Chapter 5: Why Does a Good God Allow Evil and Suffering and Things Like Pandemics?

1. When have you wondered about the problem of evil? How have you answered the question for yourself?

2. Have you ever offered one of the "slivers of the pie chart" as the whole pie in your answer? How was it received?

3. Do you agree with the author's interpretation of Job? Why or why not? Do you think that the author left out aspects of Job's story?

4. What things can we say with certainty about suffering, evil, and life after death?

5. How has the gospel helped you deal with difficult circumstances?

Chapter 6: What Do Christians Have Against Science?

1. Do you agree with the author that Christians should love science? Do you love science? If you have reservations, what are they?

2. Can you name three non-Christians you know who love science? Is that a roadblock to faith for them? How might you start—or restart—a conversation with them?

3. Do you need to do some homework about science before conversing about it? What one or two resources mentioned in this chapter could help you?

4. List the ways science benefits your life. After you complete your list, add five more ways. Give thanks to God for the advances in science during your lifetime.
5. Add scientifically minded people to your prayer list. Ask God to open doors to converse with them. Ask God for wisdom about how to talk about science with reverence and awe.

Chapter 7: Why Should We Believe an Ancient Book Written by Dead Jewish Males?

1. How much of the Bible have *you* read? It might be difficult to promote the reading of a book that you haven't even finished. Come up with a Bible reading plan that will ensure that you read all of it.
2. How have people you know worded their objections about the Bible?
3. What evidence do you see that people question authority?
4. Do you think the Bible is messy, as this chapter claims? If so, what aspects of that messiness bother you the most? How can this actually be a support of the Bible's authority rather than a criticism of it?
5. What apologetic facts do you know that support the Bible's claims about itself? If asked, could you defend why you accept the Bible?
6. Practice presenting the Bible's story line using the four-word outline: creation, rebellion, redemption, and consummation. With what part of the story do you need to become more familiar?

Chapter 8: Why Are Christians So Homophobic?

1. What "planks" should you remove from your life?
2. What influences have shaped your views of homosexuality?
3. Have you ever had any conversations about homosexuality with someone who struggles with it or embraces it?
4. How comfortable are you discussing homosexuality? Why do you think you feel comfortable or uncomfortable?

5. Which of the foundational principles mentioned in this chapter is the newest or most different to your way of thinking?

Chapter 9: What's So Good About Marriage?

1. Do you think that this chapter accurately describes how our world sees marriage and sex? What evidence have you seen to support or reject this description?
2. Do you think that the chapter accurately presented the biblical view of marriage? What other insight do you have to complete the picture?
3. Which of the pro-marriage arguments presented in this chapter might be effective with people you know? Why?
4. How would you argue the reasonableness of the biblical view of sex?
5. How does marriage point to the cross?

Chapter 10: If Jesus Is So Great, Why Are Some of His Followers Such Jerks?

1. In what forms have people posed the hypocrisy question to you?
2. Which displays of hypocrisy bother you the most?
3. Did the discussion of the kingdom of God make sense to you? Can you restate it in your own words?
4. In regard to the hypocrisy question, choose one of the responses listed—or make up one for yourself—under each of the four types of responses: a negatively worded question, a surprising statement, an honest admission, and a deep, thoughtful question.
5. Write out your own explanation of why hypocrites are in the church.

Chapter 11: The Question of Compassion

1. Can you relate to the author's attitude toward the Taliban? Toward what other groups do you sense a similar kind of contempt?
2. Why else do you think that Jesus had compassion on people, perceiving them as "sheep without a shepherd"? What did He see that we often forget?

3. Why else do you think that Paul felt the way he did in Athens? What else about idols was not mentioned in this chapter?
4. What do you think of prayers of confession like the one from the Book of Common Prayer or from John Baillie's work? How can you make contrition a part of your spiritual practice?
5. Make a list of your "ten most wanted." Ask God to work in their hearts—and yours!

Chapter 12: The Question of Anger

1. Cite examples of anger mixed with evangelism or preaching (not necessarily your own).
2. Explain how hurt, fear, or frustration trigger anger. Give some illustrations.
3. Of the triggers mentioned in this chapter, which apply to you?
4. List any relationships that require repair from damage done by anger. How can you make restitution? Confess to God any sinful anger you are aware of (1 John 1:9).
5. With whom do you have the kind of accountability relationship that could help you deal with a problem of anger?

Chapter 13: The Question of Silence

1. Why do you think that we don't listen as well or as much as we should?
2. Which of the starter questions do you feel most comfortable using? Can you think of three or four more?
3. Which of the following obstacles to good communication are you most likely to employ: "Me too!," "Oh yeah!," hot buttons, or "Yeah, right"?
4. Which Miles Davisisms are you most comfortable using?
5. Practice a conversation with a partner, using reflective listening and emotional mirroring. See how long you can go without interjecting your own thoughts or feelings. Simply try to connect and clarify so that your partner knows that you are hearing accurately.

About the Author

Randy Newman is the senior fellow for apologetics and evangelism at the C. S. Lewis Institute in the Washington, DC area. He has taught at several evangelical seminaries and at Patrick Henry College, and is currently an adjunct professor at Reformed Theological Seminary. After serving for over thirty years with Campus Crusade for Christ, he established Connection Points, a ministry to help Christians engage people's hearts the way Jesus did. He has written several books, including the award-winning *Questioning Evangelism*, as well as numerous articles about evangelism and other ways our lives intertwine with God's creation. Randy enjoys jazz and classical music, photography, art, and easy crossword puzzles. He and his wife, Pam, live in Austin, TX, and have three grown sons, two delightful daughters-in-law, and a growing number of adorable grandchildren. You can follow him online at www.randydavidnewman.com.

Let Randy Newman teach you how to respect without compromising, listen without patronizing, and share convictions without being arrogant.

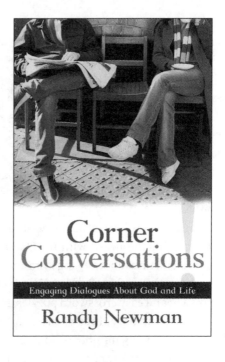

"This is a book about love and respect, written by someone who clearly loves seekers and deeply respects their heartfelt questions."
—MICHAEL E. SUMMERS, George Mason University

"Complete, realistic conversations with straight questions and answers."
—*CHURCH LIBRARIES*

Join Randy Newman as he shares surprising stories of faith that testify to the unstoppable power of the gospel.

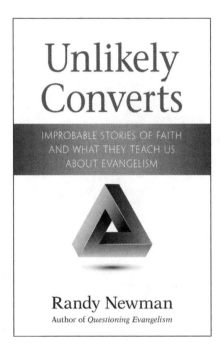

Unlikely Converts

IMPROBABLE STORIES OF FAITH
AND WHAT THEY TEACH US
ABOUT EVANGELISM

Randy Newman
Author of *Questioning Evangelism*

"Full of amazing stories of God's pursuit of the lost and practical, real-life application."
—DR. JOEL S. WOODRUFF, president of the C. S. Lewis Institute

"*Unlikely Converts* left me confident in God's creative ability to reach into difficult souls and woo them to the Savior."
—GREGORY E. GANSSLE, author of *Our Deepest Desires*

KREGEL
PUBLICATIONS